PRAISE FOR
THE MAN IN THE MIRROR

In this 25th anniversary edition of *The Man in the Mirror*, Patrick Morley examines the many difficult issues facing men in today's rapidly changing social and moral atmosphere. He helps us think about the choices we make and how those choices impact the lives of everyone around us. The book is very useful.

Ben Carson Sr., MD, emeritus professor of neurosurgery, oncology, plastic surgery, and pediatrics at Johns Hopkins Medicine and president and CEO of American Business Collaborative, LLC

Selected one of the 100 most influential books of the last 100 years, *The Man in the Mirror* had a profound impact on me when I first read it. Now Pat Morley has revised and updated it for a whole new generation of men—including you! Every man would be wise to have *The Man in the Mirror* on his shelf. That way, when you face one of these 24 problems, you can pull it down and learn God's solution.

Mark Batterson, *New York Times* **bestselling author
of** *The Circle Maker*

Patrick Morley's classic book is a must-read for every man. This important book addresses the most common problems men face and offers helpful and achievable biblical solutions to empower every man to become the person God created him to be.

**Craig Groeschel, senior pastor of LifeChurch.tv
and author of** *FIGHT: Winning the Battles That Matter Most*

Pat Morley first released *The Man in the Mirror* during the hardest, most soul-crushing time of my life. I was a new Christian, I was a young husband and father, I was a failed businessman, and I was bankrupt. God was putting my life back together, and this book was one of the tools He put in my hands. Now, more than two decades later, it's a book I'm still putting into other men's hands. If you've never read it, now's the time.

Dave Ramsey, *New York Times* **bestselling author
and nationally syndicated radio show host**

I had the privilege of publishing the first edition of *The Man in the Mirror* in 1989, along with my then-business partner Robert Wolgemuth. As a thirty-four-year-old businessman, husband, and father, I found that this book spoke to me right where I was living. It was as if Pat had been reading my mail. It gave me simple and practical solutions to the issues I was facing. Amazingly, it is just as relevant now as it was then.

Michael Hyatt, *New York Times* **bestselling author**

Only a few books are ever considered "classics." But this one qualifies. The original edition in 1989 came directly from the crucible of Patrick Morley's life as a businessman and committed Christ follower. Brilliantly written in its original publication and now wonderfully updated for a new generation of men, the book has stood the test of time ... as has the life of its author. I enthusiastically recommend this book to you.

Dr. Robert Wolgemuth, bestselling author

I believe *The Man in the Mirror* may simply be the best book written for the man who wants practical, biblical insight on how to live an abundant life every day. In this classic bestseller, Pat Morley strategically dissects what's happening to men in our culture today and then gives us specific action steps on how to live abundantly. You can read this book with confidence; it will change your life ... forever!

Norm Miller, chairman of Interstate Batteries

The Man in the Mirror has been a proven, life-changing asset to thousands of men. This updated edition carries even more pearls of wisdom for taking your manhood to a higher level. I highly recommend it.

Robert Lewis, founder of Men's Fraternity

Pat Morley is the foremost leader in discipling men in our nation and in other nations as well. His life of integrity and helpful coaching in the church has guided me personally and countless other pastors. He is both brilliant and practical as he mentors us with powerful, insightful challenges that come from God's Spirit, as well as from His Word. This book will change your life—it changed mine!

**Dr. Joel C. Hunter, senior pastor
of Northland—A Church Distributed**

Twenty-five years ago, Patrick Morley saw that men were in trouble and threw out a lifeline with *The Man in the Mirror*. Today, the principles he provides in this great resource are just as true, tried, and tested as they were a quarter century ago. I commend this book for a new generation of men who desperately need Jesus Christ.

James MacDonald, senior pastor of Harvest Bible Chapel, author of *Vertical Church*, and founder of Act Like Men conferences, jamesmacdonald.org

Paul wrote in his first letter to Timothy, "Train yourself to be godly." Where would each of us start with such an exhortation in the twenty-first century? One resource, in addition to the Scriptures, should be *The Man in the Mirror*. What an outstanding guidebook for men who really want to grow in Christ!

Brian Doyle, president of Iron Sharpens Iron

Pat Morley is arguably the world's expert on what makes men tick. Few others have helped so many men. Now he can help you too. When a man looks in a mirror and asks the tough questions, it helps to have a friend standing with him. Pat can be that friend. In *The Man in the Mirror*, he helps you answer those tough questions.

Leary Gates, corporate venture coach and president of National Coalition of Ministries to Men

If you are in a rut and looking for good advice, Patrick Morley is your man. He has years and years of real-life experience to help answer your most heartfelt questions.

Bob Buford, author of *Halftime* and *Drucker & Me*

Pat Morley is one of my favorite people—a godly man of integrity and high principle. *The Man in the Mirror* is an excellent presentation of lessons he has learned at his hearthside and in the marketplace. I recommend this book to Christians who are tired of just going through the motions spiritually and are ready to experience the rich, meaningful, and abundant life available to faithful followers of Jesus.

The late Dr. William R. "Bill" Bright, founder of CRU (formerly Campus Crusade for Christ)

I know of no other book that has impacted as many men for the gospel as this one has. It turns men's hearts toward their marriages and children. It shows men the truth of the Scriptures, helping them find a deeper relationship with Christ. As a young, hard-charging entrepreneur, I read this book, paused to take an honest look at my life, and realized that the rat race was stealing me from my family. I'm so grateful to Pat for writing—and now rewriting—this book, and I'm looking forward to seeing God continue to use this book to get hold of men's hearts.

Brett Clemmer, vice president of Man in the Mirror

The Man in the Mirror is the all-time classic book for men who want to integrate their faith into their everyday lives. Morley tackles twenty-four practical problems we all face, and he shows us how we can live as godly men in our marriages, with our children, with friends, at work, and in every other arena of our lives. Read this book. You'll be so glad you did.

Wayne Huizenga Jr., president of Huizenga Holdings

Pat hits at the very core of all that is truly important in life in a compelling way that is certain to cause the reader to challenge life priorities and practices.

Steve Reinemund, dean at Wake Forest University School of Business and retired chairman and CEO of PepsiCo

This is a significant book. It covers every key issue men face and tells it exactly like it is. *The Man in the Mirror* is a Christian handbook of success for all men. As I read it I found myself challenged, stimulated, and convicted. This book will be around for decades.

Pat Williams, senior vice president of the NBA's Orlando Magic

Over the years that I've known Pat Morley, he has greatly impacted my life through example. Now, after reading this book, I have been challenged even more. While I recommend this book for use in a small group discussion setting, I also suggest you read it as I did—a chapter a day with my Bible study. As I read each chapter, I prayed about the tough questions Pat posed and thought all day about how the Lord wanted me to respond.

Stephen Strang, founder and CEO of Charisma Media

Every once in a while someone comes along and says what I've been trying to put into words for years. This is one of those books. It's Augustine for the twenty-first century. Real. Honest. Hard-hitting. Taking on the dragons. Read this book at your own risk. It's a serendipity—one surprise after another.

**Lyman Coleman, founder of Serendipity House
and pioneer in small group ministry**

To "walk the talk" as a successful businessman is a challenge very few meet. Pat Morley walks his talk. He is a successful businessman. And he brings his wisdom and experience in a readable and understandable form in *The Man in the Mirror*. I encourage you to not only read this book but also practice its principles.

**Ron Blue, founder of Ronald Blue & Co.
and founding director of Kingdom Advisors**

This is the most stimulating book I've read in years. I believe *The Man in the Mirror* will become one of the most significant books in our generation. It is practical, relevant, and challenging.

Howard Dayton, founder of Compass—*finances God's way*

Pat Morley's "rat race" thesis hits the nail on the head. The first step in survival in this culture is to understand the problem. *The Man in the Mirror* describes it effectively. This book is solid, balanced, practical, and interesting.

Chris White, founder and president of Leadership Ministries, Inc.

Pat Morley is a class act, and *The Man in the Mirror* is a classic book. Pat was dead-on twenty-five years ago in diagnosing the issues of a man's heart. A fine wine gets better with age, and so does Pat.

Steve Farrar, author of *Point Man*

The Man in the Mirror goes right to the root of many of today's problems concerning the priorities of our lives. Besides nailing the issues on the head, it provides clear, substantiated answers from a biblical point of view. It is a must-read.

Stan Smith, former world No. 1 tennis player

A dynamite book! Finally a book that gets down to the real issues facing men in our society. Honest, practical, and clear. I recommend it to every man who has to struggle in the modern-day business world.

Dr. Steve Brown, founder and president of Key Life Network

Hundreds of thousands of men have been impacted by this powerful, yet simple message. I'm thankful I am one of those men.

**Orel Hershiser, television broadcaster
and former pitcher for the Los Angeles Dodgers**

Pat Morley is for real, and his book is for real. He deals with bottom-line living. Read it and apply it. You'll never be the same.

Dr. John Tolson, spiritual life coach, disciple maker, and author

The Man in the Mirror is the best book I've ever read about men in our culture. Pat Morley has encapsulated the trials and temptations that all men face. He challenges every man to a better quality of life.

**Dr. Charles Green, senior pastor emeritus
of Orangewood Presbyterian Church**

The Man in the Mirror gives straightforward answers to problems and fears most men have. I will be recommending this book to the thousands of men involved in Lay Renewal Ministries. It is a must-read for them.

Bob Fenn, founder of Lay Renewal Ministries

Pat Morley wrote the book I wish I had written. It's the most pertinent book for the business and professional person I've seen. I strongly urge you to read it.

Dr. Ron Jenson, founder and chairman of High Ground

Though we are inundated with religious *talkers*, there is a dearth of religious *walkers*. I thoroughly enjoyed Pat Morley's practical, business-like explanation of *his* walk with Jesus. Those who want to move from superficial faith to real faith should read this book.

Frank Brock, president emeritus of Covenant College

THE
MAN
IN THE
MIRROR

PATRICK M. MORLEY

THE
MAN
IN THE
MIRROR

SOLVING THE 24 PROBLEMS MEN FACE

25TH ANNIVERSARY EDITION

ZONDERVAN®

ZONDERVAN

The Man in the Mirror, 25th Anniversary Edition
Copyright © 1989, 1992, 1997, 2014 by Patrick M. Morley

First Zondervan edition 1997

This title is also available as a Zondervan ebook. Visit www.zondervan.com/ebooks.

This title is also available in a Zondervan audio edition. Visit www.zondervan.fm.

Requests for information should be addressed to:

Zondervan, 3900 *Sparks Drive SE, Grand Rapids, Michigan 49546*

Library of Congress Cataloging-in-Publication Data

Morley, Patrick M.
    The man in the mirror : solving the 24 problems men face / Patrick M. Morley.
       p. cm.
    Originally published: Brentwood, Tenn.: Wolgemuth & Hyatt, 1989.
    Includes bibliographical references.
    ISBN 978-0-310-33175-9
    1. Men—Religious life. 2. Men—Conduct of life. 3. Christian life I. Title.
  BV4528.2.M67 2014
  248.8'.42—dc23   2014000000

Published in association with the literary agency of Wolgemuth & Associates, Inc.

Cover design and photography: James Hall
Interior design and illustrations: David Conn

First Printing August 2014 / Printed in the United States of America

In memory of Robert, my brother,
1952-1983

CONTENTS

FOREWORD

"Mirror, mirror on the wall, who's the fairest of them all?" What greater vanity can be expressed than that of the evil queen in *Snow White*? The queen was obsessed with the desire to be the most beautiful woman in the land. She loved her mirror. She spoke to it with terms of endearment . . . until one day the mirror gave her an answer, and she didn't know which she hated more, Snow White or the mirror that refused to lie.

If a dog is a man's best friend, perhaps his worst enemy is his mirror. Well, maybe his mirror isn't really his worst enemy; it merely reflects the image of his most formidable opponent. What opponent is more dangerous than the one who knows our deepest, darkest secrets? What opponent is more lethal than the one who can probe our most vulnerable points?

The man in the mirror is me. Ouch! I suppose I should have said, "The man in the mirror is *I*." But "I" or "me," the message is the same. What I see in the mirror is what I get, like it or not. My mirror won't lie to me either.

Mirrors are marvelous contraptions. Since Narcissus fell in love with his own image while gazing at his reflection in a pond, the human race has been fascinated by mirrors. Mirrors are the friends of magicians, the enemies of aging movie stars. We have round mirrors and square mirrors, big mirrors and compact mirrors, bathroom mirrors and rearview mirrors.

The mirror was tiny Alice's magical vehicle through which she could pass into a land of enchantment. The mirror was the symbol for the apostle Paul of our dim understanding of the mysterious things of God: "For now we see in a mirror dimly, but then face to face. Now I know in part; then I shall know fully, even as I have been fully known" (1 Corinthians 13:12 ESV).

I am a Weight Watcher, a "lifetime member." At a recent meeting, a fellow member finally arrived at his goal weight after shedding sixty pounds of fat. The group leader asked him to relate how he felt after his accomplishment. He replied, "Now, I am no longer embarrassed to look in store windows. I used to avoid glancing at the store windows as I walked down the street. Every time I looked in a window, instead of seeing the merchandise displayed inside, all I could see was the reflection of my obese body. I stopped looking. Now, after reaching my goal weight, I enjoy looking in store windows again."

What do you see when you look in the mirror? I have a large stand-up mirror in my bedroom. I can't imagine why I ever parted with my hard-earned money to purchase such a loathsome thing. I use it for golf. That's right. In the privacy of my bedchamber, I swing a golf club and check my positions in the mirror. One thing is certain: It doesn't look like Jack Nicklaus in there.

The doggone mirror is insensitive. In fact, it's downright brutal. It shows me every wart, every bump in my shirt (bottom first), and every blemish.

Now Pat Morley comes along and wants a mirror that can reflect the soul. Fortunately for me and for those who read this book, Morley's mirror is gentle and kind. It tells the truth, which is scary enough, but it does so with encouragement and wisdom.

Several years ago, I wrote a biography of a man's life. Two things stick in my mind from the experience of writing that book. The first is that I discovered from probing the details of another man's life that any human life is a profound study in fascination. The unique experiences of any individual's life are genuine fodder for a gripping novel.

The second thing I discovered was this: I found myself wondering, in a fit of egomania, if anyone would ever be inclined to write a biography of *my* life. I decided that such an idea was sheer fantasy. I was convinced it would never happen.

I was astonished to discover that someone actually did undertake to write my biography. It was Pat Morley. The title of my biography is *The Man in the Mirror*. The irony is that Morley didn't even know he was writing my life story. You may be equally astonished to discover that it is your biography as well. It amazes me that Morley can write so many biographies all in one book.

I am a teacher. I am in the knowledge business. The Bible warns us that knowledge "puffs up," whereas love "builds up" (1 Corinthians 8:1). Yet, at the same time, the Bible exhorts us to seek knowledge. Such knowledge, however, is not to be sought as an end in itself. My Bible reads, "Wisdom is the principal thing; therefore get wisdom. And in all your getting, get understanding" (Proverbs 4:7 NKJV).

The goal of knowledge is wisdom. The goal of wisdom is to lead a life that is pleasing to God. This book is a book that contains uncommon wisdom. It is stirring, disturbing, and abundantly encouraging, all at the same time.

The Man in the Mirror is a book written by a man's man. It is a book written by a man, for men. While I was reading this book, the thought kept occurring to me, *I can't wait for my wife, Vesta, to read this book*. Vesta is a voracious reader. She reads more than I do. I get my best tips on what to read next from her (even with books of theology).

I want my wife to read this book, not because I think she needs to read this book. I'm the one who needed to read it. I want my wife to read this book because I know my wife will be thrilled to read it.

One last tip for you. If someone gives you this book or if you buy it yourself, be sure to read it. If you don't read it, by all means destroy it before your wife gets hold of it. If the unthinkable happens — if you don't read it and your wife does — then, my dear brother, you are in deep weeds.

R. C. Sproul, Orlando, Florida

INTRODUCTION

One evening we threw a going-away party for Ragne (RAWG-nee). For one whole year Ragne had soaked up American culture like a sponge.

A pastor from Sweden, he journeyed to America to learn how to make his own country come alive for God. I invited Ragne to attend a weekly Bible study that my wife, Patsy, and I hosted in our home. Part of Ragne's training was to participate with us. His insights, always peppered with humor, livened up our group.

On our last evening together, we went around the room and each person said their farewells to Ragne, and then we presented him with an engraved pen-and-pencil set for his desk back home in Sweden. We all grew to love that affable, Nordic teddy bear.

When all were finished, I asked Ragne to tell us the most interesting thing he had learned about Americans.

Without hesitation he said in a thick Scandinavian accent, "Well, when I first got here, everywhere I would go, everyone would always say to me, 'Ragne, so good to see you. How are you doing?'

"It took me about six months to realize — nobody wants an answer!"

Sad, but true. We have all experienced the sting of the insincere inquiry. Why doesn't anyone want an answer? For some, of course, it's just a social greeting, but for most of us we can see in this a clue into how we live.

We Americans are so busy, so overcommitted, so up to our ears in duties and debts — we just don't want to know. We have so many problems of our own that there is no time left for anyone else—we just don't have the time to "want an answer."

More than a few men are swamped—they are in over their heads. After they've taken care of their own problems, they have no capacity left over to help anyone else. They don't understand why they are so caught up in the rat race, and their lives are frequently spinning out of control.

Other men sense that something isn't quite right about their lives, but they can't put their finger on the answer. An eerie feeling lingers that they may be running in the wrong race. They see that they are more *financially* successful than their parents, but they suspect they may not be better-off.

In 1939, Christopher Morley penned the words in his novel *Kitty Foyle*, "Their own private life gets to be like a rat race." In the decades since, the term *rat race* has evolved to describe the hopeless pursuit of a good life always just out of reach—a treadmill on which we can't stop walking or we will fall off. Many of us today are trying to win the wrong race.

We could view Ragne's perceptive remark as an indictment, but instead, let's use it as a springboard to look into the problems, issues, and temptations that face the man in the mirror every day and see what practical solutions we can discover for winning the *right* race.

At the end of each chapter, I have included several *Focus Questions*. There are a number of ways you can use these questions.

- You may simply want to read them at the end of each chapter and quietly think about your responses.
- If you want to get more out of the chapter, you can write your answers down in a journal. This is an excellent way to bring clarity and resolve to your thinking.
- Finally, you may want to pull together a group of men who commit themselves to read one or two chapters a week on their own and then discuss their answers and insights in a weekly

meeting. The *Discussion Leader's Guide* at the end of this book may be helpful.

The use of the book in men's groups, Bible studies, adult education classes, or among a group of colleagues will greatly enhance its value and give you an opportunity to put what you learn into practice.

My prayer is that this book will meet you where you live — in the marketplace. Life is a struggle. And we all need Monday-through-Friday answers to Sunday's nagging questions. That said, I want you to know that this is intended to be a positive book. I believe you will be a happier, more focused man when you finish. Let's begin by taking a close-up look at the rat race.

A NEW
INTRODUCTION
FROM THE AUTHOR

The world has changed dramatically over the last twenty-five years. The once dependable consensus of Judeo-Christian values has melted away faster than a polar ice cap. Today, nearly half of our women would rather live with a man than marry him. And one-third of our children are not living with their biological dads.

The last twenty-five years have been dominated by the digital revolution. The Internet has only been with us since the mid-1990s—just long enough to have made Steve Jobs rich enough to build a $250 million super yacht that can be operated from an iPad. He died without ever being able to see it, but I did, just two days before I wrote this—a vacant ghost ship, hauntingly moored to a berth at a marina in Florida.

How did it happen that we take body searches for granted, and welcome metal detectors into our schools? Whether it's the Great Recession, Wall Street corruption, political gridlock, social media, shifting demographics, terrorism, or the Department of Homeland Security—these are but a few of the tectonic changes that have rocked our world these last few years.

Yet when it comes to what it takes to be a man, not much has changed.

Frankly, when my colleagues asked me to update *The Man in*

the Mirror, I wasn't sure it was a good idea. However, in light of the dramatic changes just mentioned, it quickly became apparent that a whole new generation of men might benefit from taking a fresh look at how to solve the 24 problems men face.

Actually, the solutions to most of the problems you and I face are surprisingly simple. But as with any skill you want to master, you have to have the right information. So my goal in this new edition of *The Man in the Mirror* is to help you address the unique challenges these 24 problems present as you find your way in the twenty-first century.

When I wrote the original edition of *The Man in the Mirror*, I wasn't a writer at all; I was in commercial real estate. Now, the fact that millions of copies have been distributed around the world — well, there's no question that God performed a miracle with that first book. And so I've resisted the urge to change those original, direct, plainspoken sentences that put into words what so many millions of men wanted — or needed — to hear in the first place. It was less about writing craft anyway, and more about what God wanted to do in men's lives — how He was moving in the world. Some who read it became Christians. Others realized they had been more cultural Christians than biblical Christians. Many reordered their priorities and, in the process, saved their marriages and families. In short, God used that book to inspire and guide an entire generation of men.

Now I'm praying that it might inspire and guide you too. What does God want to do in *your* life? If you're ready, turn the page and let's get started!

PART 1

SOLVING OUR IDENTITY PROBLEMS

CHAPTER 1

THE RAT RACE

Like a rat in a maze, the path before me lies.
Simon and Garfunkel

*You were running a good race. Who cut in on you
to keep you from obeying the truth?*
Galatians 5:7

The timer clicked, the TV screen fluttered, and the speaker blared the morning news.

"Morning already?" groaned Larry. He rolled over and squeezed the pillow tightly over his ears, not seriously thinking he could muffle the announcement of another day in the rat race. Then the aroma of coffee from the timer-operated coffeemaker lured him toward the kitchen.

Six hours of sleep may not have been the house rule growing up, but success in the twenty-first century demanded a premium from its active participants. A rising star like Larry couldn't squander time sleeping.

Curls of steam rose from the bowl of instant oatmeal; the microwave had produced predictably perfect results in perfect cadence with his thirty-five-minute wake-up schedule.

Slouched in his chair, propped against his elbow, Larry noticed the computer screen staring back at him. Last night he had balanced his checkbook after the eleven o'clock news, and, weary from the long day, he must have neglected to turn off the computer.

His wife, Carol, had a welcomed day off, so she slept in. Larry went through the rote motions of getting the kids off to school. After the two younger children had been dropped off at day care, he was alone in the car with Julie. Twelve-year-old Julie seemed troubled lately. "Daddy, do you love Mom anymore?" she asked. The question came out of the blue to Larry, but Julie had been building the courage to ask it for months. Their family life was changing, and Julie seemed to be the only member of the family diagnosing the changes. Larry reassured her he loved Mom very much.

Carol didn't plan to go back to work when she first started on her MBA degree. Bored with her traditional, stay-at-home mom role, she just wanted more personal self-fulfillment. Her favorite blogs and online articles conferred little dignity on the role of mother-tutor.

Although her family satisfied her self-esteem need for many years, other neighborhood women her age seemed to lead glamorous lives in the business world. She couldn't help but question her traditional values.

Maybe I'm too old-fashioned—out of step with the times, she thought to herself.

So two nights each week for three and a half years, she journeyed off to the local university. It was a big investment—not to mention the homework. By the time she walked across the stage to receive her diploma, Carol was convinced women had a right to pursue professional fulfillment just as much as men.

Larry, a tenacious and focused sales representative, advanced quickly in his company. Fifteen years of dream chasing rewarded him with a vice president title. The pay covered the essentials, but they both wanted more of the good life.

"I've been thinking about going back to work," Carol told him.

Larry didn't protest. She had earned extra money working in a bank at the beginning of their marriage, and the money helped furnish their honeymoon apartment. By mutual agreement, Carol stopped working when Julie was born, and ever since they had been hard-pressed to make ends meet.

Even though his own mother didn't work, Larry knew things were different now for women. Still, he had mixed emotions about sending their two small children to a day care center. But since money was always a problem, he just shrugged and kept silent when Carol announced she had started interviewing for a job.

Larry clearly understood the trade-off. More money, less family. More family, less money. Yet, they really wanted the good life.

Their neighbors bought a twenty-four-foot ski boat. Larry was surprised to learn they could own one too — for only $328 per month. By scrimping for five months they pulled together $1,000, which, when added to their savings, gave them enough for the $2,500 down payment.

Larry loved cars. His gentle dad had always loved cars. If a shiny two-door pulled up next to him at a traffic light, Larry's heart always beat faster — he could just picture himself shifting through the gears of a fancy European model. By accident he discovered that for only $424 a month he could lease the car of his fantasies — a racy import! Leasing had never occurred to him before.

Carol desperately wanted to vacation in Hawaii that year; her Tuesday tennis partner went last spring. But they couldn't do both.

"If you go along with me on this one, I'll make it up to you, Carol. I promise!" Larry told her, his infectious grin spreading across his face. She reminisced how that impish, little-boy smile had first attracted her to him. *He has been good to me*, she thought.

"Okay, go ahead," Carol told him.

His dad always loved Chevys. Larry's tastes had evolved with the times.

Carol dreamed of living in a two-story home with a swimming pool, but with the car and boat payments so high, it remained a dream for years. Larry slaved twelve- and fourteen-hour days — always thinking of ways to earn more money for Carol's dream house. When Carol went to work, they added up the numbers and were elated to see they could finally make the move.

The strain of keeping their household afloat discouraged them. There were bills to pay, kids to pick up from day care, deadlines to meet, quotas to beat, but not much time to enjoy the possessions they had accumulated.

Words from a Simon and Garfunkel song haunted Larry's thoughts: "Like a rat in a maze, the path before me lies. And the pattern never alters, until the rat dies." He was trapped.

Carol just couldn't take it anymore. She believed Larry had let her down. He was supposed to be strong. He was supposed to know how to keep everything going. But Larry was just as confused about their situation as she was.

As the U-Haul van pulled away from the house, Larry couldn't quite believe she was actually doing it—Carol was moving out. She said she just needed some time and space to sort things out. She told Larry that she was confused. The question young Julie had asked a few months earlier burned in his mind: "Daddy, do you love Mom anymore?" Yes … yes, he loved her, but was it too late? How did things get so out of hand?

THE PROBLEM

Do you know anyone who has ever won the rat race? This question deserves more than a chuckle, because, upon reflection, most of us will have to acknowledge we really don't know anyone who has.

If that's the case, then why do we compete in an unwinnable race? Frankly, I would rather win, so I would rather run in a race that has a history of producing winners. Tragically, most men don't know what race that is.

The proverbial questions of the rat race—"What's it all about?" and "Is this all there is?"—have tortured us all at one time or another.

No matter how successful we become, these questions always lurk in the shadows, just waiting to pounce on us when life's inevitable problems overtake us.

We strain to keep it all together, but the pressure is often like a tight band around our chest. Sometimes the gravity of our debts and duties weighs us down so much that our interior posture is in a slump—even if we fake it and stand tall to the world.

"What is the purpose of my life?"

"Why do I exist?"

"How do I find meaning?"

"How do I satisfy my need to be significant?"

"Why are my relationships in a shambles?"

"How did I get so far in debt?"

"Who am I trying to please, anyway?"

"How did I get caught up in the rat race in the first place?"

Confusion exists about how to achieve the desired result: the good life. We all want to improve our standard of living—that's normal. But the world in which we live has its own ideas about how to achieve the good life, ideas that are far different from God's order. Doesn't it seem like everyone has his own unique theory?

This dichotomy between God's order and the order of this world produces a strain on the Christian man trying to sort out his thinking. Are there absolutes? Do biblical principles really address the twenty-first-century, day-to-day problems we men have? Is it possible for us to sort through our problems and build a workable model to live by?

Any good business plan starts with a description of the current environment. So let's begin our look at the problems of men by first getting a handle on the environment in which we live and work. The first question we need to delve into is, "How do we measure our standard of living?"

THE "STANDARD OF LIVING" FALLACY

We Americans enjoy unprecedented material success. Yet it's deceptive to measure our standard of living in only one dimension. To comprehend the standard of living we have actually achieved, we first need to unbundle the concept of standard of living and look at some of the component parts.

On a plane trip, I sat next to a distinguished couple in their mid-sixties. Mr. Silver was the kind, gentle, grandfatherly type with a perpetual smile traced across the creases in his face. I learned they were just leaving Orlando, where they had attended their son's wedding—in a hot-air balloon. Mr. Silver was trying hard to take a philosophical view of how cavalier young people have become toward the high estate of marriage.

As we talked he reflected how all his financial dreams had been met. Yet something bothered him. Yes, his financial standard of living was up, but an eerie feeling lingered that something wasn't quite right about his life.

I happened to have with me a graph related to our discussion, so I showed it to him. He perked up and bellowed loudly, "Yes, yes, that's me! That's exactly what has happened to my life!"

Figure 1.1, the same graph I showed Mr. Silver, shows two components of our standard of living. They are on sharply different vectors. While our *material* standard of living has soared over the last century, our *moral/spiritual/relational* standard of living has plummeted. They have, more or less, traded places.

Without respect to why, are we better-off than we were even just twenty-five years ago? How about schoolchildren? Is government improving? What do you think about television standards? Are marriages stronger? Are families healthier? Do people respect authority more than they used to? Is society more civil? Is Wall Street more honest? Is sexual immorality on the increase or declining? Are movies more wholesome? Again, without respect to why, common sense tells us that American culture is slowly but surely unraveling.

Perhaps you're old enough to remember *The Cosby Show*, traditional families, prayer rather than metal detectors in schools, and TV without explicit sex. Yes, there were problems. But they were Chevrolet problems for Chevrolet families who lived in Chevrolet neighborhoods and had Chevrolet paychecks. Life was gradual, life was linear: Chevy, Buick, Cadillac, gold watch, funeral.

The desire for instant gratification, however, has taken the place of deferring to a time when we can pay cash for our wants. Today, men are consumed by desires to buy things they don't need, with money they don't have, to impress people they don't like. Where do these desires come from?

The technology explosion of the last few decades marks our era as the pinnacle of human potential and achievement in all of history. We are blessed with technological enhancements in our creature comforts, our travel, our communications, and our jobs. Do you remember how tedious it was to find information before Google? And what would we do without Wikipedia? Can you recall when there wasn't "an app for that" to load onto your pocket mobile device?

But at the same time we have run up the score, we have also injured most of our players. The changes come quickly, game plans have to be altered, our best players get no rest, and tired players injure the easiest. Yes, we are prosperous, but at what price? We have a winning score, but most of us are tired. As individual members of the team are injured, the team as a whole begins to lose its rhythm, courage, and will.

Men today are worn-out. Many who chased their dreams have lost their families. Too many children have grown up with an absentee father. Still, the invoices for the debts to accumulate the things we didn't need and don't use arrive in the mailbox like clockwork at the first of each and every month.

At a time when we are experiencing such unprecedented advances on so many fronts, why has the moral fabric of our nation gone threadbare? America was founded by men who sought spiritual freedom to worship God. Where are the descendants of these men? Was their courage not hereditary? The most lasting satisfaction of life is in our relationships, so why are we trading them in for careers with companies that will drop us like hot potatoes if we miss our quota? Our standard of living must be measured in more than one dimension.

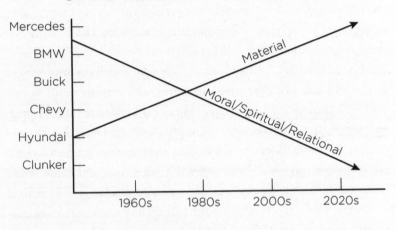

STANDARD OF LIVING UNBUNDLED

Figure 1.1

THE DOMINANT ECONOMIC THEORY IN AMERICA

The material prosperity we enjoy is a modern miracle. Think about the now tiny homes that sprung up after World War II. Television was new then (color telecasts didn't begin until 1953). No one had a computer yet (Steve Jobs wasn't even born until 1955). Greyhound was how America traveled, the interstate highway system didn't exist, space exploration was an abstract idea, nuclear power was a mystery, Madison Avenue was still in its infancy, and a millionaire was an anomaly.

Think of it. God has blessed this nation with the greatest think-ers, leaders, and implementers in history. He has granted prosperity that would make even Solomon burn with envy! But how did it come about? Have you ever wondered how, in the few short decades since the end of the Great Depression (1942) and World War II (1945), America achieved such a remarkable standard of living? Even the Great Recession that started in 2007 couldn't stop our economic juggernaut for more than a few years.

The dominant economic theory in America for the past century or so has been _consumerism_. The dictionary defines consumerism as "the economic theory that a progressively greater consumption of goods is beneficial." Is this true? Is a progressively greater consump-tion of goods beneficial? Whether true or not—and I think not— we know from glancing at ads and TV commercials that American industry applies this theory diligently in its business plans.

In the 1950s, Vance Packard wrote a book, _The Hidden Persuad-ers_, which shocked and alarmed the nation. He discovered, and blew the whistle on, a large-scale effort to channel our unconscious habits and manipulate our purchasing behavior. The Madison Avenue pin-stripers formed an unholy alliance with the practitioners of psychol-ogy to manipulate the American consumer.

At the end of World War II, our industrial machine had the capacity to produce far greater amounts of products than people were buying. So the pin-stripers probed the question of how to stimulate people to buy more, and the science of motivation research was born.

Have you ever wondered why, after only two or three years, you begin to itch for a shiny new car? Why don't we simply drive our cars until they stop running before we buy new ones? The answer, a creation of the unholy alliance, is termed _psychological obsolescence_.

Madison Avenue figured out how to make us feel ashamed to own a slightly used car. We are _programmed_ to consume, because _the dominant economic theory employed in America is that a progressively greater consumption of goods is beneficial._

In late 1955, the church publication *Christianity and Crisis* commented grimly on America's "ever-expanding economy." It observed that the pressure was on Americans to "consume, consume and consume, whether we need or even desire the products almost forced upon us." It added that the dynamics of an ever-expanding system require that we be "persuaded to consume to meet the needs of the productive process."[1]

Don't you find it intriguing that this prophetic 1955 statement could readily be a comment on life in the twenty-first century? As succinct and powerful as the observations of Packard, *Christianity and Crisis*, and others are, the financial clout of industry overwhelmed these wise observers. Their warnings were drowned out by the din of advertisements for new, improved soapsuds and sleek, shiny cars. Just turn on your computer or tablet — consumerism dominates the economic process. But how are we influenced to be part of consumerism?

THE INFLUENCE OF THE MEDIA

No greater influence impacts our thinking than the media. Unfortunately, the media in America is controlled by secularists, so the slant of most print and digital copy, programming, advertising, and news portrays a secular worldview.

The secular worldview will be explored in the next chapter, but let's use this working definition for now: Secularists believe that man establishes his own moral values apart from the influence of anyone (including God), and he self-determines his destiny — he is "the master of his own fate."

The problem with such a worldview is that it has no absolutes; everything is relative — it has no eternal reference point. We can make up our own rules as we go. But how do we know if sexual promiscuity or pornography is immoral or not? Why shouldn't we cheat in business? Why should family life be valued higher than career?

Legendary news reporter Ted Koppel said in a prophetic commencement address at Duke University in the 1980s, "We have reconstructed the Tower of Babel and it is a television antenna. A thousand voices producing a daily parody of democracy in which everyone's opinion is afforded equal weight, regardless of substance or merit. Indeed, it can even be argued that opinions of real weight tend to sink with barely a trace in television's ocean of banalities."[2]

And of course, we can now add bloggers, Facebook, Twitter, and other social media to the list. This relativistic approach means we need to guard our minds more carefully, because so many kooky ideas are floating around.

Through the media and advertising, which relies heavily on subliminal suggestions, we are consciously and unconsciously lured to go for the Madison Avenue lifestyle. The secret of fanning our smoldering desires and wants has been elevated to a scientific approach. The economic goal of all media is, after all, to sell products and services!

Our problem may be more what our unconscious minds are exposed to than how our conscious minds operate. According to Wilson Bryan Key in his book *Subliminal Seduction*:

> The conscious mind discriminates, decides, evaluates, resists or accepts. The unconscious, apparently, merely stores units of information, much of which influences attitudes or behavior at the conscious level in ways about which science knows virtually nothing. The vast communication industry realized long ago the resistance to advertising which develops at the conscious level. However, there is little, if any, resistance encountered at the unconscious level, to which marketing appeals are now directed.[3]

You see, we can at least somewhat defend ourselves at the conscious level, but most of consumerism's appeals are directed to our unconscious mind.

Perhaps the only way to overcome this dilemma is to reevaluate our sources of entertainment and information. Personally, when I was a young father, I virtually stopped watching television and tried to read more books. First Corinthians 6:12 offered me a credo worth adopting:

> "I have the right to do anything," you say—but not every-thing is beneficial. "I have the right to do anything"—but I will not be mastered by anything.

My concern for myself was that my unconscious mind would be mastered in an area in which I had no ability to resist. The same is true for you. Our unconscious minds have no walls around them and no sentinels at the gates.

Watch TV commercials one evening and ask yourself, *If these commercials are true, then who am I, and what am I?* The life por-trayed on the tube loves pleasure and sensuality, doesn't deny itself anything, and has a right to whatever goal it sets. I believe you will come to the same conclusion I did.

Wouldn't we all like the models for our children to be the sac-rifices and contributions of famous scientists, artists, thinkers, mis-sionaries, statesmen, builders, and other heroes and saints? They are out there, but we are usually not going to find them through popular media.

THE BEAUTIFUL, WRINKLE-FREE LIFE

Today, a lack of contentment pervades the life of the American consumer. That's because consumerism and media influence have caused a basic shift in values.

The desire for things appears to have become more important than having a meaningful life philosophy. Some researchers have been able to dramatically illustrate this shift in values by data min-ing the American Freshman Survey that has tracked the life goals of first-year college students every year since 1966. They decided to group the survey results by generations: Boomers (born 1946–1961),

Gen Xers (born 1962–1981), and Millennials (born after 1982). They found that the number of students who want to be very well-off financially increased from 45 percent of Boomers to 71 percent of Gen Xers to 74 percent of Millennials. At the same time, those desiring to develop a meaningful philosophy of life fell from 73 percent of Boomers to 47 percent of Gen Xers to 45 percent of Millennials. On the positive side, helping others who are in difficulty has held steady (66 percent, 64 percent, and 65 percent, respectively). And raising a family has experienced a slight uptick (65 percent, 71 percent, and 75 percent, respectively).[4]

Unfortunately, more of us are trying to achieve the Madison Avenue lifestyle (let's call this *the beautiful, wrinkle-free life*) than the economy will support. The lifestyle image we strive for is a *media-generated, artificial standard of living*. The media creates the lifestyle image that the producers of goods and services want to sell. It is unrealistic. It is artificial. And only a weary few achieve it.

Men who pursue the Madison Avenue lifestyle — and to some extent we all do — find it either unobtainable, unable to be maintained, or not worth maintaining at all.

The result of failing to achieve or maintain the beautiful, wrinkle-free life produces an excruciating level of anxiety. The more we are exposed to our consumeristic society, the more our lack of contentment intensifies.

Figure 1.2 shows two types of pressure produced by pursuing the beautiful, wrinkle-free life. First is *media-generated standard of living anxiety*: "I went for it but couldn't find it." This is the extent to which our total spending still didn't achieve the lifestyle level we set as our goal.

Eliminating the anxiety produced by the media-generated standard of living is virtually impossible if we have bought into the Madison Avenue lifestyle because, as Solomon wrote, "Whoever loves money never has enough; whoever loves wealth is never satisfied with their income" (Ecclesiastes 5:10). The more we get, the more we want. Anxiety is the natural by-product of chasing the beautiful, wrinkle-free life.

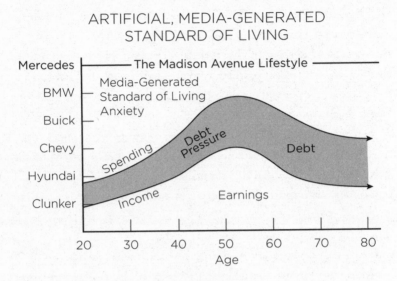

Figure 1.2

The second is *debt pressure*. In Figure 1.2, notice the difference between our *spending* and our *income*. To the extent that our spending exceeds our income, we must accumulate *debt*. We can create a standard of living for ourselves two ways: income and debt. The fundamental method of providing for our families is work. Our productivity has a value, which is the income we earn. The other method is by borrowing money from the future income we expect to earn.

Borrowing has become a national pastime. Easy credit seemed like a good idea—at least until the housing bubble burst and caused the Great Recession in 2008. If we could control our passions, it would be wonderful. Mixing easy credit and consumerism together, however, produces a highly combustible formula. In pursuit of the good life, we are lured to stretch a little further for happiness, made possible by credit.

Essentially, we have exchanged our traditional values for a murky sort of prosperity, financed by a remarkable increase in productivity and by a suffocating load of consumer, mortgage, student, and public debt.

THE RAT RACE DEFINED

We can define the rat race as the pursuit of this beautiful, wrinkle-free life. Since there are no winners, the aftermath of running the race and losing takes a heavy toll.

The double whammy of media-generated standard of living anxiety and debt pressure is enormously depressing. Not only do we have the tension of not reaching the lifestyle we set as our goal, but we also have the pressure of the debt we accumulated trying to get there. The debt makes us bitter and angry because we realize we played the part of a fool and deceived ourselves. Not only that, but our relationships end up fractured. The rat race boils down to the conflict between who we are created to be and who we are tempted to be. Could we define the rat race any more succinctly?

If the pursuit of money and possessions stood alone as an issue, we might be able to rationalize some of our money lust. But every balance sheet has two sides, and the other side of this balance sheet is relationships.

When we choose the rat race, fracture lines soon appear in our relationships, and crumbling is not far behind. Unfortunately, all too often, in pursuit of the good life, *men leave a trail of broken relationships.*

The way in which we measure our standard of living indicates the race we have decided to run. The American Christian faces a true dilemma. We can choose the rat race, or we can choose to not love this world and "throw off everything that hinders and the sin that so easily entangles" and "run with perseverance the race marked out for us" (Hebrews 12:1).

We each make our own choice, but the pressure to make the wrong choice is intense and should not be underestimated. As my first Bible study leader was fond of saying, "You can choose your way, but you can't choose the result." The cause and effect nature of our choice brands us.

DOING THE NEW JOB

I learned in business school that the number one reason men fail when they are promoted is that they keep doing the old job. In other words, since what they have done in the past is comfortable, they simply continue the old job description instead of taking on the new challenges.

The same is true in the spiritual realm. The number one reason men fail when promoted to "follower of Christ" is that they keep doing the old job. Instead of penetrating the issues of their lives and responding biblically, they continue to live an impotent life as if nothing had ever happened. Maybe they clean up their language a little, but essentially there's no change.

Perhaps it's time that Christian men in America check out of the rat race. It's an unwinnable race. Isn't it time we started doing the job we were promoted to when we first trusted Christ? "Therefore, if anyone is in Christ, the new creation has come: The old has gone, the new is here!" (2 Corinthians 5:17). We are promised a new spiritual nature, but we must be faithful to do our part—to do the new job.

Is it time for you to start doing the new job? Are you tired of the rat race? Are you concerned that you may be on your way to a life filled with regrets?

With this description of the environment in which we live, let's now turn to the specific problems men face, see what solutions might be available, and see if we can't discover a new track on which we can run in a race that counts.

———————————— FOCUS QUESTIONS ————————————

1. "Most men are caught up in the rat race."

   ❏ Agree ❏ Disagree. Why?

2. If the rat race is an unwinnable race, why do you think so many men run in it? What are they trying to accomplish?

3. In what ways has your material standard of living gone up since you were a child? In what ways do you think your moral/spiritual/relational standard of living has been affected?

4. It appears that many men have been lulled into mental and spiritual complacency. How have consumerism and the media impacted your own values and the way you spend your time and money?

5. Madison Avenue works hard to define for us *who* and *what* we are, usually in terms of *the beautiful, wrinkle-free life.* What practical steps can you take to free yourself from its influence?

CHAPTER 2

LEADING AN UNEXAMINED LIFE

The life which is unexamined is not worth living.
Socrates, quoted by Plato in *Apology*

Let us examine our ways and test them,
and let us return to the LORD.
Lamentations 3:40

I used to watch *Dempsey and Makepeace*, a British TV show that was on for a couple of years in the 1980s.

He was Dempsey—a tough New York cop. After a reliable police informer reported that the mob had placed a contract on Dempsey's life, his boss sent Dempsey—a gruff, head-busting maverick—to London for safekeeping.

She was Makepeace—a very feminine, very British, very proper English policewoman. They become partners. Together they played the lead roles in what turned out to be a classic English cops-and-robbers program.

On the lead-in at the top of each week's show, they ran away from burning cars that exploded in the background. They dove to the pavement so they wouldn't be sprayed by machine-gun fire. They rolled across the ground and returned gunfire at the bad guys. You knew an hour of nonstop action was on the way! Then the screen suddenly quieted, and the camera zoomed in on a close-up of Dempsey's knotty face. He glared straight into the camera lens for what seemed like a long time. And then, very matter-of-factly, he summarized his view of the world: "Life is hard, and then you die."

Dissolve to a commercial.

You didn't get the impression Dempsey represented the profound intellectual sort, but there is a certain ring of truth to what he said. Dempsey took life one episode at a time, never giving a thought to what tomorrow might bring.

A lot of us are like Dempsey.

There comes a day, though, when we each want the *real* answers to the questions Dempsey raised: "Why is life so hard?" and "What happens when I die?"

THE PROBLEM

When we progress along the trajectory we set for ourselves, we don't give much thought to the *why* questions of life. But when we hit the target and are still not satisfied, the questions start to come. "Who am I? Why do I exist? Is this all there is? If I'm so successful, why do I feel so empty?"

And if we *don't* hit our target, the list of questions grows even longer. "Why me, God? If You love me, where are You when I need You? Why won't You bless me? How could this happen to me?" Our hurt feelings slowly give way to anger and bitterness, or fear and guilt, or some of each.

After all is considered, the number one shortcoming of man is that *we tend to lead unexamined lives. Most men have not carefully chiseled their worldview by a personal search for truth and obedience to God.*

Instead, we rush from task to busy task, but we don't call enough time-outs to reflect on life's larger meaning and purpose. Rather, we live myopically from day to day to day; we live under the tyranny of today's problems. Our lives, like Dempsey's, are consumed in action as we react to the seemingly endless menu of options that vie for our attention, time, and money. But as Gandhi said, "There is more to life than increasing its speed."

Spiritually, too many of us are just "playing church" — just going through the motions. We show up for worship services, but the message we come away with doesn't do for us what it does for some of the other men. We don't know exactly why, and before we spend much time thinking about it, our minds wander to the work problems chewing at our gut. We speed off to the next busy task, and by Monday afternoon, the memory of Sunday is as distant as the memory of last year's vacation.

As a lawyer or electrician is no better than the effort he puts into keeping up with his profession, so is the Christian no better than the effort he puts into self-examination of life's big questions.

NOT EVERYONE THINKS LIKE I DO

A friend astonished me with a comment at lunch one day. He was telling me his views on abortion. He was foreign-born, with a sense of history, and I had always admired his business skill.

He suggested it was better to kill the unborn than to allow them to be born unwanted into a life of suffering. He did not argue that the unborn are not human beings. Rather, since they would be neglected and possibly abused, he reasoned the unwanted are mercifully spared when terminated before birth. Of all the reasons I've heard for abortion, this one stands alone as the most patently absurd. This friend — wealthy and influential — was making important commercial decisions shaping the life of our community.

Why do men think the things they think, say the things they say, and do the things they do? Each of us has a worldview. For most of us, our worldview results more from where we were born, who our parents were, and what schools we attended than a careful examination of issues. Yet our worldview influences every thought we have, every word we speak, and every action we take.

TWO WORLDVIEWS

As we grow and mature, our worldview develops from our many experiences and relationships. There are two predominant worldviews in America today. One view, the *secular worldview*, believes man is the central figure in shaping events. The second view, the *Christian worldview*, believes God is sovereign and active in everyday life.

The secularist believes man is intrinsically good, masters his own fate, determines on his own the boundaries of his achievements and knowledge, and is unconstrained by moral standards—apart from those he chooses at his sole discretion.

The Christian, on the other hand, believes an all-powerful God created the heavens and the earth. This living, omnipotent God possesses all knowledge, and because of His great love for us, He established absolute moral standards for our protection. He is holy, loving, and personal.

Often confused about the differences between these two worldviews, Christian men frequently apply the wrong set of principles to their problems. We seem to have a fragmented understanding of how to live as Christian men.

In today's world, Christians have seen things in bits and pieces instead of in totals. We have sounded alarms over the breakdown of the family, pornography, gun violence, racism, poverty, and abortion. But as Dr. Francis Schaeffer pointed out, we "have not seen this as a totality—each thing being a part, a symptom, of a much larger problem."[5]

This "larger problem" is the basic shift in values mentioned in chapter 1. It's a fundamental change in how we view life and the world as a whole. We have moved away from traditional Judeo-Christian values toward a worldview that lets us self-select values based on whether they serve our self-interests. Like a child loose in a candy store, *we* pick our values, *we* determine our own fate, *we* captain our own ship.

These two worldviews, secular and Christian, are on a collision course. They inevitably produce opposite results. To understand the differences between the two is the key first step to resolving the questions of the unexamined life.

We often don't even *see* these dramatic differences. I'm sure you have seen a daring circus performer riding two horses at the same time. He has one foot firmly planted on the back of each horse. He can do this because they are so close together. If the two horses begin to move apart from each other, though, the performer must pick one or the other to ride.

So it is in our spiritual journeys. At first these two worldviews don't seem that far apart. Unless we carefully examine our lives, we tend to see the Christian worldview and the secular worldview close together, like our two circus horses. However, when we begin to take a closer look, we start to see unmistakable contrasts.

We begin to see how dramatically different — even totally opposite — they are. As they come into sharper focus, they move farther and farther apart, and we eventually reach a point, like the daring circus performer, at which we must choose one or the other.

The choice between a Christian worldview and a secular worldview is a choice between God's race and the rat race.

THE RESULTS OF LEADING AN UNEXAMINED LIFE

John and Betty started out like most Christians. For seven years I watched them struggle with lifestyle and worldview issues. They sincerely wanted the peace and contentment that comes from knowing Christ personally. Yet they experienced a constant tension because of their material appetites. Betty, in particular, always wanted more.

They lived in a comfortable home, but like so many of us, they clutched the hope of buying their dream house. John knew the payments weren't manageable, but Betty seemed so anxious to take the leap. Eventually they plunged in and bought a real showplace.

John just couldn't seem to satisfy Betty's appetite for possessions. He worked hard enough, but Betty honestly believed he was unambitious. When John worked on Christian tasks, Betty felt he was copping out on his responsibility to work and save for the family they talked of starting.

Two years later, Betty went home during the summer to visit her parents for a few weeks. One day Betty phoned home.

"I've taken a job," she said simply.

"What does that mean?" John managed to ask, with a lump in his throat.

Betty didn't respond in terms of their relationship, but spoke only of her ambition to earn more money. They eventually filed for divorce, and their lawyers leveled off at each other. They lost the house they bought to the mortgage company.

How can a Christian couple go so far astray? The secular worldview competes directly with the Christian worldview. Since Christians are in a minority, we are often proselytized by the majority message of consumerism and materialism that is trying to convert us to a secular lifestyle. That's right — the disciples of the other worldview work just as hard as Christians do to make converts!

CHRISTIANS IN CAPTIVITY

Yes, these two predominant worldviews exist, but how many of us have drawn a sharp contrast between the two? How many of us have carefully chiseled ours by a search for truth? Or is our worldview more the product of our environment and circumstances?

Colossians 2:8 tells us, "See to it that no one takes you captive through hollow and deceptive philosophy, which depends on human tradition and the elemental spiritual forces of this world rather than on Christ."

The secularists have been doing a much better job of influencing our culture than we Christians. School prayer was made illegal in 1961, abortion was made legal in 1973, and the major networks stopped censoring their TV programming in 1989. Since those watershed decisions, virtually every other valued institution has experienced significant erosion.

Today, Christians in America are a minority. Christians are as much a minority, and their values and views are as impotent, as any minority group at any time in modern history. Why is this? Because we lead unexamined lives, many good men — Christian men — have been taken captive "through hollow and deceptive philosophy, which depends on human tradition and the elemental spiritual forces of this world." In other words, many of us are Christians in our spirit but secular in our practice. We have become a generation of cultural Christians.

We have seen things in bits and pieces instead of in totals. Archaeologists search the ruins of long-forgotten civilizations looking for, among other things, shards. A shard is a piece of broken pottery that the archaeologist studies. Then he visualizes what the object must have looked like by projecting from the broken pieces.

This is how we should lead our lives. We should look at every shard — every idea and theory we discover flowing through our minds — and see which worldview it represents. Too often we see events and circumstances as unrelated and isolated when, instead, we should try to visualize how they fit into the bigger picture of our worldview.

In his book *The Closing of the American Mind*, Dr. Allan Bloom spoke to the issue of leading an unexamined life. He made a compelling case for replacing the openness of our times, what he termed "the openness of indifference," with "the openness that invites us to the quest for knowledge and certitude."[6]

Dr. Bloom built the case that our society's "openness" is not one that pursues the truth with dogged determination, but an openness that presses to be "open to all kinds of men, all kinds of lifestyles, all ideologies." The only enemy is the man not open to everything.

The man who thinks like this is so blind that he can't tell you whether our daring circus rider is on horses or donkeys, nor could he tell you if one is better than the other—even if he were lucky enough to notice a difference.

This is not openness that examines its beliefs in pursuit of moral truth and good, but openness that finds its virtue in saying yes to everything—anything goes. The Christian's openness comes from his search for truth and absolutes. The secularist's openness exists because he makes up the truth in his own "best thinking" and has no absolutes. He thinks it doesn't matter what you believe, as long as you're sincere.

This captures one aspect of leading an unexamined life. We can know much, but if we do not use our knowledge to elevate ourselves—our mind, our soul, our spirit—to the highest level of moral good we can attain, then we are poor stewards of that knowledge. And we become Christians in captivity, held captive by the secular worldview, "captive through hollow and deceptive philosophy."

If we are going to live by the Christian worldview, we must recognize, first, that ours is a minority view and, second, that we are responsible for our own lives. Christ aches for us to turn to Him and follow His plan. But we are the ones who must decide to do it. *The first step to knowing God's plan for our lives is the commitment to see ourselves as we really are.*

THE TWO YOUS

There are two yous—the *visible* you and the *real* you. The visible you is the you that is known by others. We know intuitively from our experiences how to act and speak to fit in with our peer groups. We often act differently from one peer group to the next.

In high school, I was involved in three different peer groups. One was the jock crowd. When I worked out with the athletes, I talked tough and wouldn't smoke or drink.

Another peer group was the academics. I had been an honor student and liked these highbrows. We would discuss Darwinian theory and talk about the importance of science to the future of mankind.

The third group was the hell-raisers. All weekend long I would smoke, drink beer, cruise the drive-in restaurants, and look for girls. Frankly, I was a nervous wreck around campus. When I walked the halls with one peer group, my eyes constantly darted around. I feared seeing a friend from a different peer group—then I would be exposed as an impostor!

Even though I portrayed three different people at school, a fourth Pat Morley showed up at home every day after school. I was a walking identity crisis!

The visible you is the known you. It is never the real you. We have learned to speak and act in ways that allow us to cope with our world and peacefully coexist. We work hard to project a certain image of ourselves to others.

The real you is the you that is known by God. We are who we are in our minds first, before we speak or act. Our speech and actions are the result of our thinking. Scripture tells us, "The heart is deceitful above all things and beyond cure. Who can understand it?" (Jeremiah 17:9). To protect our self-image, we kid, trick, and fool ourselves into believing the *visible* you is somehow *real*. To see ourselves as we really are, we must acknowledge our inability to do so without God's help.

The mind is where the battle takes place. It's the battle between the majority view and the minority, Christian view. Ephesians 6:12 describes this battle for the mind: "For our struggle is not against flesh and blood, but against the rulers, against the authorities, against the powers of this dark world and against the spiritual forces of evil in the heavenly realms."

Because we don't take this invisible war seriously, many of us are losing the battle for our minds. But we can win them back by committing ourselves to self-examination through studying the Scriptures. You can know the real you, the you that is known by our God. Let's look at a promising tool to help us in the quest to understand ourselves.

"LOOK AT THE FISH"

Ralph Waldo Emerson listed Louis Agassiz second in his journal of the men he most admired, after Carlyle and before the likes of Thoreau and Oliver Wendell Holmes. Agassiz had a magic touch with people. At a young age, he gained an international reputation as a natural scientist.

Swiss born, he arrived in Boston in 1846 with boundless imagination and enthusiasm. He accepted a teaching post at Harvard University, where he conducted seemingly infinite investigations of fishes and fossils.

As great as the genius of Agassiz was in the study of fossils and fishes, his genius as a teacher was of far greater significance. He trained a whole generation of scientific men who achieved important stature of their own. Agassiz developed his own original method of instruction, which gave his students an opportunity to learn to think for themselves and to work out their own problems.

I first learned of Agassiz when I attended an executive education program at the Harvard Business School. The professors revere Agassiz and have immortalized him in the culture. His ideas on instruction are an integral part of the famous Harvard Business School case study method. The lesson for the man who would like to examine his life is considerable.

One of Agassiz's students, who later became a professor of near equal popularity, Mr. Scudder, gave this account of Agassiz's method:

> It was more than fifteen years ago [from 1874] that I entered the laboratory of Professor Agassiz ... He asked me a few questions about my object in coming ... "When do you wish to begin?" he asked.
>
> "Now," I replied.
>
> This seemed to please him, and with an energetic "Very well!" he reached from a shelf a huge jar of specimen in yellow alcohol.
>
> "Take this fish," said he, "and look at it ... By and by I will ask what you have seen." In ten minutes I had seen all that could be seen in that fish, and started in search of the Professor—who had, however, left the Museum ... Half an hour passed—an hour—another hour; the fish began to look loathsome. I turned it over and around; looked it in the face—ghastly; from behind, beneath, above, sideways, at a three-quarters' view—just as ghastly. I was in despair; at an early hour I concluded that lunch was necessary; so, with infinite relief, the fish was carefully replaced in the jar, and for an hour I was free.
>
> On my return, I learned that Professor Agassiz had been at the Museum, but had gone and would not return for several hours ... Slowly I drew forth that hideous fish, and with a feeling of desperation again looked at it ... I pushed my finger down its throat to feel how sharp the teeth were. I began to count the scales in the different rows, until I was convinced that that was nonsense. At last a happy thought struck me—I would draw the fish; and now with surprise I began to discover new features in the creature. Just then the Professor returned.
>
> "That is right," said he: "A pencil is one of the best of eyes. Well, what is it like?"
>
> He listened attentively to my brief rehearsal ...
>
> When I had finished, he waited as if expecting more, and then,

with an air of disappointment: "You have not looked very carefully ... look again, look again!" And he left me to my misery ...

I ventured to ask what I should do next.

"Oh, look at your fish!" he said ... And so for three long days he placed that fish before my eyes, forbidding me to look at anything else, or to use any artificial aid. "Look, look, look," was his repeated injunction.

This was the best entomological lesson I ever had—a lesson whose influence has extended to the details of every subsequent study; a legacy the Professor has left to me, as he has left it to many others, of inestimable value, which we could not buy, with which we cannot part ...

Agassiz's training in the method of observing facts and their orderly arrangement was ever accompanied by the urgent exhortation not to be content with them.

"Facts are stupid things," he would say, "until brought into connection with some general law."

At the end of eight months, it was almost with reluctance that I left these friends and turned to insects; but what I had gained by this outside experience has been of greater value than years of later investigation in my favorite groups.7

The main reason we lead unexamined lives is that we do not take time to "look at the fish," carefully looking for more and more. We can always see so much more, if we will only take the time to look. "Take this fish and look at it." Soon we discover that Professor Agassiz's criticism is just—we have not examined our lives carefully. With any good fortune we will soon be able to say, "No, I am certain I don't see it yet, but I see how little I saw before."

By the end of this book I hope it will be with Mr. Scudder's reluctance that you leave this study and turn to some new area of self-examination. With the Bible as your resource book, you will be able to find God's principle for every aspect of your life. You will be able to bring the bits and pieces of your life into connection with the general laws of God.

CONCLUSION

Have you been leading an unexamined life? Have you ever understood the dramatic differences in worldviews? Do you understand why you think the things you think, say the things you say, and do the things you do?

Or, like Dempsey, have you been taking it one day at a time?

"Okay," you say, "I'm convinced. I have decided there is more to know about the real me — the me that is known by God. What's the next step?"

There was a pastor who wanted to get to know a church visitor who was a sports enthusiast. Since the pastor liked boxing, he invited the man to a boxing match, to which the man had never been. Just before the fight started, one of the boxers made the sign of the cross.

"What does that mean?" asked the man.

The pastor quickly replied, "It doesn't mean a thing if the guy can't box."

Let's move on, then, and gain the skills we need to win the battle for our minds. The rest of this book will provide you with a framework to think about specific problem areas of your life — a framework to look at the fish.

———————— FOCUS QUESTIONS ————————

1. What would you like on your tombstone to summarize your life?

2. Which of your experiences and relationships do you think have had the greatest impact on how you think, speak, and act? In what ways have they influenced you for good? For bad?

3. Of the two worldviews, what percentage of each are you? Example: 60 percent Christian worldview, 40 percent

secular worldview. Describe the thinking that led you to your answer.

4. Are you the kind of person who gives thought to the *why* questions of life, or are you content with life as it is? What are some of the risks of leading an unexamined life?

5. There are two yous — the *visible* you that is known by others and the *real* you that is known only by God.

   ❑ Agree ❑ Disagree. Explain your answer.

6. Are you willing to allow God to show you yourself as you really are? What are some of the things you might find out about yourself?

7. The secret of knowing something well is to keep "looking at the fish." What kind of commitment would you be willing to make to self-examination in terms of time and effort?

CHAPTER 3

BIBLICAL CHRISTIAN OR CULTURAL CHRISTIAN?

A whole new generation of Christians has come
up believing that it is possible to "accept" Christ
without forsaking the world.
A. W. Tozer

Anyone who listens to the word but does not do
what it says is like someone who looks at his face
in a mirror and, after looking at himself, goes away
and immediately forgets what he looks like.
James 1:23–24

We've got a problem. Remember Larry and Carol—our couple from the first chapter? They're Christians.

"What!?" you say. "You've got to be kidding!"

I'm not kidding. In fact, I submit to you that the forces at work in Larry and Carol's lives are the rule and not the exception among Christian households today. Going one step further, I would also tell you that after meeting with thousands of men, I can't name more than a handful of men whose marriages are working the way they are supposed to.

In groups where I have made the adventurous statement, "I don't personally know ten men whose marriages are working like they are supposed to," I have never had anyone challenge me on it, nor has the body language ever shown any individual resistance to such a notion.

"Well, how could that happen to a Christian couple?" you may ask.

It's easier than you might first think.

THE PROBLEM

As we've seen, our material standard of living is up, but are we really better off? As I said in the introduction to this book, many men sense that something isn't quite right about their lives, but they can't quite put their finger on the answer. An eerie feeling lingers that they may be running in the wrong race. They see that they are more *financially* successful than their parents, but they suspect they may not be better off. What is really going on?

As we noted in the first chapter, a century of consumerism and media influence has caused a basic shift in values. Overall, we live in a culture dominated by the secular worldview.

The real problem we have is that it's not just happening to Larry and Carol and Mr. Silver — *it's happening to us too.*

TWO IMPOVERISHED VALUES

In his epic book *How Should We Then Live?* theologian Francis Schaeffer noted how changes in art, music, drama, theology, and the mass media have negatively affected our values.

Dr. Schaeffer underscored that the majority of people have adopted two impoverished values: *personal peace* and *affluence.* His perceptive analysis was immediately adopted as a consensus view because it had, and still has, the ring of truth. Here are his working definitions of those two values:

> Personal peace means just to be let alone, not to be troubled by the troubles of other people, whether across the world or across the city—to live one's life with minimal possibilities of being personally disturbed. Personal peace means wanting to have my personal life pattern undisturbed in my lifetime, regardless of what the result will be in the lifetimes of my children and grandchildren. Affluence means an overwhelming and ever-increasing prosperity—a life made up of things, things, and more things—a success judged by an ever-higher level of material abundance.[8]

Our spirits sense the truth of Dr. Schaeffer's observations, don't they? They give us a framework that helps explain a great deal of what we see happening in the world around us.

We saw in chapter 1 how we are lured into these two values by pursuing the Madison Avenue lifestyle.

But we also have the lingering problem of Larry and Carol—how could a *Christian* couple become so desperately entangled in these bankrupt, impoverished values? And the conspicuous question—how does it happen to us?

A THIRD IMPOVERISHED VALUE

Christianity is flourishing. There are more Christians today in America than ever before, both as a percentage and in total numbers. Roughly one in three Americans indicate they have asked Jesus to forgive their sins and grant them the gift of eternal life.

Here's the question: *If religion is such a big part of our lives, why isn't it making more of an impact on our society?* The sad reality is that claims of religious commitment run high, but impact is at an all-time low. At the very point when Christians have felt comfortable to come "out of the closet," our culture has sunk into a moral sewer.

So why is our culture in such turmoil? The answer is simple: While Christianity is flourishing, our culture is no longer guided by Christian values. Some people call this a post-Christian culture.

Here's what's interesting: While one in three are evangelical today, in 1800 only one in *fourteen* of America's 5.3 million citizens belonged to an evangelical church.[9] So while the number of Christians in America has grown dramatically, Christianity has *always* been in the minority in America.

Yet we once operated under the moral consensus of Judeo-Christian principles. Movies, television, literature, and other instruments of culture adhered to the morals of this consensus. That consensus has been breaking up for more than a hundred years and has accelerated rapidly over the past twenty-five years. So, while Christianity itself continues to flourish, secular culture no longer rests on Judeo-Christian values.

Essentially, Christianity and non-Christianity are both growing, but in different directions. So don't make the mistake of saying that Christianity is not working. It is! It is non-Christianity that is not working. Where our culture is wholesome, it is because of Christians and non-Christians who still hold to Judeo-Christian values. Everything else is a moral mess. Don't make the mistake of judging Christianity by the failures of non-Christianity.

Here's the problem: Although Christianity is flourishing, many of us who are Christians have gotten caught up in this increasingly bankrupt culture. We have adopted many of the values of the world around us. Maybe it's the new sexual ethics of cohabitation or pornography, rampant greed and materialism, or winking at the needs of the poor. Galatians 5:9 explains why adopting these values is a problem: "A little yeast works through the whole batch of dough." So when we try to have the best of both worlds, we exchange the truth of God for a lie and the glory of God for idols, we do what seems right in our own eyes, we get engrossed in the secular world, and we worship created things instead of the Creator.

When we don't run a good race, the unfortunate result is that a third impoverished value evolves: *cultural Christianity*. Cultural Christianity means pursuing the God we want instead of the God who is. It is the tendency to be shallow in our understanding of God, wanting Him to be more of a gentle, grandfatherly type who spoils us and lets us have our own way. It is sensing a need for God, but on our own terms. It is wanting the God we have underlined in our Bibles without wanting the rest of Him too. It is God relative instead of God absolute.

Cultural Christianity is Christianity made impotent. It is Christianity with little or no impact on the values and beliefs of our society. When the secular worldview is merged into the Christian worldview, neither one survives.

Cultural Christianity requires God to grant us personal peace and affluence to prove He loves us. It is God love, but not God holy. Actually, God loves us so much that He will cleanse the cultural Christianity from our lives, like the silversmith purifies silver by burning off the dross.

We often want God to be adjustable, like the transformer toys that children play with. We want him to adapt to our whims instead of us adapting to Him. Look for a moment at your own lifestyle. To what extent do you think these three values—personal peace, affluence, and cultural Christianity—describe your own life? What has been the result of this adaptive, cultural religion?

TWO KINDS OF CHRISTIANS

The ease with which people now associate themselves with religion has produced two kinds of Christians: *biblical Christians* and *cultural Christians*.

When we "look at the fish" in self-examination, perhaps the first observation we make is that among those who identify themselves as Christians, we lead sharply different lifestyles.

None of this is new, of course. It's only that the cycle has come around again. Jesus was the first to clarify the different types of people who would or would not associate with Him. The parable of the sower reveals four groups of hearers of the Word of God.

Group 1—The Non-Christian

"Those along the path are the ones who hear, and then the devil comes and takes away the word from their hearts, so that they may not believe and be saved."

Luke 8:12

Christ makes clear the point that not everyone who hears about salvation will believe.

Group 2—The Cultural Christian: Type "C"

"Those on the rocky ground are the ones who receive the word with joy when they hear it, but they have no root. They believe for a while, but in the time of testing they fall away."

Luke 8:13

Modern thinking is correct in believing that once a man is saved he is always saved. Christ affirms this by saying, "My sheep listen to my voice; I know them, and they follow me. I give them eternal life, and they shall never perish; no one will snatch them out of my hand" (John 10:27–28).

Modern thinking breaks down, though, by advertising to people that all they need to do is "pray a prayer" and they will be saved—born again. Everyone, it seems, has "prayed a prayer"! Prayer doesn't save; faith saves. More on this in the next chapter.

Type "C" stands for *counterfeit faith.* Among us are some who profess to be Christians, but in reality they are not Christians at all; they are cultural Christians—type "C." They have a counterfeit faith—a faith that is not a genuine faith in Christ. Jesus said, "Not everyone who says to me, 'Lord, Lord,' will enter the kingdom of heaven, but only the one who does the will of my Father who is in heaven" (Matthew 7:21).

The apostle Paul urges, "Examine yourselves to see whether you are in the faith; test yourselves. Do you not realize that Christ Jesus is in you — unless, of course, you fail the test?" (2 Corinthians 13:5).

Without sounding a false alarm, but in love, I encourage every man who finds himself to be a cultural Christian to consider whether his faith is merely a defeated faith or a counterfeit faith. If counterfeit faith is the condition of your life, don't be discouraged. God loves you with an everlasting love and wants to reconcile with you. In the next chapter we will look at how you can get on, or get back on, the right track.

Group 3 — The Cultural Christian: Type "D"

> "The seed that fell among thorns stands for those who hear, but as they go on their way they are choked by life's worries, riches and pleasures, and they do not mature."
>
> Luke 8:14

Early on, I noticed what many others have also observed about the purchasing habits of evangelical Christians compared to society at large: The majority of the time there is no difference. Why is this significant? Spiritually, if there is no difference in the way we as Christians live, then what is there about us that will recommend Jesus to those who don't know him yet? From a practical point of view, the typical U.S. family has right around $100,000 in household debt.[10] When as Christians we spend like the "typical family," we also will be bogged down with debts and run the race to acquire material possessions. As a result, the worries that follow choke the Word and make it unfruitful in our lives.

Sadly, there is little marginal difference between the way many Christians spend their money and the way non-Christians spend theirs. For a group whose primary commission is to be salt and light to a broken, confused world, this example does little to present a viable alternative to empty lifestyles.

Type "D" stands for defeated faith. The type "D" cultural Christian lives in defeat. There is little, if any, marginal difference between his lifestyle and the lifestyle of the man who makes no claim to be in Christ. He has never understood, perhaps because he has never been told, the difference between what it means to be a cultural Christian versus a biblical Christian. This book will be especially helpful for the man who falls in this category. This is the category I flirted with before God brought me to my senses.

Group 4 — The Biblical Christian

> "But the seed on good soil stands for those with a noble and good heart, who hear the word, retain it, and by persevering produce a crop."
>
> Luke 8:15

Biblical Christians don't live by their own ideas, but by penetrating, understanding, and applying the Word of God. By the Spirit, they experience the success and peace to which we each aspire.

A biblical Christian is a man who trusts in Christ, and Christ alone, for his salvation. As a *result* of his saving faith, he desires to be *obedient* to God's principles out of the overflow of a grateful heart (see Romans 1:5). Obedience doesn't save us; faith does. This explains why some men can be cultural Christians — they have a saving faith, but they have not obediently made Christ Lord over all their lives. They have not allowed the Holy Spirit to empower them.

People who associate themselves with Christ, then, fall into two broad categories: *biblical Christians* and *cultural Christians.* Among cultural Christians are those who have a *counterfeit* faith and those who have a *defeated* faith. Here's another way of putting it:

- Biblical Christian — a genuine faith (obedience)
- Cultural Christian
    Type "C" — a counterfeit faith (not genuine faith)
    Type "D" — a defeated faith (no power)

Why is there so much confusion about what it means to be a Christian?

AN AMBIGUITY OF TERMS

Because so many people have chosen to identify themselves as Christians, an ambiguity has developed about what it really means to be a Christian. It's a little like calling yourself a Republican or a Democrat. The label reveals far less about what you think and believe today than it did fifty years ago.

C. S. Lewis, in his 1943 book *Mere Christianity*, points out how words can be spoiled for their intended purpose. The word *gentleman* originally meant something exact — to be a gentleman you had to have a coat of arms and own property. To be called a gentleman was not a compliment, but a statement of fact. Over time, however, the term evolved into a way of complimenting a man instead of giving information about him. As a result, Lewis pointed out, *gentleman* is now useless for its original meaning — it has been spoiled for that purpose.[11]

The term *Christian* has also evolved to have broad and various intended meanings by those who use the term. A man is either a Christian or he is not. That fact is what it is, and no adjective is now, or ever will be, required to describe a true Christian. But because of the current ambiguity surrounding the term, thinking in terms of *cultural* or *biblical* is a useful way to explain the wide differences in what professing Christians think, say, and do. As Lewis pointed out, a Christian is a Christian, but he may be a good one or a bad one.

What does it mean to be a cultural Christian today?

LESSONS FROM ELEMENTARY SCHOOL

Do you remember your elementary school teacher demonstrating the principle of diffusion? She started with a clear glass of water. Then with an eyedropper she took some red food dye from a bottle and squeezed one drop into the glass. Within moments, the water was tainted with a pinkish hue as the dye permeated the water in the glass.

To be a cultural Christian in your parents' generation was to be like a clear glass of water with one drop of red dye. In other words, the secular culture was not that different from the Christian culture. That was before the days of Internet pornography, abortion on demand, explicit sex during prime-time TV, songs that degrade women, and a drug culture that's hard to avoid. So a man could be a cultural Christian and still be somewhat close to a Christian worldview and values.

To be a cultural Christian today is like having the whole bottle of red dye poured in the glass. The secular culture today is so polluted that to be a cultural Christian today means that your worldview and lifestyle are not tainted a pinkish hue but are contaminated by failed, impoverished values, three in number:

1. Personal peace
2. Affluence
3. Cultural Christianity

FROGS IN HOT WATER

Malcolm Muggeridge told the story about how to cook a frog. If you take a pot of boiling water and toss a frog in, the frog will immediately feel the heat and leap out of the pot. But if you start with a pot of cold water, put the frog in it, and slowly turn up the heat, the frog won't notice the change in temperature and won't leap out—he'll be cooked.

Like an unsuspecting frog in a cold pot, our values have been slowly "cooked" over the past few decades. If someone had been cryonically frozen one hundred years ago and we brought that person back to life today, he would jump out of this boiling pot we have created so fast our heads would spin!

Why don't we scream our lungs out over abortion on demand, illegal drugs, the federal deficit, and corruption? We don't jump up and down because over a period of years, like the unsuspecting frog that didn't notice the changing temperature, many of our values have gradually eroded—been "cooked"—and many of us have become cultural Christians.

Many of us have bought into our modern culture lock, stock, and barrel. Too often our values and beliefs reflect the bankrupt values of a shallow, hurting society. Instead of offering hope to a weary world, they look at us and think, "Well, I just don't see how Christ has made that much difference in your life. If that's what it means to be a Christian, then I'll just stay where I am."

The question for us all should be: *Is there any marginal difference between the way I live and the way the broken, hurting world lives? Does my life offer hope or disillusionment?*

Jesus said to one group of Christians, "I know your deeds, that you are neither cold nor hot. I wish you were either one or the other! So, because you are lukewarm—neither hot nor cold—I am about to spit you out of my mouth. You say, 'I am rich; I have acquired wealth and do not need a thing.' But you do not realize that you are wretched, pitiful, poor, blind and naked" (Revelation 3:15–17). Is Jesus saying this to you? Are you lukewarm, slowly being cooked—like the frog? If your answer is yes, then you have been living the life of a cultural Christian.

TOO BUSY

Ron Jenson rented a travel camper and traveled around the country with his wife while working on his doctoral thesis. His task was to interview 350 Christian leaders. At the end of this tour, he made a discouraging observation. He said, "I found a great deal of zeal for God's work, but very little passion for God." The one exception he found was Cru founder Bill Bright, who wept openly as he spoke about his love for Jesus.

Many of us are busy "doing" but are not keeping our personal relationship with God in tune. We can become so busy for Christ that we live in defeat in important areas of our personal lives. Christ said to another group of Christians, "I know your deeds, your hard work and your perseverance. I know that you cannot tolerate wicked people, that you have tested those who claim to be apostles but are not, and have found them false. You have persevered and have endured hardships for my name, and have not grown weary. Yet I hold this against you: You have forsaken the love you had at first" (Revelation 2:2–4). Is Jesus saying this to you? Have you become so busy with your own agenda that you have lost your passion for God? If your answer is yes, then you have been living the life of a cultural Christian.

Perhaps you have never before thought about what kind of a Christian you are. Or perhaps you have known you have not lived as you should, but you have not known how to make a change. Whichever the case, let's contrast the life of a cultural Christian and the life of a biblical Christian for clues about how to live. It has been said that understanding the problem is half the solution.

MARKET-DRIVEN VERSUS PRODUCT-DRIVEN

Former Chief Justice of the United States Supreme Court Frederick Moore Vinson once said, "Nothing is more certain in modern society than the principle that there are no absolutes."

Cultural Christians often think truth is relative—that it changes over time as circumstances change. The biblical Christian accepts Jesus' statement, "I am the way and the truth ..." (John 14:6). He finds no fault in old teachings having modern application. The lack of a hi-tech appearance to the Scriptures is a source of strength and encouragement, not embarrassment.

The biblical Christian is persuaded that the Bible, though often filled with mystery, reveals a personal God who has unchanging, absolute principles and precepts.

THAT MAY NOT BE SUCH A GOOD IDEA!

Every day, men of enormous intellect uncover new ideas that we embrace. I wonder who the genius was who first figured out that the federal government could borrow money? Have you ever considered that a majority elected Adolf Hitler to the leadership of the Nazi party?

The cultural Christian lives by his own ideas and the ideas of others. The 51 percent majority rule is the law of his mind. The biblical Christian lives by the Word of God and the counsel of the Holy Spirit.

Is the biblical Christian, then, ever allowed to question Scripture? Yes, of course. However, there is a difference between wrestling with a Scripture to understand the truth of it, to penetrate it, and to grasp its full depth and meaning versus wrestling with it to decide whether or not you think it's true. The first wrestling is seeking the terms of surrender. The second wrestling is a contest of our will against the will of God—a specific act of disobedience.

I met a man here in Orlando whose wife became a Christian. She felt the Lord was calling her to leave her family and take a public relations job in New York City. He was shattered. She wasn't open to the counsel of God's Word, and a disaster resulted. The biblical Christian will never live against the Word of God.

LOOKING OUT FOR NUMBER ONE

Who is number one in your life? The answer may reveal whether you are a cultural or biblical Christian.

Steve and his wife sold their businesses, he enrolled in graduate school out of state, and they purchased a home near the university.

When they went to close on the new house, the mortgage company wanted him to falsify some financial information.

"I can't do that," he told them.

"It's no big deal. Everybody does it," was the reply.

"I don't think you understand; I can't do that."

"It just goes in the file; nobody will ever even look at it. Besides, if you don't, then we can't give you the loan."

Steve really believed God had led them to the decision to return to school. Now his peace was shattered. To complete the move he would have to compromise his integrity. The decision was really quite simple: "Who will I put first in this decision—my own desires or Christ?"

We must often make similar decisions. Do we interrupt our personal peace by putting Christ first? Do we cheerfully accept a setback in our standard of living? Or do we go ahead because "everybody does it"?

Steve decided to return to school locally instead of moving out of state on a lie. To put himself first would have been easy. Who would know? Who would even care? He decided to put Jesus first, and he couldn't be more at peace.

Many Christian men have adopted the three impoverished values of our time: personal peace, affluence, and cultural Christianity. They become number one in their own lives. The biblical Christian puts his relationship with Jesus at the top of the list. He strives to "seek first his kingdom and his righteousness..." (Matthew 6:33).

Obedience is the trademark of a biblical Christian. That is how we demonstrate our love to God and truth to a weary culture.

How can a man become a biblical Christian? If you have been a cultural Christian, how can you make the change?

SELF-EXAMINATION

The man who has been living as a cultural Christian can change by examining the *influences* on his life and the *values* he has adopted.

If you think you have been a cultural Christian, then examine the influences on your life. Look at the church you attend. Is it a biblical church? How about your friends—what worldview do they represent? What forms of entertainment, media, art, and music do you expose your mind to?

Look at the values you have lived by. Are they biblical or cultural values? Today's society embraces the three impoverished values of personal peace, affluence, and cultural Christianity.

PATIENT FOR CHANGE

When I became a Christian, I asked God for help on two serious, practical problems I struggled with. The first was cursing. Almost instantly, without any help or assistance from me, the cursing ceased. My wife mentioned one day, "Pat, you hardly swear at all anymore."

I was flabbergasted. I had made no conscious effort to stop, nor was I aware that a change had even occurred.

The other struggle was with my temper. I would become too angry. Many regrettable words escaped from my mouth. Although the Lord quickly helped me with cursing, the temper problem lingered for five long, tearful years. Virtually every day I would have to ask forgiveness. There were many tears and long prayers pleading with God for help. But five years passed before my level of anger became a normal person's level of anger.

Here's the point: We didn't get to be the men we are overnight, and we may need to allow some time, perhaps a long time, before we will see our lives the way we want them to be.

A LOOK IN THE MIRROR

The man in the mirror will never change until he is willing to see himself as he really is and to commit to know God as He really is.

This objectivity anchors a man; it gives him the clarity of thought he needs to be a biblical Christian.

Is the man looking back at you in the mirror a cultural Christian or a biblical Christian? These pages are dedicated to helping each of us self-examine and reshape our values and beliefs so we can be biblical Christians in a weary, broken world.

FOCUS QUESTIONS

1. Think of a Christian couple you know who is having marriage problems. In what ways do you think their conformity to cultural values has contributed to their struggle?

2. Dr. Francis Schaeffer says that modern society has two impoverished values: personal peace and affluence. Do you agree with Dr. Schaeffer? Why or why not?

3. In what ways have you pursued the values of personal peace and affluence?

4. Are you more financially successful than your parents? Is the quality of your personal life more successful than your parents? Why or why not?

5. How would you define *cultural Christianity*?

6. After reading this chapter, would you call yourself a *biblical* Christian or a *cultural* Christian? Why?

7. If you are a cultural Christian, how do you think you became that way? What do you think are the factors that contributed to your worldview?

8. If you are a biblical Christian, what advice would you give to a cultural Christian that might help him get on the right track?

9. Where is the "red dye" in your life? What do you need to do to get it out?

CHAPTER 4

SIGNIFICANCE: THE SEARCH FOR MEANING AND PURPOSE

The mass of men live lives
of quiet desperation.
Henry David Thoreau

"I have come that they may have life,
and have it to the full."
Jesus, John 10:10

Freeport, the Bahamas. Howard Hughes, the richest man in the world. The Xanadu, a ten-story condominium on the ocean.

Who isn't fascinated by the lives of the rich and famous? Howard Hughes, perhaps the most eccentric of wealthy men, fled to the Bahamas in self-exile.

Shunning public contact for the last twenty years of his life, Hughes once refused to appear before a Senate subcommittee, but instead spoke to them by phone from his top-floor penthouse at the

Xanadu. Mormon guards, hired for their honesty, quarantined Mr. Hughes from contact with outsiders in his impregnable stronghold.

As I walked up to the imposing front door of the penthouse compound, I noticed a small porthole window covered with several strips of 3M reflective film. It seemed odd that such a makeshift arrangement would greet visitors at the threshold that led to the richest man in the world.

Howard Hughes was dead, but two years later his estate had still maintained the four penthouse condominiums that he had converted to a fortress for himself.

Nervous as a cat, I peered through the film-covered window but couldn't see a thing, even though the edges were starting to peel up. Just then the elevator chime startled me, and I jumped around to see a maid coming out of the elevator cab.

She gave me the evil eye, but I put on my best smile and told her how much I admired Mr. Hughes, and since he was deceased, did she think it would be all right for me to go in and look around?

She hesitated, still suspicious, but I could tell she saw some humor in my silly request, so I picked up the gab. Finally she shrugged, as if to say why not, and took me in.

I don't know what I expected, but what I saw was a shock! I imagined the richest man in the world would import opulent chandeliers and expensive rare art. I visualized seeing the fingerprints of some famous European designer in the decor.

The sparse, austere furnishings made it look more like a rustic mountain cabin. Worn, threadbare, olive-green plaid cushions rested in cut-rate-priced wooden couch frames. The bathroom fixtures looked like those you would find in a cheap motel.

The further I penetrated into Hughes's secret world of intrigue, the louder my heart pounded. My legs went adrenaline-weak, that same feeling you get after a near miss on the expressway. As I crept through the boardinghouse-like rooms, I romanticized Hughes eating, sleeping, making important intercontinental calls, and wiring cables. I could almost see him sitting at his desk scribbling out his famous handwritten notes to subordinates.

His wealth and power and fame were unmatched by any other man of his time. Yet this final hideaway, where he sequestered himself from reality, was a stark reminder that money is a mortal god. Howard Hughes died a prisoner in the citadel of his own power, betrayed by his fame. His impact began to fade into the dusty pages of history the instant his flesh turned cold.

THE PROBLEM

What do you think is a man's greatest need? Someone recently mentioned they would like their tombstone to read, "He made a difference." Whether we speak of achieving our full potential or only of surviving to the next paycheck, men invariably talk about their need to be significant. A man's most innate need is his need to be significant—to find purpose and meaning:

"I want to make a difference."

"I want my life to count."

"I want my life to have meaning."

"I want to have an impact."

"I want to make a contribution."

"I want to do something important with my life."

"I want to conquer, achieve, excel, prove myself."

"I want to be somebody."

"I want my life to be significant."

The difference in men is in how we go about satisfying our need to be significant. Some men, eager for the spoils of this life, pursue significance by gratifying only their own ambitions. Others, trained by the Scriptures, find it by obeying God.

How we each answer the questions *"Who am I?"* and *"Why do I exist?"* determines how we pursue our significance. Our answers divide us succinctly into two groups: those who pursue significance in appropriate ways and those who pursue significance in inappropriate ways. Our desire to satisfy this need can take us close to or far away from the things of God.

Authentic, lasting significance is hid with Christ. Jesus said, "I am the vine; you are the branches. If you remain in me and I in you, you will bear much fruit; *apart from me you can do nothing*" (John 15:5, italics added). That is to say, a man cannot find significance in any lasting way apart from Christ. So, if a man is in Christ, and submitted to God's plan and purpose, then he can satisfy his greatest need in a way that endures. Otherwise, his efforts, like Howard Hughes's, will return to room temperature within hours of his death.

A MAN'S HIGHEST HOPE

Ted is a charmer; his broad smile is contagious. He has attained social stature and financial independence. As the chairman of a large enterprise, he is powerful and influential—and he has many friends.

He owns several homes and has been a genuine contributor to the welfare of our community. It's hard not to like Ted. He has pursued significance and found it, according to his own rule book. But has he really? The answer depends on how you define the term.

What is the highest hope of a man who does not have Christ? Most men will never see their name in the newspaper. If you were a really great man—someone of national reputation—what would be the most you might expect from history? At the very best, if you were a giant in your time, the most you could expect would be a few pages on Wikipedia. Just look up Howard Hughes.

A man's ultimate desire is for immortality. "He has also set eternity in the human heart" (Ecclesiastes 3:11). That's part of what we mean when we say we want to be significant. We want "something" to survive us. In our search for immortality, how do we live on? Is it in our accomplishments, our legacy to our children, or a couple of paragraphs on Wikipedia? Some wealthy men finance hospital wings and have university buildings named for them to achieve a measure of immortality.

How we decide to answer the questions *"Who am I?"* and *"Why do I exist?"* is a choice between two time lines—one that's eighty years long and one that lasts forever.

If we do not ultimately find our significance in Christ, then we will not survive the threshold between this world and the next. Our highest hopes will come to a screeching halt. It would be better if we had never been born.

INAPPROPRIATE WAYS OF FINDING SIGNIFICANCE

No one can question that many of us get caught up in the rat race—the conflict between who we are created to be and who we are tempted to be. Many people satisfy their need to be significant without Christ. The difference in the *quality* and *durability* of that significance, however, is monumental. Why settle for the crumbs under the table when you can join in the feast? Yet many of us pursue significance in ways that are inappropriate. Let's look at some common ways the world defines significance.

Fame: Short Memories

Once my daughter and I went with friends to the U.S. Open tennis tournament. Moments before the women's championship final match began, they introduced the great women champions of yesteryear, from the oldest to the youngest.

These former champions were not introduced to just any crowd, but to enthusiastic New Yorkers! Yet as the first elderly woman was escorted to center court, there were only a few polite claps from a handful of fans. Then as the announcer introduced the next one, the applause picked up a little. This continued, with each former star gaining an increment of more applause.

Finally they introduced someone whose name I recognized, and I joined in the applause. By the time they called Billie Jean King's name, the applause turned from polite to robust. But when they called out Chris Evert, the great lady of tennis, the stands went wild with thunderous approval!

As I sat in the stands observing this, I couldn't help but think how the first doddering old lady had been the Chris Evert of her year. But just fifty years later, she was receiving only a few polite claps from a handful of fans. I wondered if she thought her significance would endure? And I wondered how many years it would be before Chris Evert was forgotten, worthy of only a few polite claps from a handful of courteous fans.

Memories are short. When we try to answer the question "Who am I?" in terms of our fame and worldly accomplishment, we select an identity that will fade like sun-bleached furniture.

Possessions: Unsatisfied Eyes

For Christmas one year, I bought my wife an expensive, solid-gold Swiss watch. I must confess I didn't do this charitably out of a desire to honor her. My actual motive was a bit more sinister.

You see, I wanted an expensive, solid-gold Swiss watch myself, but didn't feel like I could just go out and buy one. I had a problem. Patsy and I had exchanged watches as wedding gifts, and the watch on my wrist was the one-and-the-same, sentimentally engraved wedding gift.

I needed a dignified plan to dispose of the watch I already wore. I thought about it for years. Finally, I got a break. My wife's thirteen-year-old watch started to die. A plan started to take shape. If I bought Patsy an expensive new watch, then I could buy the companion watch after a reasonable amount of time passed.

Why did I want the new watch? Did I need it? No, I just wanted a symbol to let people know I had arrived. We all use our possessions to send signals for us that we are significant—we are "somebody."

The advantage of flashing our stuff is that we don't actually have to be tacky and say something self-serving.

The most fleeting significance comes from things. Once I purchased a new luxury car. I will always remember how the metallic-blue paint glistened in the sun, and the aroma from the white leather seats was like a sweet perfume to a young materialist.

About three weeks after I bought it, the novelty began to wear off, and I noticed the same car, but in a different color. I wished I had bought the other color instead!

When possessions and money become a surrogate for our real identity, who we are is tied to things that rust and rot away.

POWER: WHAT'S HIS NAME AGAIN?

Former Secretary of the Interior Donald Hodell remarked about the obscurity of former Cabinet members. As a member of President Reagan's Cabinet, he reminded his department heads not to be too enamored with their titles. He pointed out that no one remembers former secretaries — much less, important department heads. He quipped, "Some people working in the bowels of this department don't even remember who the former secretaries were!"

Men who achieve significant positions of responsibility and authority in this life run one of the greatest risks. _The risk is to identify who you are as a person with the position._ The heartache comes when you no longer have the position, and you realize people were not interested in you because you were _you_ but because of the position you held, which they believed could benefit them in some way.

Answering the "Who am I?" question in terms of our position betrays a faulty definition of significance.

The ability to control people, the ability to influence the big decisions, the ability to change the course of history — these have been chief ways of satisfying a man's need to be significant from the earliest days of recorded history.

The most visible arena in which men seek power is the political arena. Yet as intensely as men lust for power in elective office, the pursuit of significance through power equally tempts business, labor, military, and religious leaders.

The thrill of closing the big deal, the power to allocate massive resources to a project, the ability to persuade a prospect to buy your product even at higher prices than your competitors'—these accomplishments are intoxicating and give the aura of power. We can begin to believe we have special abilities mere mortals are not endowed with!

A retired man said, "We come into this world as babies, and that's the way we go out. I used to be able to pick up the phone and talk to anybody I wanted to. Enjoy your power while you can, because once you retire, they don't return your calls anymore."

The Game of Tens

If you think a man can find lasting significance through the pursuit of fame, possessions, or power, then take this pop quiz to test your "significance IQ":

1. Can you name the ten wealthiest men in the world?
2. Can you name the ten most admired men in America?
3. Can you name the ten top corporate executives in America?
4. Can you name the last ten Presidents of the United States?
5. Can you name the last ten Nobel Prize winners?
6. Can you name the ten members of the President's current Cabinet?

The Game of Tens is a ruthless, heartless, but objective illustrator of the folly of pursuing significance apart from Jesus Christ. Can you think of any other Tens to guess? Even the highest achievers of our society are, as James wrote, mist that appears for a little while and then vanishes (see James 4:14).

To go a step further, play the Game of Tens this way:

1. Name your ten best friends.
2. Name ten family members who love you.
3. Name the ten most memorable experiences of your life.
4. Name ten people who you think will attend your funeral.
5. Name ten questions you want to ask God.

THE SELF-GRATIFICATION/ SIGNIFICANCE DISTINCTION

Our society — as the scales have tipped toward individual rights and away from Judeo-Christian values — has immersed itself in pursuit of self-gratifying activity. Focus on personal peace and affluence has largely replaced deeply held, self-sacrificing convictions (and the resulting community-building causes) that benefit the human condition. But the path to significance is bigger than the individual.

We often only spend our energies to satisfy ourselves rather than to serve others. *Significance is not possible unless what we do contributes to the welfare of others.* If what I do is only for my self-gratification and pleasure, then I will never derive a lasting sense of purpose and meaning from it. On the other hand, when I embark on a task that will pass the test of benefiting others, a sense that what I am doing is important grows within me. And if I make helping others my practice, a state of significance results.

One day I was riding by our new church as it neared the completion of construction. As a building committee member, I swelled with significance as I imagined the generations of children who will remember that facility as a focal point of their childhood activities.

I did not serve on the committee to make me feel better about myself or to improve my self-image. I served to make a contribution to others, and, in a sense, I had to deny myself to make the contribution of time. The result is a knowledge that I am leading a life of significance.

Christ put it this way: "Whoever wants to be my disciple must deny themselves and take up their cross and follow me. For whoever wants to save their life will lose it, but whoever loses their life for me will find it. What good will it be for someone to gain the whole world, yet forfeit their soul?" (Matthew 16:24 – 26).

The difference between self-gratification and significance is found in the *motive* and *attitude*, not in the *task*. Two men working side by side in an office can fulfill the exact same job description, yet have entirely different impacts.

One fellow runs on the fast track. It's a race uphill, always fighting for the next rung on the ladder, climbing higher, grabbing glory. The other man finds great reward in mentoring younger associates. He counsels, exhorts, and encourages. Everyone knows he is a Christian, but he doesn't smite his colleagues with his biblical knowledge.

These two men actually perform the same tasks. The attitudes and motives, however, distinguish one as only a seeker of self-fulfillment and self-gratification. The other is experiencing a significant, meaningful life, contributing to others in love and faith.

Here's the *significance test*: "Does what I am about to do contribute to the welfare of others in a demonstration of faith, love, obedience, and service to Christ?" That's putting wheels on denying ourselves, taking up our cross, and following Jesus. If we sacrifice our lives in this way, the irony of Scripture is that we save ourselves. Accumulating wealth, power, influence, and prestige are self-gratifying, but none of this will satisfy a man's need to be significant in a lasting way.

BEING A DOER

The smell of fall was in the air, and the small town of Wittenberg, Germany, was just beginning to bundle up for the winter. Over at the university, a young, unassuming scholar was asking himself the question, "How can a man find favor with God?"

The deeper he penetrated this question, the greater his frustration and outrage with his beloved church grew. This young monk didn't

idol is anything you think you can't live without

want to be a rebel, yet the abuses he observed in his own church drove him to record the injustices he saw.

One disgraceful practice to increase church revenue was to accept payment for the forgiveness of sins. In other words, one could sin and obtain forgiveness for that sin by payment of money to the church — without repentance.

In 1508 this young man, who took his original studies in law, began teaching his beliefs at the University of Wittenberg, attracting students from all over Germany. His disgust came to a head in 1517 when John Tetzel, a representative of the Pope, came to Germany selling certificates pre-signed by the Pope, offering a pardon of all sins to whomever procured one. A man could even buy them for relatives!

Over the years, a vision of God's purpose for the young man's life took shape. On October 31, 1517, a trembling Martin Luther marched to the front doors of the Castle Church in Wittenberg, where he posted ninety-five theses, soon to become famous throughout the world.

It was a turning point of all Christian history, the result of one man unsatisfied with what he saw when he looked at the man in the mirror. "Do not merely listen to the word, and so deceive yourselves. Do what it says. Anyone who listens to the word but does not do what it says is like someone who looks at his face in a mirror and, after looking at himself, goes away and immediately forgets what he looks like" (James 1:22 – 24).

He decided not to merely listen to the Word of God, but to become a doer. Over the next forty years, half of the churches in Europe became Protestant, beginning the Protestant Reformation. Social, political, and economic structures were reformed; even the Roman Catholic Church made changes.

Certainly young Martin Luther had no idea of the impact — the significance — his life would have. But because he was willing to study the Bible, to let God speak to him, and to be a doer of the Word, he was able to be used by God. Because he believed God, he found *significance*, and God gave young Luther a *purpose* for his life.

In your search for significance, have you sought a purpose for your life by studying the Scriptures? Any one of us who desires to satisfy his need to be significant must study the Scriptures and ask God to show him His purpose for his life. Then he must faithfully be a doer of what God tells him.

FAITHFULNESS

Today Europe is a post-Christian continent. Many of the great, ornate churches of the leading cities are museums and tourist attractions. What would have happened if, in each generation, a handful of men had the same courage to be doers of the Word like young Martin Luther? God's order would have been continually reestablished. Why hasn't it happened? The answer must be, at least in part, that there were not enough faithful men.

Many think America is headed in the same direction as Europe— if it's not already there. Does America have a handful of faithful men who will stand in the gap and work to make sure that doesn't happen? Wouldn't you like to be one of them?

At lunch one day, a deeply committed man related his discouragement with his profession, and his belief that God might have a full-time ministry for him. At the time, he led a Bible study and was responsible for discipling six men. To his own surprise, our discussion revealed he was not being completely faithful to his responsibilities to care for these men.

He came to the conclusion on his own: "Why should God give me a greater job when I am not yet a faithful doer of the job He has already given me?" You and I would never consider promoting someone who wasn't doing the job they already had!

Now he is achieving significance without a career change. What's the difference? His faithfulness to do the job God had already given him.

Does your life feel impotent? Are you achieving your full

potential? Or are you stuck in a quagmire of insignificance? If you are not experiencing the full measure of significance you desire, then apply these diagnostics to your life:

1. Am I trying to win the rat race?
2. Do I fully understand how God keeps score?
3. Am I leading a life of faith, love, obedience, and service?
4. What is my highest hope?
5. How did I score on the Game of Tens?
6. Am I pursuing significance or self-gratification?
7. Am I disillusioned with materialism?
8. Has my passive indifference contributed to the decaying state of the nation?
9. Have I been looking for significance in inappropriate ways?
10. Am I willing to pay the price if the cost of being a Christian in society goes up?
11. Am I a talker or a doer?
12. Have I been faithful with what God has entrusted to me?
13. Do I regularly study God's Word so He can show me the purpose for my life?
14. Am I contributing to God's agenda? Do I even know what God's agenda is?
15. Am I a cultural Christian or a biblical Christian?

If you are dissatisfied with the thrust of your answers, then let me encourage you to pause for a moment. Acknowledge to God that you have sinned, and thank Him for forgiving your sins through the sacrificial death and resurrection of Jesus. If you have been a cultural Christian with a "defeated" faith, ask Christ to take control of your life; rededicate yourself to Him. If you have been playing games with God, confess that to Him. If you have been guilty of the sin of partial surrender — trying to have your cake and eat it too — totally surrender yourself to Him. Ask Him to lead and guide you by His Spirit to a purpose for your life that will give you lasting significance. And then ask Him to give you the power to be faithful. Take a moment and do this right now.

If you have never placed your faith in Jesus Christ, or if you have been a cultural Christian with a "counterfeit" faith, there will never be a better time to receive Christ than right now. Christ offers the only lasting significance. He gives us an identity that never fades, rusts, or rots away. As He said, "Apart from me you can do nothing."

How many really big decisions will we each make in our lifetime? Certainly, the decision of whether or not to become a Christian ranks right at the top. Can you think of anything worse than coming to the wrong conclusion about Christ?

If you sincerely desire to become a Christian, then invite Him into your heart and life. We receive Christ by faith and repentance. Prayer is an excellent way to express faith. Here is a suggested prayer:

Lord Jesus, I acknowledge that I have been attempting to find significance in an inappropriate way. As a result, I have sinned against You. Thank You for dying on the cross for me and forgiving my sins. As an act of faith, I invite You to come into my life and direct me. Take control of my life, and make me into the kind of man You want me to be. Amen.

If this prayer expresses your desire, why not kneel wherever you are and invite the living God to take up residence in your life. True significance is hidden with Christ. Apart from Him we can do nothing.

If you prayed and invited Christ into your life, you can be sure you have just made the most important decision of your life. You will learn more about what to do next as you read on.

——————————— FOCUS QUESTIONS ———————————

1. A man's greatest need is his need to be significant.

   ❑ Agree ❑ Disagree. Explain your answer.

2. The difference in men is in how they go about satisfying their need to be significant.

❏ Agree ❏ Disagree. What are some of the main ways men try to satisfy this need?

3. How do you keep score? At the end of the day, how do you measure whether or not it has been a successful day? How does your method compare to the way God keeps score?

4. How did you score on the Game of Tens? What truth does this game underscore?

5. What is the difference between self-gratification and significance?

6. What Martin Luther did was simply to live out his conscience. Why do you think more men don't do the same?

7. What would you do differently if you decided to be another Martin Luther, one of this generation's handful of faithful men?

8. Did you receive Christ or rededicate your life to Him? If yes, what are the next two or three steps you should take as a result?

CHAPTER 5

PURPOSE: WHY DO I EXIST?

Man's chief end is to glorify God,
and to enjoy Him forever.
Westminster Shorter Catechism

The LORD foils the plans of the nations;
he thwarts the purposes of the peoples.
But the plans of the LORD stand firm forever,
the purposes of his heart through
all generations.
Psalm 33:10 – 11

The most surprising thing about Tom's call wasn't that he was crying; it wasn't even that he was fifty-eight years old and crying. But his candor really got my attention — Tom is one of Florida's most prominent attorneys.

"My life has no meaning — no purpose," he began. "It's as though I've been chasing the wind all these years."

He attended a leadership prayer breakfast we sponsor every Thanksgiving. For the next six months he couldn't stop thinking about what he heard. Tom found the message of Jesus intriguing and called to say he was interested in the whole story. We made an appointment to talk about it.

As Tom unfolded the story of his life, the vast array of accomplishments on his résumé awed me. He was a man of stature. His list of credits revealed a Who's Who in the legal field. I would have imagined him to be a satisfied man, were it not for the stream of tears that diluted the value of those achievements.

Tom had reached the pinnacle of professional success, yet still ached for a sense of purpose in his life. He had attained the rung on the ladder every young lawyer aspires to, but he found that the ladder only reached up into clouds of disillusionment. Success created more questions for him than it answered.

Tom spent a lifetime pursuing the god he wanted. Then one day, he woke up and realized he didn't have the slightest idea who God really is. Aware of just how unfulfilled he was, and not knowing why, he had accepted an invitation from a friend to our prayer breakfast.

Maybe God will have some answers, he thought.

What interested Tom most was the peace he saw in some of the men involved with the prayer breakfast. Over the six months that followed, he was surprised to learn these men attributed their sense of peace and purpose to a "personal relationship" with God through Jesus Christ.

"I've always attended church," he insisted.

"We're not talking about attending church, although that's important. What we're talking about, Tom, is a relationship with the living, personal God."

"We are not talking about working your way into God's favor, but acknowledging it's impossible to work your way in. The only way into God's favor is to receive the free gift of eternal life that comes by trusting Christ with your life."

"Well, I've been a faithful churchman for over thirty years," he said. "Are you trying to tell me I've wasted all those years? I just can't believe you would even suggest such a thing!"

"Tom, if church has been such an important part of your life, why are we together today talking about your feelings of emptiness and lack of purpose?"

Tom is not alone. He lived the first fifty-eight years of his life without giving much attention to why he thought, said, and did things. He attended church because it was the expected thing to do, not because of a deeply held conviction. Many men are like Tom—just going through the motions.

THE PROBLEM

Do you enjoy setting and meeting goals? I do—I find achieving goals intoxicating! A number of years ago I set a goal of achieving a certain income level. I felt a deep sense of personal satisfaction when I finally reached my goal. But after a few weeks, the novelty wore off, and I wanted more.

One of the most perplexing problems men face is that met goals tend to become an unrelated string of hollow victories, increasingly frustrating as more and more are achieved. That's the problem with goals: You have to keep setting new ones, because achieving them doesn't provide any lasting satisfaction.

The fleeting satisfaction of a met goal begs the question: "Is there something bigger for my life than the routine of setting and meeting goals?"

Before we set goals, we would do well to answer the questions, "Why do I exist? What is the purpose of my life?" To be satisfying, our goals need to reflect our examination of life's larger meaning. The plain truth is that most men either don't know their purpose in life, or their purpose is too small. A man can do nothing more important than to wrestle with the purpose of his life.

IDENTITY VERSUS PURPOSE

There are two aspects to finding significance. The first one answers the fundamental question, "Who am I?" which we concentrated on in the last chapter. The other answers life's second big question, "Why do

I exist?" We derive meaning and identity from understanding *who we are* in Christ. It's a *position* we occupy. It's a *relationship* with God, not a thing to be found through fame, fortune, and power.

On the other hand, God has a purpose for our lives—a mission, a destiny—which is *why we exist.* It is the other half of our search for significance. Once you settle the issue of who you are, the next question is, "What does God want me to do with my life?"

The only purposes that will survive are ones linked to God. "Many are the plans in a person's heart, but it is the LORD's purpose that prevails" (Proverbs 19:21). Once we understand the direction He wants us to take—our purpose—then we can set goals to move us in that direction.

GOALS VERSUS PURPOSE

What is the difference between a *goal* and a *purpose*? A goal is a specific objective we want to accomplish. We will know when we have achieved it, such as with buying a home or saving a certain amount of money to retire. Some insist that goals are "hard," that they must be measurable and require a specific completion date. Others believe goals can be more "soft"—qualitative, not just quantitative.

For example, if you want to become a more loving person, measuring whether or not you have achieved a more loving spirit is subjective. Nevertheless, becoming more loving is a worthwhile goal. So I suggest we cast off strict definitions of a goal except to say that we should be able to determine whether or not we have achieved it.

Purposes, on the other hand, answer life's larger questions—not "What do I do today?" but "Why do I exist?" and "What are my functions in life?" They reflect our examination of life's larger meaning. Our purpose is what God wants us to do long-term. Once we know this purpose, we can set goals to advance us toward the answers we give to these questions.

Purposes are threads of continuity that we weave into the

long-term view of our lives. Goals come and go, but purposes survive because they are long-term; they pertain to the *why we exist* part of our lives. They relate to how we perceive *the theory of our lives*.

Purposes are a place to begin. They help us focus our lives and give them direction so our goals do not become an unrelated string of hollow victories.

THE WHAT/WHY DISTINCTION

One spring, we decided to enroll our daughter in a Christian elementary school for the upcoming fall. That was our goal—what we had decided to do. The broader question to ask is, "Why did we pursue this goal?" We believe one of God's purposes for our lives is to give our children a heart for God. It's bigger than a goal for us. It's a thread of continuity we are weaving into everything we do with both of our children. We believe it's one of the primary reasons we exist, one of our functions as Christian parents.

As we looked at the theory of our lives, we believed the goal of a Christian education fit into the purpose—the direction—we have discerned for our lives. When we looked at why we existed as parents, we felt giving our children a "spiritual edge" was worth it. The *goal* (*what*) was the school enrollment. The *purpose* (*why*) was to work toward giving our children a heart for God.

Goals are *what* we do. Purposes are *why* we do what we do. When you set a goal, do you ever ask yourself, "Why am I pursuing this goal?" The answer to this question reveals your purpose. This distinction between *what* we do and *why* we do what we do is an important one. If we can examine each goal we set in clear view of why we want to achieve it, then we can set goals that build toward our understanding of God's purpose for our lives rather than for our own motives.

ETERNAL PURPOSE VERSUS EARTHLY PURPOSE

The Westminster Confession of Faith endures as one of Christianity's most comprehensive statements of faith. The Westminster Assembly, first called by an act of the English Parliament on June 12, 1643, had as its objective to clarify the doctrines of the Christian faith by careful examination of the Holy Scriptures. King Charles I had placed the civil and religious liberties of England in serious jeopardy, and Parliament mustered to battle the absolutist monarch by creating the Assembly.

The Westminster Shorter Catechism, an important product of the Assembly, asks and answers 107 essential questions that form the basic tenets of the Christian faith. Profoundly, the first question asked is, "What is the chief end of man?" We might rephrase it, "What is the purpose of man?" or "Why does a man exist?"

The answer is at once both eloquent and simple: "Man's chief end is to glorify God, and to enjoy him forever."

We can draw a distinction between God's *eternal* purpose for us and His *earthly* purpose. In Matthew 6:31 – 33, Jesus tells us, "So do not worry, saying, 'What shall we eat?' or 'What shall we drink?' or 'What shall we wear?' For the pagans run after all these things, and your heavenly Father knows that you need them. But seek first his kingdom and his righteousness, and all these things will be given to you as well."

The *kingdom* of God is an *unseen* realm, while the *righteousness* of God is the *seen*. We are instructed to seek both the seen and the unseen. God has an eternal purpose for us that is part of the unseen kingdom of God. He also has an earthly purpose for us as we live in the tangible, seen world.

In the Catechism's answer we find both God's eternal purpose — to enjoy Him forever — and His earthly purpose — to glorify God. God's eternal purpose for us is to seek His kingdom, by which we enjoy Him forever. And His earthly purpose for us is to seek His righteousness, by which we glorify God. As the chief end of man, this means we are to give priority above all else to the knowing and the doing of God's eternal and earthly purpose for us.

Eternal Purpose

When Jesus tells us to seek His kingdom, He is telling us to seek eternal life. The kingdom of God is an unseen kingdom. Jesus said, "My kingdom is not of this world ... But now my kingdom is from another place" (John 18:36).

The unseen kingdom is a volunteer kingdom. Jesus does not force Himself on us; rather, through Jesus, we are offered a new birth. This new birth is into a realm that lasts forever.

God's eternal purpose for us is to enjoy Him forever. This is the most important part of our relationship with God. If God did not have as His purpose to give us eternal life (so that we can enjoy Him forever), then our faith would be futile. Our faith would not be enough to get us beyond the threshold of death.

Foremost in our thinking about why we exist is to seek God in His unseen kingdom so that we can pass forth to new life, like a butterfly bursting forth from a cocoon (see John 6:38 – 40; Ephesians 1:9 – 11; 3:11).

Earthly Purpose

God's earthly purpose for us is why we, the "eternal" man, continue to exist here (instead of God's just beaming us up). This is a subject about which Christian men are really hungry: *Why am I here, God? What do You want me to do with my life?* We are all hungry to know our earthly purpose.

God's universal earthly purpose for us is to glorify Him, and Jesus tells us to do that by seeking God's righteousness. What is God's righteousness? His righteousness is His moral character. He is perfect in doing right, and the reason we exist is to emulate the perfect example of Christ's life. In this way we accomplish the first half of the chief end of man—to glorify God.

How do we pull this off? The truth? We can't. But when we abide in Jesus, He will give us the desire and power to imitate His example. Philippians 2:13 puts it like this: "It is God who works in you to will [*desire*] and to act [*power*] in order to fulfill his good purpose." And our part? Philippians 2:12 gives the answer: "Continue to work out your salvation with fear and trembling." We work—but like a child whose father has wrapped his hand around the youngster's hand to show him how it's done. So search, strive, aspire, and yearn to understand—and then trust that God will direct your steps to find His "good purpose" for your life.

Different levels of earthly purpose exist. Let's look at three levels that will help us build a framework for our own understanding.

Universal Purpose—Level One

There is a sense in which all men are alike, and God gives all men the same *universal* earthly purpose. We can break this down into two areas:

1. Who God wants us to *be*.
2. What God wants us to *do*.

The universal part of our earthly purpose is to be a certain type of man in character (being) and conduct (doing).

God "has saved us and called us to a holy life—not because of anything we have done but because of his own purpose and grace" (2 Timothy 1:9). His eternal purpose is to save us, and His earthly purpose is for us to glorify Him by leading a holy life characterized by faith, love, obedience, and service. We have no input in establishing this universal purpose—it is for all men.

Personal Purpose — Level Two

There is a sense in which each of us is unique, and God gives each of us a specific call on our lives. In other words, God has a personal, unique, and specific purpose for your life just waiting to be discovered. Could anything be more exciting?!

How can we discover God's personal purpose for our lives?

I believe every man should prepare a *Written Life Purpose Statement* that encompasses what he discovers as God's *personal earthly purpose* for his life.

This statement is intensely personal, and I don't think it's relevant whether or not it makes sense to other people. Your Written Life Purpose Statement is like a mission statement for a business, only in this case the business is your life.

God's Word reveals His known will. If possible, your purpose should spring from Scripture so you can have confidence it conforms to the will of God.

My first Written Life Purpose Statement was from Philippians 3:10: "I want to know Christ and the power of his resurrection and the fellowship of sharing in his sufferings." I adopted this at a time when I desperately wanted to know Christ more intimately and personally.

I don't mean just to know *about* Him, but to really *know* Him, and all that that means. I wanted to penetrate His power — to really understand the significance of His resurrection. And I wanted to know the fellowship of sharing in His sufferings — not just to read about His sufferings, but to share in sweet fellowship with the living God because I was willing to suffer for His sake.

I decided to change my Written Life Purpose Statement on February 1, 1986. All of my adult life I have been tormented by migraine headaches. After trying every conceivable modern and medieval remedy, I discovered I am allergic to everything I put into my mouth — literally. I have never been tested for anything to which I am not allergic — except the glycerin in which they mix the allergens.

Over several years I eliminated certain foods from my diet and measured the intake of others and, on a trial-and-error basis, have been able to reduce these daily migraines to a few headaches a week, which are manageable with medication.

The passage of Scripture that helped me survive those many years of tearful, agonizing pain is 1 Peter 4:1–2, without which I am quite certain I would have gone bonkers! The verses encourage, "Therefore, since Christ suffered in his body, arm yourselves also with the same attitude, because he who has suffered in his body is done with sin. As a result, he does not live the rest of his earthly life for evil human desires, but rather for the will of God."

The prospect that, because of the suffering I had to endure in my body, I might overcome sin and spend the rest of my earthly life for the will of God ministered to me deep inside the speechless chambers of my tortured soul. I found new depths of courage and strength to plunge forward in hope.

When I began to improve after fifteen years of sometimes hopeless despair, I felt a new purpose for my life taking shape. At first it was without form, and words wouldn't describe it. But as time passed, as I meditated on Scripture, and as I asked God to reshape in me a new purpose for my life, I was drawn repeatedly back to 1 Peter 4:1–2. One morning, years of deep, unutterable groanings flowed spontaneously from my heart through my pen onto the title page of my Bible: *I want to spend the rest of my earthly life for the will of God.* I really meant it—still do.

I relate the shaping of my own Written Life Purpose Statement so you can see its simplicity, yet gain an appreciation for the often grueling price at which it is born. Crafting this Written Life Purpose Statement is the hardest kind of work, exacting and exhausting, but well worth the effort. Once settled, it is a constant reminder of why you exist. It describes in a general and overarching way what your life is all about. It points the way to the meaning and significance we all yearn for. Like a gyroscope, it will help you stand upright whenever you are knocked off balance. Like a compass, it points the way. It answers the questions, "Why do I exist?" and "What do I do with my life?"

At the end of this chapter is a worksheet you can use as a guide for developing a Written Life Purpose Statement. Sometimes the process is more important than the product. I believe it's in the fleshing out of different ideas, verses, and thoughts that the real sense of God's earthly purpose for your life will move from *abstract* to *personal*. Why not give the worksheet a try?

Other Life Purposes — Level Three

In addition to your Written Life Purpose Statement, which is the overarching purpose for your earthly life, you can drop down a level and develop written purpose statements for important areas of your life.

Think through the reasons you exist. As you uncover nuggets of wisdom about different areas, jot them down, and begin to shape a record of what God is saying to you about the *why* part of your life. Keep a file on your desk or computer into which you can toss the ideas you jot down. If something occurs to you while reading the rest of this book, make a note of it and save it. Here is a list of some specific areas to consider:

- relationship with God
- relationships with family (wife, children, grandchildren, parents)
- other relationships
- use of gifts (serving others, witnessing, encouraging, etc.)
- work life

Goals and activities are how we put specific actions to our purposes. They are a natural result of a carefully examined life. When we determine God's purposes for our lives, whether level one, two, or three, our goals and activities are focused on doing the known will of God — His good, pleasing, and perfect will.

Example: *Purpose*: To be an encourager
Goal: Take one man to lunch each week
Activities: Write notes, call hurting men

Example: *Purpose*: To give my children a heart for God
Goal: Enroll Jen in Christian school
Activities: Daily prayers, Bible story reading

Our purposes will change over time—not quickly, like goals, but over a longer horizon; children grow up, men retire, and new spiritual gifts develop. So we need a measure of flexibility, and we need to periodically review where God has put us by His sovereign will.

THE APOSTLE PAUL: A LIFE WITH PURPOSE

He was an aristocrat from the tribe of Benjamin, of pure Jewish descent, a Roman citizen, a Greek, an esteemed religious leader. He would certainly be a great leader had he been born in the twenty-first century.

Though conceivably the greatest man who ever lived after Jesus, the apostle Paul's early destiny was to become to the early Christians what Heinrich Himmler was to German Jews in the 1930s. Himmler, the head of the Nazi Gestapo, personally orchestrated the annihilation of millions of Jews in Nazi Germany.

Before Paul's conversion, Scripture records that he entered the homes of Christians, tore people (including women) from their homes, and imprisoned them. He had men scourged in the synagogues and tortured in an attempt to cause them to blaspheme.

He was present at the stoning of Stephen and, by his own confession, voted the death sentence for unknown numbers of Christians. He was a notorious man, known for evil. Blaise Pascal once wrote, "Men never do evil so completely and cheerfully as when they do it from religious conviction." That was Paul!

Apart from the grace and mercy of God, young Paul, in the

manner of Himmler, might well have exterminated Christianity from the face of the earth. I wonder what part this may have played in God's decision to convert Paul to faith in Christ?

After Paul's conversion on the road to Damascus, a thankful turning point in history, the Jews conspired to kill him in Damascus. The Grecian Jews tried to kill him in Jerusalem. He was beaten and flogged, ridiculed and persecuted. He was frequently imprisoned. In a town named Lystra, the townspeople actually stoned him and left him for dead!

His own remarks attest to the hardship of his life.

> Five times I received from the Jews the forty lashes minus one. Three times I was beaten with rods, once I was pelted with stones, three times I was shipwrecked, I spent a night and a day in the open sea, I have been constantly on the move. I have been in danger from rivers, in danger from bandits, in danger from my fellow Jews, in danger from Gentiles; in danger in the city, in danger in the country, in danger at sea; and in danger from false believers. I have labored and toiled and have often gone without sleep; I have known hunger and thirst and have often gone without food; I have been cold and naked.
>
> 2 Corinthians 11:24–27

To the same degree that Paul persecuted the Christians, he was persecuted in return. It was not an easy-street life. For Paul, following Christ and God's purpose for his life was not an option, not a cushy desk job, but a mandate to *exist* and *function* in the way God directed, whatever the cost.

Paul records in Colossians 1:28–29, "He is the one we proclaim, admonishing and teaching everyone with all wisdom, so that we may present everyone fully mature in Christ. To this end I strenuously contend with all the energy Christ so powerfully works in me."

Can you think of a more succinct way of stating your purpose? To my knowledge, Paul didn't have a Written Life Purpose Statement, but if he had, I think this may have been it! Paul's earthly purpose, the way he glorified God, was to present every man fully mature in Christ (see also Acts 9:15).

Why didn't Paul just give up? Why did he endure such opposition? Because he had tasted the kingdom of God and His righteousness, which comes from having His Spirit and knowing His purpose for his earthly life. He had known the exhilaration of Christ's power flowing through his weak, decaying, mortal body, and everything else by comparison seemed meaningless, hollow, and paltry.

The story of Paul's life gets me excited! Doesn't this story inspire you to discover God's purpose for your life? Doesn't it make your glands pour overdoses of adrenaline into your bloodstream? *God, this is how I want my life to be! God, this is the kind of purpose I want for my life! God, let me know this kind of destiny, this kind of intensity, this kind of commitment! God, show me why I exist here on this earth.*

The truth is, *God has a special purpose for your life.* It may be different from the one you are pursuing now. If you have never known God's purpose for your life, or if you have been playing games and gotten off track with God, or if you sense God is calling you to a deeper commitment to Him and a new purpose, then let me suggest you go before God in prayer, confess your lack of meaningful purpose, and ask Him to begin to shape in you an understanding of His eternal and earthly purposes for your life. Here is a suggested prayer:

Lord God, I acknowledge that You are a sovereign God. I praise You because You have ordered eternal and earthly purposes for me. I confess that I have not sought and have not done Your purpose for my life, or I have forgotten the sense of destiny and purpose I once knew and felt. Forgive me for pursuing my goals without seeking Your purpose. Show me the reasons I exist. Help me discover Your purpose for my life, through the study of Scripture and prayer, to which I now pledge myself to do on a regular basis. Amen.

DEVELOPING A WRITTEN
LIFE PURPOSE STATEMENT

Use this worksheet as a guide to help you discover God's personal purpose for your life. Your reward will be a sense of destiny about your life. Photocopy or remove this worksheet and keep it inside your Bible.

Follow these practical steps:

1. Ask God, in prayer, to reveal your personal earthly purpose to you. Read Psalm 32:8 and claim it as a promise that He will answer.

2. Search the Scriptures for verses that capture your sense of God's purpose for your earthly life; record verses that give a special sense of meaning and purpose, picking out verses that are big enough to last a lifetime. Here are some you can begin to explore: Joshua 24:15; Proverbs 3:5 – 6; 30:7 – 9; Ecclesiastes 12:13; Micah 6:8; Matthew 6:33; 22:37 – 40; 28:19 – 20; John 4:34; 15:1 – 9, 15; 17:4; Acts 1:8; 20:24; 1 Corinthians 10:31; Ephesians 2:10; Philippians 3:10.

   Other verses:

   _____

   _____

   _____

   _____

3. Go slow and wait for God to reveal Himself. Be patient; it may take some time.

4. Once you find a verse you believe expresses God's earthly purpose for you, rephrase it in your own words. Write a draft Written Life Purpose Statement here:

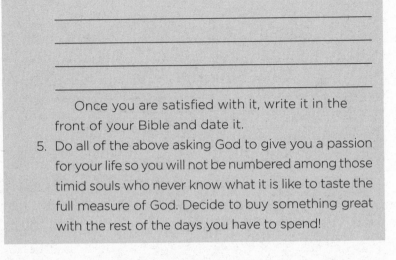

Once you are satisfied with it, write it in the front of your Bible and date it.

5. Do all of the above asking God to give you a passion for your life so you will not be numbered among those timid souls who never know what it is like to taste the full measure of God. Decide to buy something great with the rest of the days you have to spend!

———— FOCUS QUESTIONS ————

1. What is the best part of achieving your goals? What is the frustrating part of achieving goals?

2. Do you have a clear understanding of your life purpose? What is it? Are you satisfied with it? How can the Developing a Written Life Purpose Statement worksheet help you?

3. Read Psalm 32:8 and Philippians 2:13. Will God show us His purpose for our lives? How do you think He will do so?

4. Read Proverbs 16:9; 19:21; and 21:30. According to these verses, how is the outcome of our goals and plans determined? How should this influence our thinking?

5. Does failure to reach your goals make you angry at God? Describe one major unmet goal. Why do you think God didn't grant your request?

6. The apostle Paul had a remarkable sense of life purpose. Do you think you can have the same sense of mission, purpose, and destiny in your own life? Why, or why not?

CHAPTER 6

THE SECRET OF JOB CONTENTMENT

The most outstanding characteristic
of Eastern civilization is to know contentment
whereas that of Western civilization is not
to know contentment.
Hu Shih

I have learned the secret of being content
in any and every situation.
Paul, Philippians 4:12

Chariots of Fire, the fact-based, Oscar-winning movie, depicts the quests of Harold Abrahams and Eric Liddell to win gold medals in the 1924 Olympics, a feat they both accomplished.

The difference between Abrahams and Liddell is transparent: Everything Abrahams did was for himself, while everything Liddell did was for the glory of God.

Eric's sister, Jennie, mistook her brother's love of running for rebellion against God and pressed him to return to the mission field in China, where they both were born and their parents lived. One day his sister was upset because he had missed a mission meeting, so Eric decided to have a talk with her. They walked to a grassy spot overlooking the Scottish highlands.

Clutching her arms, trying to explain his calling to run, he said, "Jennie, Jennie. You've got to understand. I believe God made me for a purpose — for China. But He also made me fast! And when I run, I feel His pleasure!"

That is in sharp contrast to a scene later in the movie, one hour before the final race run by Harold Abrahams. While his trainer gave him a rubdown, he lamented to his best friend, "I'm twenty-four, and I've never known contentment. I'm forever in pursuit, and I don't even know what it is I'm chasing."

Both men won a gold medal, but only one of them enjoyed it. Do you feel God's pleasure in what you do? Or, as it did Abrahams, does contentment elude you?

THE PROBLEM

Are you getting what you want out of your job? Is your work rewarding? According to Gallup's 2013 "State of the American Workplace" report, fully 70 percent of working Americans don't find their work rewarding.[12] Unfortunately, research reports have shown for decades that only 20 to 30 percent of Americans find their work inspiring. A lack of contentment pervades the workplace.

In hot pursuit of the good life, most men don't find God's pleasure but, instead, find contentment elusive and mysterious. Their "if onlys" betray a lack of satisfaction with life. "If only I had gotten that promotion." "If only that big deal had gone through." "If only I had married someone else." "If only I could have another chance." *"If only, if only, if only . . ."*

No one wins the rat race — it's an unwinnable race. The main arena for the rat race is the workplace. Men, made for work, *must* feel a sense of accomplishment and satisfaction in their work, or contentment will elude them. If a man is unhappy in his work, *he is unhappy everywhere.*

Rather than knowing job contentment, many men lack direction or don't understand God's will for their vocation. They are not doing what they really would like to do but work on because they are trying to maintain a lifestyle, impress other people, win the rat race, please family, build an empire, acquire things, or live out their fantasies.

Other men, willing and anxious to do God's will, don't understand how God views vocation or have been led to believe vocation is an unholy pursuit.

IS WORK A CURSE ON MAN?

You may be surprised to learn that work is not the result of the fall of man. Yes, God did curse the ground because of the sin of Adam and Eve, but God established work as a holy pursuit *before* they sinned. "The Lord God took the man and put him in the Garden of Eden to work it and take care of it" (Genesis 2:15).

Later, when Satan tempted Adam and Eve and they succumbed, God cursed the ground and prescribed that "through painful toil you will eat of it all the days of your life" (Genesis 3:17). So it is the ground that is cursed, not work. Work is a holy vocation — it is how God intended us to occupy our time in the perfection of His creation plan. The holiness of vocation is as close to the fabric of Christianity as the dye is to the cloth.

THE SECRET OF JOB CONTENTMENT

An out-of-town investment partner and I reviewed by phone the terms of a good-sized transaction I was negotiating with a third party. We had been going over the contract terms for over an hour when out of the blue he said, "Man, I love this!"

"Love what?" I asked.

"The adrenaline. I love the adrenaline! This is what business is all about! This is war, it really is war! I wish I could be there with you to negotiate—I love the rush!"

I assured him I would happily trade places, because the other party was a very tough customer.

Most men who *do* like their jobs usually like the thrill of the deal or the satisfaction of beginning and completing a project. We are made to enjoy the thrill—to feel God's pleasure in our work.

Unfortunately, that is not the whole purpose of work, and many of us are tempted to become "deal junkies"—living to please ourselves (like Harold Abrahams), going from one deal fix to the next in search of contentment. The thrill takes on new meaning, though, when we do it for the glory of God. There is more to job contentment than shooting up on adrenaline.

What is the secret of job contentment? A few paragraphs ago, I posed the question, "Are you getting what you want out of your job?" As is so often the case, the answer is hidden in the question.

The secret of job contentment is not getting what you want, but redefining what you need. The distinction between wants and needs has always been an integral part of Christian thought. Most men, like Harold Abrahams, only think of what they want and are discontent. Others, like Eric Liddell, redefine their needs, live to please God, and "feel His pleasure."

Are you willing to redefine what you need? Three principles leap off the rustling pages of Scripture when we are willing to redefine what we need to achieve job contentment. Let's take a look.

REDEFINING OUR AMBITION

What is your career ambition? Is it to be significant in your industry, to be an authority figure, to make a lot of money, to win prestige, to gain respect, to be important, to be "somebody"?

Pursuing these desires is no sin, and God certainly wants us to find a sense of dignity and destiny in our vocation. Yet the secret of job contentment is not getting what we want, but redefining what we need—to please God (like Liddell) rather than just ourselves (like Abrahams). So what is God's ambition for our vocation?

> We instructed you how to live in order to please God ...
> Make it your ambition to lead a quiet life: You should mind your own business and work with your hands, just as we told you, so that your daily life may win the respect of outsiders and so that you will not be dependent on anybody.
>
> 1 Thessalonians 4:1, 11–12

I have always been very ambitious. There was a time when I worked totally for my own ambitions. When I became a Christian, I dedicated myself to Christ and asked Him to bless my ambitions. But they were still *my* plans for my life, not God's.

He allowed me to bumble along. When I was blocked from a goal, it never occurred to me that God was saying no. Instead, I would charge off in another direction, looking for a way around the obstacle.

When the Tax Reform Act of 1986 passed, my ambitions collided with the stark reality of the real estate equity market, or, should I say, the disappearance of the real estate equity market. Overnight, and I mean *literally* overnight, equity was a dead topic. No one, but no one, would talk to me. With many large development projects unfunded, I suddenly realized what I wanted simply wasn't going to happen.

The result? My ambition collided with God's plan for my life, and the glory days were replaced with agonizing months upon months of working out problems. People had to be laid off, expenses slashed, lenders contacted—a very humbling experience. I had spent seven years borrowing wheelbarrows full of money, and it eventually took another seven years to satisfy all my debts.

I found out that the secret of job contentment was not getting what I wanted, but *redefining what I needed.* What I wanted was an ever-expanding business, but what I needed was to crucify my ambition. Since then, I've been a lot quieter, minded my own business, and worked hands-on in the business—and now ministry—once God helped me understand *His* ambition for me.

As a result of that seven-year wilderness experience, I decided I wasn't making any more plans for myself. If God wants me to pursue a plan, then He will have to show me clearly that it's His ambition for my life, not mine. I know what I need; I need to redefine my ambition. My ambition now is that I will do anything God wants me to do.

CONTENTMENT IN HARD TIMES

This brings up another subject. Is it possible to have the walls crashing down around you and still experience contentment?

I would never have thought so, but I was surprised to learn we can be content in the depths of suffering—not mere inconvenience, but severe, agonizing suffering. The issue, I learned, is that our circumstances don't determine our contentment, but our faith and trust in God do. Paul wrote, "I have learned the secret of being content in any and every situation, whether well fed or hungry, whether living in plenty or in want. I can do all this through [Jesus] who gives me strength" (Philippians 4:12–13). No one is going to be bubbly when times are tough, but neither do we have to be discontent.

Even in my darkest hours, when it seemed the full force of my adversaries and my own sins would surely crush me completely, there was a peace and a knowing that I was in the center of God's will for my life—not at first, but when I humbled myself, confessed, and redefined my ambition. And this peace came even when I was still under the heavy hand of His discipline.

If we are in the center of God's will for our lives, we can bear up under any amount of stress. But when we are out of God's will, then even unbridled success can taste sour and bitter.

The Holy Spirit teaches us all things and reminds us of everything Christ told us (see John 14:26). In a mysterious, unexplainable way, He tells us when we are in the will of God—even though our emotions may be overwhelmed with sorrow.

You've heard of "sweet" sorrow? The Holy Spirit is the author of sweet sorrow. In the depths of our calamity, pain, anguish, and suffering, the Spirit of Christ ministers to us and tells us that what we are facing is part of God's plan for our lives—a plan for good, not evil (see Jeremiah 29:11; Romans 8:28).

One of the most remarkable statements ever made by a human being was that of the apostle Paul when he wrote, "That is why, for Christ's sake, I *delight* in weaknesses, in insults, in hardships, in persecutions, in difficulties. For when I am weak, then I am strong" (2 Corinthians 12:10, italics added).

Even when we cannot see a light at the end of the tunnel, and even though our emotions are frayed, we can know contentment in hard times by the inaudible voice of the Holy Spirit. "Not only so, but we also glory in our sufferings ... because God's love has been poured out into our hearts through the Holy Spirit, who has been given to us" (Romans 5:3, 5). We can delight in the fellowship that comes from sharing in Christ's sufferings. With a God so gracious as this, shouldn't we let Him be the boss of our lives?

REDEFINING OUR BOSS

Who is your boss? Do you work for yourself, or are you employed by someone else? Whether you are self-employed or work for a large or small company, chances are you are striving "to be your own boss."

Everybody, it seems, wants to be their own boss—to be independent and call their own shots. Employment is just one more area in which our desire to be independent collides with God's plan for our

lives. Job contentment does not come from getting what we want—
"to be our own boss"—but from redefining what we need.

Paul wrote:

> Slaves [employees], obey your earthly masters [employers] in
> everything; and do it, not only when their eye is on you and
> to curry their favor, but with sincerity of heart and reverence
> for the Lord. Whatever you do, work at it with all your heart,
> as working for the Lord, not for human masters, since you
> know that you will receive an inheritance from the Lord as a
> reward. It is the Lord Christ you are serving.
>
> Colossians 3:22–24

To be content requires us to redefine our boss. It is the Lord we
are serving. Of course, we still have an earthly boss, whether an
employer or our customers, but the ultimate boss is God. We are to
serve our earthly boss because he holds God's proxy as our employer.
But God still owns the company—He owns everything. He has the
final interest in all things.

Shortly after I went into business for myself, my partner and I
dedicated our company to God. I read a book, *God Owns My Business*,
by Stanley Tam, and gave it to my partner. He read it as well
and was equally excited. So we called a board of directors meeting
and went to Burger King for lunch (that's the only place we could
afford to eat). We made God the senior partner, and we became
the junior partners. Then we endeavored to run our decisions by
Him—not perfectly, but we tried. After my partner sold out to me
five years later, I continued with God at the helm. It was His company. He was the boss, and we trusted Him to meet our needs. We
also worked very hard.

In order to be content, we must redefine who our boss is. The
boss we usually want is "me"; the boss we need is God. Not only do
we need a new boss, but we also need to change our own role.

REDEFINING OUR ROLE

Steve sold his eighty-employee company to a large national concern. In the course of the transaction, he decided to stay on as a branch manager, even though he didn't have to. Most people never even knew there had been a change of ownership, because there was no *visible* change, but the change in authority structure, reporting relationships, and goals was total and complete. Steve's *role* changed sharply. What he did parallels the central idea in one of Jesus' parables.

Jesus said:

"Suppose a king is about to go to war against another king. Won't he first sit down and consider whether he is able with ten thousand men to oppose the one coming against him with twenty thousand? If he is not able, he will send a delegation while the other is still a long way off and will ask for terms of peace. In the same way, those of you who do not give up everything you have cannot be my disciples."

Luke 14:31–33

When an ancient king decided to fight, he had to recognize that if he lost, he would die. But when a king surrendered, the opposing king would leave him in place. Just like in Steve's case, there was no visible change, but the authority structure was completely different.

What does Jesus mean when he says, "In the same way, those of you who do not give up everything you have cannot be my disciples"? This seems like a hard teaching—it *is* a hard teaching! But it doesn't mean we are to sell all of our possessions and go to China. Instead, it means we are to "surrender" everything we have to Christ. He will leave us in place, like the surrendering king, to rule over what was once ours but has been willingly surrendered to Him. Essentially, we sell out to Jesus and stay on as the branch manager. He becomes the final authority, sets policy, and determines goals—and we report to Him.

The secret of job contentment is not getting what you want but redefining what you need—to redefine our role from owner to steward. He becomes the owner, even though He asks us to stay on as the branch manager and look after things.

DAILY SURRENDER

After fifteen years of striving to be known for excellence as a business planner, I came to a startling realization. I am convinced God simply does not want to give it to us more than one day at a time. It's a biblical idea:

> Now listen, you who say, "Today or tomorrow we will go to this or that city, spend a year there, carry on business and make money." Why, you do not even know what will happen tomorrow. What is your life? You are a mist that appears for a little while and then vanishes. Instead, you ought to say, "If it is the Lord's will, we will live and do this or that."
>
> James 4:13–15

When we strive to control the future with our own plans, we choke off God's plans for our future.

One day at a time. He wants us to redefine our ambition, our boss, and our role and surrender to Him completely—one day at a time. "Therefore do not worry about tomorrow, for tomorrow will worry about itself. Each day has enough trouble of its own" (Matthew 6:34).

When the rush of adrenaline flows through our veins for a meeting that went especially well, a project completed with excellence, a big deal that closed, or that great feeling at the end of a day well spent, let's remember the source of such pleasure—work is a holy vocation. Following the principles discussed here is the most rewarding path for each of us to find job contentment.

Redefine:
1) Ambition
2) Boss
3) Role
4) Surrender

FOCUS QUESTIONS

1. What is something you do that really makes you "feel God's pleasure"? What work tasks give you a deep sense of personal satisfaction?

2. Read Genesis 2:15, and then Genesis 3:17. Did you think work resulted from the fall of man? Since it is the ground that was cursed and not work, how does this affect your view of work?

3. Read Luke 14:33. How do you think Jesus intends for us to implement this command into our lives?

4. What is your ambition? Will it survive your physical death? Will it pass the Luke 14:33 test?

5. Read 1 Thessalonians 4:1, 7, 9–12. What should be "more and more" the ambition of a genuine Christian? (See also Colossians 3:22–24.)

6. What area of your life have you not yet surrendered to Christ? Are you the owner of your career or the branch manager?

PART 2

SOLVING OUR RELATIONSHIP PROBLEMS

CHAPTER 7

BROKEN RELATIONSHIPS

Happy families are all alike; every unhappy family
is unhappy in its own way.
Leo Tolstoy

Your wife will be like a fruitful vine
within your house;
your children will be like olive shoots
around your table.
Yes, this will be the blessing
for the man who fears the LORD.
Psalm 128:3 – 4

Our children were young—one a preschooler and one elementary age. The business had finally started to do reasonably well.

People who before wouldn't give me the time of day suddenly acted friendly. When I was just getting started, I tried to introduce myself to a bank president at a Chamber function. But first he glanced around the room to spy out someone of stature. Only after he could see that no one important was available did he speak with me. I don't think he thought I could tell what he was up to. Then after I started to have some success, that same bank president acted like we were long-lost buddies.

The mail started to bring invitations to join organizations and attend functions—community benefit events, societies, dinner parties, service organizations. Money was always involved. I couldn't believe the pressure we felt to join up. How do we pick? On what basis do we prioritize our yeses and nos? For a long time I said yes to just about everything. Then the reality of what we were becoming started to dawn on us.

We were about to buy into a network of shallow relationships built on the sole foundation of commercial gain. Time with our kids, who needed us most and whom we love most, was about to get buried under an avalanche of avarice. And the ones who were going to get our time obviously only wanted a relationship as long as we were successful.

Patsy, the proverbial woman of intuition, was first to see what was happening, but I was blind as a bat, telling her, "We've arrived!"

"Yes," Patsy added, "but at the wrong place."

One evening as we reviewed our calendar and a stack of time-consuming opportunities, the thought came, *Why not prioritize everything we do on the basis of who's going to be crying at our funeral?* We did it. The results saved our family.

This simple question—Who's going to be crying at my funeral?—cuts out time wasters with the accuracy of a laser. Why should you and I give ourselves to people who don't love us, at the expense of those who do? Prioritizing this way keeps us focused on our biblical priorities.

THE PROBLEM

Let's be honest. Work can be intoxicating. At the office we don't have to deal with unpredictable female emotions and whiny kids. Work holds two attractions: not only is it a place to escape to, but the thrill of the deal awaits us there.

Yet no amount of success at work can compensate for failure at home. Many men are succeeding in their work but failing in life. So many of us are hurting silently in our relationships with our wives, children, parents, business associates, and friends. Many times we wound those we love the most. And our own spirits are wounded too, but we don't know how to stop the bleeding. Christian men have no special inoculation against this kind of pain.

In pursuit of the good life, most men leave a trail of broken relationships. Our secular culture has incited man's natural, selfish inclination to pursue fame and fortune into a strange, unstable cauldron of ambition and visions of grandeur. All too often this concoction explodes in his face, scattering what should be his most treasured possessions—his relationships—like the irretrievably shattered fragments of a precious vase, an heirloom that was destined to be a joy of future generations, linking one generation to the next. Somehow the broken shards, like Humpty Dumpty, just can't be put together again.

What we need most is not a sticky glue to desperately repair the shattered pieces of our broken relationships, but a cool resolve to catch the vase, now tumbling through the air, before it bursts into a thousand little bits.

As a young businessman, I made it a habit to always ask older men what their greatest regrets were, hoping I could glean some wise tips for my own life.

While their regrets varied all over the map, there were two that showed up on virtually every man's list. First, a man would say, "I was so busy taking care of company business that I never put my own financial house in order. Now I'm fifty-five, and I have to do in ten years what I should have done in forty."

Then he would add, "I was so busy trying to improve my family's standard of living that, before I knew it, my children were grown and gone, and I never got to know them. Now they are too busy for me."

What will your regrets be? Are you willing to pay the price for running in the rat race? *No amount of success at work can ever be enough to compensate for failure at home.*

WHY DO MEN SCORE SO LOW IN RELATIONSHIPS?

Many have observed that men are generally more task-oriented, while women are generally more relationship-oriented. I have certainly found this to be true in my own experience. When someone asks me to lunch, my first question is, "What do you want to talk about?" I'm usually thinking, *If I can find out what the agenda is, maybe I can handle it with a five-minute call instead of a one-hour lunch.*

When one of my wife's friends calls for lunch, she asks no questions. Women will get together just to be together. Men find that thought inconceivable. We work off agendas.

God gave men the natural inclination to be task-oriented. This is usually referred to as the *creation mandate* or *cultural mandate*—the mandate to fill, subdue, and rule the earth (see Genesis 1:28). When we strike the right balance between task and relationship, we find peace. But when our relationships are out of balance, our insides ache.

Most men start chasing the good life with clear thinking and pure motives. Our goal? To improve the standard of living for our family. The task is a means to an end. But we get so involved with the task—and it can be exciting—that we lose sight of why we are working so hard. We become confused, and what originally was a means to an end becomes the end itself.

For example, to improve his family's income, Brian started a trucking company. One truck. Short hauls. Mostly around town. Business picked up. Eventually he was leaving before sunup and getting home after dark. One night, his wife told Brian that earlier that day their five-year-old son, Sean, asked, "Mommy, where does Daddy live?" At first he chuckled. But then he realized he had gotten the ends and the means mixed up. What was supposed to be the means to a better life had become the end. To his credit, Brian made the adjustment—although it took him a couple of years of vigilance to get his schedule back to a normal workweek.

The culture we live in places a higher value on possessions and accomplishments than on people and relationships. Our society does little to dissuade our confusion about the desired end result. Instead of encouraging and nurturing family and relationship values, our culture suggests that professional achievement and financial success are the measure of a man. When is the last time you met a man whose first inclination is to describe himself in terms of the impact he is having on his children? As someone who works with men as a vocation, I can tell you that not many do—although we're steadily seeing more and more men putting family over career.

Still, most men describe themselves in terms of their work and financial achievements because that's what they value most. Our culture has persuaded most men that significance is related more to our balance sheet and our title than to teaching our children and cherishing our wives.

Unfortunately, we are all self-centered. Developing an interest in the welfare of others is a cultivated skill. Without the power of Jesus Christ, only a handful of people would be interested in others. "For everyone looks out for their own interests, not those of Jesus Christ" (Philippians 2:21). Yet, we are exhorted, "In humility, value others above yourselves, not looking to your own interests but each of you to the interests of the others. In your relationships with one another, have the same mindset as Christ Jesus" (Philippians 2:3–5).

If we don't look out for our own interests, we're crazy! No one else is going to take responsibility for our lives! The problem occurs when we live according to our flesh—our sin nature—and only look out for number one.

This can grow into a circular problem. If no one else looks out for my interests, then I must. And if I spend all my time looking out for my own interests, then I don't have any time left over to help anyone else.

If every man had that same outlook, wouldn't this world be a big mess? Everyone would be an island of self-interest. Thank God that millions of Christians do look after the interests of others and not just their own. More of us need to.

By having the same attitude as Jesus Christ, we can break with the self-interested, secular view of the world. Our score in relationships will improve so much we might even make the dean's list!

GRUMPY MEN

How we are behind the closed doors of our own private castle is how we *really* are. That's the *real* you and the *real* me. We can fabricate an image for our work associates and friends, but when the shades go down, the man we really are comes out of the shadows.

We trap ourselves into thinking that our grouchiness and abusiveness with our wife and kids is excusable; they just don't understand us. "If they only knew what we men have to put up with in the course of a workday, they would break their necks to help make our lives more bearable!" Instead, they don't understand, so we make their lives unbearable too.

Dr. Henry Brandt, a Christian psychologist, said, "Other people don't create your spirit; they only reveal it." Our wives don't make us grumpy; we are a grumpy person looking for a place to grump! It's time to stop blaming our families for our bad attitudes and confess they are just the scapegoats for the character issues we have not yet sorted out for ourselves.

When I acknowledged that my wife was not the cause of my

anger and frustration, it unlocked the door to her friendship. When I began to include her by sharing my deepest thoughts and hurts with her instead of taking out my frustrations on her, a new friend started to show up when I came home every day.

The key to our relationships is this: *People know if you are for them or not.* We can say whatever we want, but people figure out the truth in time. If we tell our wives we love them, but spend Monday night at softball practice, Wednesday night at the church, Saturday on the golf course, and the rest of the time watching TV, they can tell if we are for them or not. Time is *everything* to a relationship. Let's change our ways and give time to whom time is due.

CONCLUSION

Why are we men so blind to the problems that exist in our relationships? I know, for myself, that I get so absorbed in watching the ground immediately in front of me for the next two or three steps that I forget to glance up to see if I'm going in the right direction.

No area of a man's life has more potential for improvement than his relationships. Most men, in pursuit of the good life, leave a trail of broken relationships. We hurt silently in our relationships. We get intoxicated with our work, and in our light-headedness, we abuse the ones we love.

No amount of success at work will ever be adequate to compensate for failure at home. We each need to do a gut check and answer the question, "Do my wife and children know I am for them by the way I spend my time?" How we spend our time is an act of the will—a decision. We are the sum of our decisions; we decide who is first, second, and third in our lives. If we fail in this area, we fail completely.

Here's the big idea for this chapter: *If you don't have enough time for your family, you can be 100 percent certain you are not following God's will for your life.* Let's look more specifically at our relationships with our wives and children.

———————————— FOCUS QUESTIONS ————————————

1. Most men are hurting silently in their relationships.

   ❑ Agree ❑ Disagree. Explain your answer.

2. One primary reason for broken relationships is men's pursuit of an ever higher standard of living.

   ❑ Agree ❑ Disagree. Explain your answer.

3. Why do men get so wrapped up in their work that they forget to be good husbands and fathers?

4. Have you found the pursuit of a higher standard of living to be worth the price? Give an example.

5. Comment on this statement: "No amount of success at work can compensate for failure at home."

6. Why do you think men score so low in relationships?

7. How we are behind the closed doors of our own private castle is how we really are. How are you behind closed doors? What changes would help your family life?

8. Do you feel you are a good communicator at work? Compare your communication skills at work with how you are doing with your wife and kids.

CHAPTER 8

CHILDREN: HOW TO AVOID REGRETS

My child arrived just the other day; he came
to the world in the usual way. But there were
planes to catch and bills to pay; he learned
to walk while I was away.[13]
Sandy and Harry Chapin

Fathers, do not exasperate your children;
instead, bring them up in the training
and instruction of the Lord.
Ephesians 6:4

The salmon nearly leaped onto their hooks! That was a far cry from the previous day, when the four anglers couldn't even snag their lines in the rocks.

Disappointed but not discouraged, they had climbed aboard their small seaplane and skimmed over the Alaskan mountains to a pristine, secluded bay where the fish were sure to bite.

They parked their aircraft and waded upstream, where the water teemed with ready-to-catch salmon. Later that afternoon, when they returned to their camp, they were surprised to find the seaplane high and dry. The tides fluctuated twenty-three feet in that particular bay, and the pontoons rested on a bed of gravel. Since they couldn't fly out till morning, they settled in for the night and enjoyed some of their catch for dinner. Then they slept in the plane.

In the morning the seaplane was adrift, so they promptly cranked the engine and started to take off. Too late, they discovered one of the pontoons had been punctured and was filled with water. The extra weight threw the plane into a circular pattern. Within moments from liftoff the seaplane careened into the sea and capsized.

My friend, Dr. Phil Littleford, determined that everyone was alive, including his twelve-year-old son, Mark. He suggested they pray, which the other two men quickly endorsed. No safety equipment could be found on board—no life vests, no flares, nothing. The plane gurgled and submerged into the blackness of the icy morning sea. Fortunately, they all had waders, which they inflated. The frigid Alaskan water chilled their breath.

They all began to swim for shore, but the riptide countered every stroke. The two men alongside Phil and Mark were strong swimmers and they both made shore, one just catching the tip of land as the tides pulled Phil and Mark out of the bay toward the open sea.

Their two companions last saw Phil and Mark as disappearing dots on the horizon, swept arm in arm out to sea.

The Coast Guard reported they probably lasted no more than an hour in the freezing waters—hypothermia would chill the body functions and they would go to sleep. Mark, with a smaller body mass, would fall asleep first in his father's arms. Phil, a strong swimmer himself, could have made the shoreline too, but that would have meant abandoning his son. Their bodies were never found.

What father wouldn't be willing to die for his son? If we are willing to go so far as to die for our children, why is it that we often don't seem willing to live for them?

THE PROBLEM

Family life has changed a lot in the decades since I was a boy. In the late 1950s, the average number of children in the American home was 3.7; today it's about 2.0.[14] But more remarkable than the change in family size is the change in family values.

Let's face it. Being a godly man, husband, and father has never been more challenging. Our kids are under tremendous pressure to try drugs, alcohol, sex, and all kinds of risky behavior. On a positive note, fewer and fewer teens are experimenting with sex, affirming that abstinence is a message that resonates.[15]

When we adopt the three impoverished values of personal peace, affluence, and cultural Christianity, dads get spread too thin. As a result, the emotional pain young people experience is overwhelming. Dr. James Dobson, the respected Christian psychologist, cited research done by Dr. Urie Bronfenbrenner. Wanting to determine how much time middle-class fathers spent in contact with their kids each day, researchers asked these men to estimate the amount of time spent each day with their one-year-old kids. The average response was fifteen to twenty minutes.

However, in the social sciences, it's common for people when self-reporting to exaggerate the good they do. So the researchers attached microphones to the shirts of the kids to record actual parental interaction. The results are shocking. The average amount of daily time each dad spent with his kids was *thirty-seven seconds*, an average of 2.7 daily encounters of ten to fifteen seconds![16]

Unfortunately, this scene replays in millions of homes across America every day. Christian homes are just as susceptible to this malady. Compare these thirty-seven-second encounters with the fact that the same child watches four hours of TV each day[17] — much of it morally bankrupt — and we can anticipate a frightening, apocalyptic future.

One current thought, used to justify leaving children unattended while both parents pursue professional fulfillment, is that it's the *quality* of time, not the *quantity*, that's important. A *Fortune* magazine article, "The Money Society," suggests differently:

> Psychoanalysts find that many money addicts are children of parents too preoccupied, overworked, or withdrawn to respond with the appropriate oohs and ahs to baby's smiles and antics. The children consequently never stop looking for the withheld applause and pleased response, and money helps them get it — even takes the place of it ...
>
> But, says Dr. Arnold Goldberg, a Chicago psychoanalyst, "The ante always goes up because the need is never satisfied. The kid wants a human response; money is a nonhuman response." Some of these people ... end up in Goldberg's office complaining that their life has no purpose.[18]

If, as we discovered in the last chapter, one of the two greatest regrets of men in their fifties is that they never got to know their kids, what practical steps can we take to be the exception to the rule? What are some realistic ideas we could try out on our own young ones to show we are willing to live for them?

FREEDOM TO BE KIDS

I've loosened up over the years, but I am a perfectionist by nature. I like things to be just so. This doesn't mix well with tiny creatures drooling over everything in sight.

When our two children were both toddlers, I was always uptight about the new scratches that showed up daily in our coffee table. This was a real point of contention with my wife, who could not care less about such matters. My blood boiled when I spotted a new nick in the luster of the smooth-grained wood.

Finally, Patsy couldn't take it anymore and said, "You leave my children alone! I'll not have you ruining a million-dollar child over a $300 table!"

Wow! It finally connected with my brain. I was more interested in a $300 table than the emotional welfare of my kids. I asked Patsy to forgive me and told her, "Let them do whatever they like to anything in the house. When they are grown, we'll buy a whole new houseful of furniture."

We dads need to give our kids the freedom to be kids. One day my daughter was crying over some neighborhood spat. I barked out four quick, easy steps to solve the problem. That may work great at the office, but it just made her cry louder.

"Dad," she sniffled, "from now on [sniff], when I'm crying [sniff, sniff], would you please not say anything that's logical?"

Growing up is harder on kids than adults. Let's give them the freedom to be kids. Our approach, Dr. Dobson says, should be to just help them get through it.

PROTECTION FROM THE WORLD

When we allow our children to be indiscriminately exposed to the secular worldview, we risk losing their fragile, impressionable minds to secular values. This approach to parenting carries with it the presumption that our children can discriminate between right and wrong, good and evil. This is incorrect.

During the period when I originally wrote this book, popular singer George Michael sang on his single, "I Want Your Sex," that "sex is natural, sex is fun, sex is best when it's one on one." Overnight, the song shot up to number two on the charts. After Michael's Orlando concert the newspaper reported, "During the hit song [his opening number], he thrust his hips and gazed adoringly at girls in the front row ... mostly thirteen to nineteen years old ..." Our children don't automatically make the right choices!

In the late 1980s, George Michael's song was censored. Today it would be prime-time. In the moral devolution that has become our current era, female stars have joined the parade into decadence.

Miley Cyrus twerks away while millions of parents are trying to raise honorable boys and self-respecting girls. Men, there's a battle raging for the hearts and minds of our children.

The largest response I've ever had to a Facebook post came after Beyoncé's Super Bowl act. I wrote the following:

I AM SAD TODAY

My wife and I watched Beyoncé together. In the middle of the halftime show Patsy said, "She has such a beautiful smile." I assured Patsy there was not a man on the planet who was looking at her smile. If you ever wondered why Herod offered Herodias "up to half my kingdom" in Mark 6:23, now you know. The President's wife said she admires Beyoncé. I get it. Beyoncé is a wonderful human being. But she and all her admirers are confused. Beyoncé is simply an exotic dancer with a great voice and, yes, a beautiful smile. It's a terrible message to send young people. Last night I became a dinosaur. It makes me sad, but I would rather be a dinosaur than a politically correct party to glorifying lust.

On a positive note, my wife and I used sexually explicit songs and performances as a platform to openly discuss our views on sex with our children and contrast them with the secular view. In fact, we talked openly about everything because we found they already know about everything anyway. The goal is *protection*, not *insulation*.

And with the Internet, your children know about everything too — more than you think, and perhaps too much. For example, Christian writer and speaker Anne Marie Miller, herself a recovering pornography addict, finds more students looking at pornography at younger ages and with greater frequency. And guess where our children are learning about porn? Here's how Miller explains it:

Remember the first time you, as a parent, saw pornography? Likely it was a friend's parent who had a dirty magazine, or maybe you saw something somebody brought to school. Now, when a student hears a word or phrase they don't understand, they don't ask you what it means (because they fear getting in trouble). They don't ask their friends (because they fear being ashamed for not knowing) ... They go straight to Google Images. In almost all of the stories I heard, this is how someone was first exposed to pornography— Google Image searching.[19]

Children, not wise but foolish, discriminate best between what makes them feel good and what makes them feel bad. Unfortunately, for this generation of latchkey children, sin feels good. The duty and role of fathers includes protecting our children from evil as well as teaching them righteousness.

Our children are entitled to more from us than a laissez-faire approach to parenting. A man must take hold of the reins of spiritual leadership in his home. Children need to be guided into the value system we want for them.

Value systems and *belief systems* are primarily influenced by parents, teachers, coaches, professors, pastors, peers, music, movies, and television. We need to ensure our children are exposed to the people and media that stand for the values and beliefs we want. If not, we should make a change. The fragile minds of young people can't distinguish the merit of the values and beliefs presented to them, and they will tend to adopt whatever they are exposed to.

Four hours a day of television against thirty-seven seconds of conversation with Dad is a statistic we need to reflect on.

We need to influence our children as much as possible as early as possible, because once they become teenagers, their friends (peers) exert more influence on them than any other single factor. Teaching our children what to look for in a friend, and placing them in environments where such young people can be found, is a gigantic contribution to the stability of their beliefs and values. Think about this. What are those young people who *remain* virgins doing with their time that's different? How can we encourage our kids to do the same?

 Short of purposed, planned effort on our part, our kids will self-select the values that they unwisely think will make them feel the best. Too bad that many things that feel good at first deeply scar the lives of millions of our young people each year—drugs, alcohol, and sex lead to addiction, STDs, and unplanned pregnancies.

Each of us owes our children the protection from calamity that we alone can provide, just as God our Father provides it to us. Syrupy permissiveness will only appeal to the foolishness that is bound up in the heart of a child (see Proverbs 22:15). These days, when we misjudge, we tend to underprotect, not overprotect.

ENCOURAGE, DON'T EMBITTER

Mothers love and stroke their children. Angry fathers handle the discipline. This image of dads may not be fair, but when we do err, this is how we usually go astray. Colossians 3:21 confirms that this is a problem by its inclusion in the Bible as one of very few instructions given only to fathers: "Fathers, do not embitter your children, or they will become discouraged."

Angry fathers are everywhere. I once heard a dad scream at his elementary-age son, "Why don't you act your age!"

Actually, that's exactly what this youngster was doing—acting his age. What his dad really meant was, "Why don't you act like a grown-up!"

Gordon MacDonald told a story about James Boswell, the famous biographer of Samuel Johnson. Boswell frequently mentioned a special childhood memory—a day of fishing with his dad. Apparently Boswell's life had been deeply etched for the better on this single day, for he constantly referred to the many matters his father had tutored him about on that one occasion.

Many years later someone stumbled across the following entry in his father's journal — words penned by Boswell's dad: "Gone fishing today with my son; a day wasted."[20]

I believe this is a positive story about Boswell's father. Whatever personal feelings he had, he must have effectively suppressed them since his son profited so much from the day. Sadly, we often express our selfish displeasure and ruin the day for everyone.

Instead, Boswell had been deeply encouraged by the mundane affair, and the memory became a cornerstone of his entire life. We don't have to be the sweetest guy in the world to have an impact on our kids. What seems like a bore and a waste of time can be a great inspiration to them. They just need our time and attention.

If we can learn to control our selfish desires, not lose our tempers so often, and encourage our kids, they will inherit a great legacy from us.

NO REPLACEMENT FOR TIME

A favorite song of mine, "Cat's in the Cradle," took on special meaning during a sneak attack on my emotions one evening. Patsy and I signed up for a parenting class led by Lyle and Marge Nelsen, the very successful parents of four children. Before the class began, they invited us all to a family picnic. During the day, our "shutterbug" leader snapped dozens of candid photos.

On the first night of our class, Lyle and Marge set up a projector and played "Cat's in the Cradle" while flashing pictures of *my* children on the screen! Talk about impact.

One day I was reflecting that my twelve-year-old daughter would be in college at eighteen, so two-thirds of her time with her mom and me was gone. Then it occurred to me that, at twelve, she spent more time with her friends than with the family.

The more I thought about it, I realized that 85 to 90 percent of our time together had already gone by. It's best to get your time in now if you have youngsters, because those weeks turn into years faster than a speeding bullet, and then their friends become very important to them.

If your children turn out well, all of your other problems will fit into a thimble. But if you end up with regrets over the time you didn't give your children, it's a pain that never goes away, as the following piece, taken from an essay I once read that was written by a dad and submitted to an advice column, illustrates.

WHERE DID THE YEARS GO?

I remember talking to my friend a number of years ago about our children. Mine were five and seven then, just the ages when their daddy means everything to them. I wished that I could have spent more time with my kids but I was too busy working. After all, I wanted to give them all the things I never had when I was growing up.

I loved the idea of coming home and having them sit on my lap and tell me about their day. Unfortunately, most days I came home so late that I was only able to kiss them good night after they had gone to sleep.

It is amazing how fast kids grow. Before I knew it, they were nine and eleven. I missed seeing them in school plays. Everyone said they were terrific, but the plays always seemed to go on when I was traveling for business or tied up in a special conference. The kids never complained, but I could see the disappointment in their eyes.

I kept promising I would have more time "next year." But the higher up the corporate ladder I climbed, the less time there seemed to be.

Suddenly they were no longer nine and eleven. They were fourteen and sixteen. Teenagers. I didn't see my daughter the night she went out on her first date or my son's championship basketball game. Mom made excuses and I managed to telephone and talk to them before they left the house. I could hear the disappointment in their voices, but I explained as best I could.

Don't ask where the years have gone. Those little kids are nineteen and twenty-one now and in college. I can't believe it. My job is less demanding and I finally have time for them. But they have their own interests and there is no time for me. To be perfectly honest, I'm a little hurt.

It seems like yesterday that they were five and seven. I'd give anything to live those years over. You can bet your life I'd do it differently. But they are gone now, and so is my chance to be a real dad.[21]

As the saying goes, no one says on their deathbed, "I wish I had spent more time at work."

GUARDIANSHIP THROUGH PRAYER

Seven couples, all new Christians, started to meet in a prayer group. The results of their prayers were so dramatic that I verified their story with three separate sources. They all corroborate each other.

It seems these naive new Christians discovered a verse of Scripture and decided to claim it as a promise from God. The verse states, "Believe in the Lord Jesus, and you will be saved — you and *your household*" (Acts 16:31, italics added).

Between the seven couples they had twenty-three children — none of whom were Christians. Each week the couples would faithfully pray for the salvation of their beloved children. Over the course of two years, all twenty-three kids committed their lives to Jesus Christ.

In a Denver crusade, Dr. Billy Graham spoke about this verse of Scripture, indicating they had learned that in homes in which a child came to Christ first, 25 percent of the time the entire family became Christians. When the wife came first, 40 to 50 percent of the time the entire family accepted Christ. But in families where the father came to faith in Christ first, the entire family came to faith in 60 percent of the cases.

The principle of Acts 16:31 excites me to no end! What better way to equip our children for a meaningful life than by praying for their eternal salvation? *No single undertaking will ever come close to that of assisting in the salvation of our children.*

You pray for yourself, don't you? You understand the need you have for protection from temptation and the need for forgiveness, wisdom, grace, mercy, courage, and hope. You recognize the importance of expressing praise, honor, glory, and gratitude to the Lord.

Who prays for your children? Are not the needs of our fragile children even greater than our own? *We can make no greater contribution to the well-being of our kids than to intercede for them in daily prayer.*

Over the years I built up a regimen of prayer subjects for my children. It's an eclectic assortment from many sources. One source was the parenting class just mentioned. Another was a tape by Gordon MacDonald. The Bible has given me several prayer subjects for my kids. And my own broken heart has ached for my kids to be spared some of the anguish and pain I have had to bear.

Here is a list of the subjects I accumulated. You may find some adaptation of this list helpful:

- a saving faith (thanksgiving if already Christian)
- a growing faith
- an independent faith (as they grow up)
- their strength and health in mind, body, and spirit
- a sense of destiny (purpose)
- a desire for integrity

- a call to excellence
- an understanding of the ministry God has for them
- my commitment to set aside times to spend with them
- a thirst to acquire wisdom
- protection from drugs, alcohol, and premarital sex
- the mate God has for them (alive somewhere, needing prayer)
- a passion to glorify the Lord in everything

Can you think of anything in the entire world more important than for your children to place faith in Jesus Christ and to experience God's wonderful plan for their lives? Through prayer and the example of your own life, you can have confidence that, by God's grace, they will.

No man would be unwilling to die for his children. How much more important it is to live for them.

———————— FOCUS QUESTIONS ————————

1. The problems that kids face growing up today are not that much different from the problems I faced growing up.

   ❑ Agree ❑ Disagree. Why?

2. Do you give your children the freedom to be kids, or do you try to make them act older than they actually are? Give an example in which you expected more from your children than you should have.

3. Do you become angry with your children too often? What changes could you make in your attitudes and expectations that would lower your temperature?

4. Comment on this statement: "It's not the quantity of time but the quality." React to the statement, "I've never heard anyone on their deathbed say, 'I wish I had spent more time at work.'"

5. Most men do not regularly pray for their children.

   ❑ Agree ❑ Disagree.

   Do you regularly pray for your children? If not, why? Are you willing to make prayer a regular habit?

6. Our children's value system and belief system are influenced by us, teachers, coaches, professors, pastors, peers, music, movies, and television. How active have you been in monitoring these influences? What changes should you make?

7. Once our children become teenagers, their peers become the primary influence on their lives. What can we do before they become teenagers to best prepare them for the teen years? What can we do while they are teenagers to help them get through those tough years?

CHAPTER 9

WIVES: HOW TO BE HAPPILY MARRIED

Let the wife make the husband glad
to come home, and let him make her sorry
to see him leave.
Martin Luther

Husbands, in the same way be considerate
as you live with your wives, and treat them
with respect as the weaker partner and
as heirs with you of the gracious gift of life,
so that nothing will hinder your prayers.
1 Peter 3:7

You've seen them at restaurants. They look a little alike, in a strange sort of way. His eyes are distant, and she never looks up from her food. During the course of dinner, the only words they speak are to the waiter.

They've been married for more than thirty years, but they scarcely know each other. As the children were growing up, ball games and school plays kept everyone on the run. Now they have time on their hands, but they don't really have a personal relationship. They don't know how to talk to each other.

THE PROBLEM

Most men are not *un*happy with their marriages, but they've never learned how to really enjoy their wives. They have a problem expressing and feeling love. In a written survey I conducted, I found that men were deeply troubled by the ability to love. Marriage is hard work, the exacting kind of work in which all the little blemishes are noticeable.

Women can be hard to understand. Sigmund Freud, the father of psychoanalysis, posed this interesting question: "Despite my thirty years of research into the feminine soul, I have not yet been able to answer ... the great question ... What does a woman want?"

Why did Freud find this such a difficult question to answer? Why do *we* find it such a difficult question to answer? The easier road for most men is to throw themselves into their jobs. We can hide behind our game face at work. Then we don't have to figure out our wives, or let them in on our weaknesses and fears.

Many couples live together more as roommates than partners. Their social and sexual needs are met, but intimacy as friends never develops. Yet, as men, we each need a friend we can let our hair down with, someone we can really trust. Too few men ever find that friend.

THE ROLE OF THE WIFE

Sam intuitively knew his wife held him in low esteem. He had not achieved the same station in life her father held, and though she never actually said anything, Sam sensed her contemptuous pity.

One of a man's deepest needs is to be respected. Maybe you remember a girl you dated who said, "You don't respect me!" when you went for that first-date kiss. But a man's need to be respected far exceeds a woman's need, though a woman also needs to be held in high regard.

The importance of respect is highlighted in the Scripture passage that outlines how wives are to treat their husbands. "The wife must respect her husband" (Ephesians 5:33).

How can a woman show her husband respect? The Ephesians passage about Christian households begins with God's foundational instruction to wives. "Wives, submit yourselves to your own husbands as you do to the Lord" (Ephesians 5:22). Your wife's duty is to submit to you, which is the ultimate expression of respect.

To yield to another is impossible unless you respect them. You can be forced to *obey* someone, but not to *respect* them. Men need the respect of their wives to have self-esteem. So the wife must submit to her husband, which is nearly impossible unless she respects him. Several surveys indicate that power struggles between spouses is a leading cause of divorce.

Your wife's submission to you is to be in the same manner, or equal to, the way she submits to Christ. Don't you think that puts a pretty large responsibility on you as the husband? If she submits to you as if you were Christ Himself, then can you treat her any less than the way Christ would treat her?

Women like to take exception to this concept of submission. It just seems archaic to many women; modern thinking derides such a notion as antiquated. Contemporary women, it is argued, are on the move as much as men. The Greek word translated as "submit" carries the idea of "to subordinate, to obey, or to submit one's self to." The goal of this instruction is not to reduce women to servants and doormats, but to provide an authority structure in the marriage.

The opposite of *submit* is *resist*. To know the value of submission, we need look no further than the consequences of resistance.

In any business organization, high productivity and good morale result from a clearly defined authority structure and good relationships. As long as the employees submit to the authority structure, the organization prospers. When employees don't know or don't follow the authority structure, morale gets low, productivity goes down, and sometimes labor organizes to deal with unresponsive management.

When our marriages don't run by God's authority structure — whether it is our wife's fault or our own — "morale" and "productivity" go down. Some women even join feminist groups — marriage's version of the labor union.

Figure 9.1 shows a continuum between submitting and resisting. Where is your wife on this continuum? If she is not a submitting wife, how has your "management style" contributed to her morale? Have you promoted "good relationships" at home?

THE ROLE OF THE WIFE

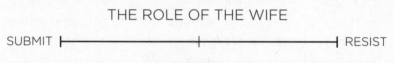

Figure 9.1

If the wife's role is to submit and operate under an authority structure, then the husband's responsibility is to create an environment for good relationships. Let's look at the biblical responsibility of the husband.

THE ROLE OF THE HUSBAND

Don hid deep feelings of guilt from his wife. He couldn't tell her he loved her, because he didn't *feel* any love toward her. And his integrity was too high to lie about something so important, so he said nothing at all.

The scriptural instruction to us as husbands is to love our wives: "Husbands, love your wives, *just as* Christ loved the church and gave himself up for her to make her holy ... *In this same way*, husbands ought to love their wives as their own bodies" (Ephesians 5:25 – 28, italics added).

Most men do not yet understand how Christ loved the church

(the people of God), and so they find it doubly difficult to love their wives in a way that they don't understand.

The Greek word for how men are to love their wives is the same word used in the Bible to describe God's own love for the world. "For God so *loved* the world that he gave his one and only Son" (John 3:16, italics added). It's also the same kind of love we are to have for God. "*Love* the Lord your God with all your heart and with all your soul and with all your mind" (Matthew 22:37, italics added).

What kind of love is this? The kind of love Scripture directs us to is *volitional* love rather than *emotional* love. Scriptural love is *agapao* love, which means to love in a moral sense; it is a deliberate act of the *will* as a matter of principle, duty, and propriety.

The English word *heart* doesn't communicate the full weight of its intended meaning without further explanation. The heart, the inner self, is comprised of three parts, as shown in Figure 9.2.

The *intellect* is the *rational man*; the *will* is the *volitional man*; and the *feelings* are the *emotional man*. We are to love our wives volitionally, as an act of the will by choice. Fortunately, we are not instructed to *feel* in love with our wives.

THE HEART

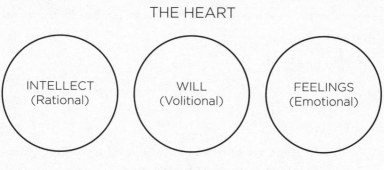

Figure 9.2

That "loving feeling" *may* be there, or it may not. But love is not a feeling, and we are to love our wives first as an act of our will. After that, feelings will come, but they will come and go. In fact, they will come and go regularly. But the love we demonstrate is a decision made as a deliberate act of the will. *Biblical love is a decision, not a feeling*.

Figure 9.3 shows another continuum, this time for men. At one end is love, and at the opposite end is hate. Hate in its worst form goes by the name of *indifference*. Where would you place an "X" for yourself?

THE ROLE OF THE HUSBAND

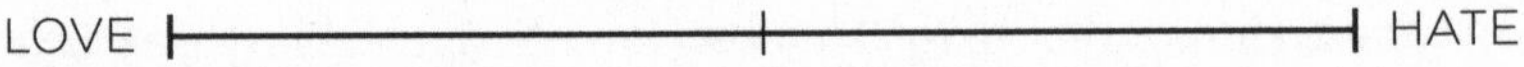

LOVE ├──────────────────────┼──────────────────────┤ HATE

Figure 9.3

Now that we have looked at the role of the husband and wife, let's look at the four types of marriages that can be created when we mix men and women together.

FOUR TYPES OF MARRIAGES

If a woman can submit or resist, and if a man can love or hate, then how many marriage combinations can we come up with? The answer is four. Figure 9.4 shows how marriages can fall into four general categories:

- Hate and Resist
- Hate and Submit
- Love and Resist
- Love and Submit

Naturally, these are only meant to be helpful working generalizations. An infinite number of shades and degrees are possible, depending on where each partner puts the "X" on their continuum, but most marriages can be placed in one of these four broad categories. Let's look at each of them individually.

FOUR TYPES OF MARRIAGES
Ephesians 5:22-23

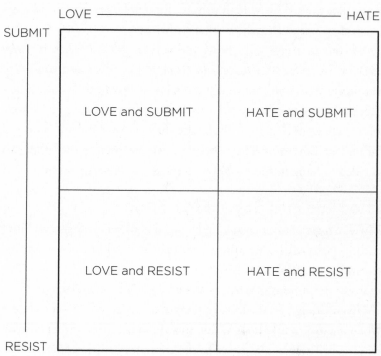

Figure 9.4

The Hate and Resist Marriage

The worst possible marriage is the one in which both partners are unhappy, and both aim for their own selfish way. Though they weren't married, think of Han Solo and Princess Leia in *Star Wars*, or Scarlett and Rhett from *Gone with the Wind*. The idea behind a Hate and Resist marriage is an angry husband married to a berating wife.

In the Hate and Resist marriage, the wife nags her man, idles the day away, and contends with her husband's authority. Her disrespect for him displays itself at social functions, at which she makes sarcastic remarks about him, which he hears for the first time.

He treats his wife harshly and doesn't consider her feelings when making family decisions. Animosity and disrespect characterize his demeanor toward his wife in private, though he pretends to like her when they attend church or other gatherings.

If your marriage falls short, and you are still together, it is not likely a true Hate and Resist marriage. Why? If it was a true Hate and Resist marriage, you would probably be divorced by now. If neither partner tries to make the marriage work, a divorce is inevitable. Most marriages that are still together but not working are Hate and Submit or Love and Resist, because one partner or the other has decided to hang in there and try to make the marriage work.

The Hate and Submit Marriage

My wife married me because I convinced her I was a Christian. Since early childhood she had always prayed she would marry according to God's will. Within weeks of our wedding day, it was crystal clear that our definitions of what makes a Christian were different.

Even though I said I was a Christian, there was no correlation when it came to my thought life, speech, or actions. I didn't nourish or care for Patsy in any way. On the contrary, I expected her to wait on my every whim.

Patsy continued to submit to me, irrespective of my response. The Bible suggests the wife can win her husband by godly behavior, which is exactly what happened in our marriage. She continued to respect me, to manage our home, and to pray for me. Within six months, I surrendered my life to the Lord.

If you've ever seen *All in the Family* reruns with Archie and Edith Bunker, you've got the caricature of this marriage—Archie, the opinionated, domineering emperor of his row house, and Edith, the submissive mouse who gets run over by Archie's belligerent demands.

If this sounds like your marriage (it's the most common type of marriage that is not working), you can turn it around by following the biblical commands for husbands (see the section titled "Love Her as the Family Prophet, Priest, and King" below). This area of life is so overrun by the Enemy that I want to restate those teachings here and challenge you to tear out or photocopy this page, tape it to your dashboard, and memorize these Bible verses:

> Husbands, love your wives and do not be harsh with them. (Colossians 3:19)

> Husbands, in the same way be considerate as you live with your wives, and treat them with respect as the weaker partner. (1 Peter 3:7)

> Anyone who does not provide for their own relatives, and especially for their own household, has denied the faith and is worse than an unbeliever. (1 Timothy 5:8)

> In this same way, husbands ought to love their wives as their own bodies. He who loves his wife loves himself. After all, no one ever hated their own body, but they feed and care for their body, just as Christ does the church. (Ephesians 5:28–29)

The Love and Resist Marriage

The feminist movement originally fueled the Love and Resist marriage syndrome. In times past, we might have pictured this marriage as a wimpy little guy dominated by a screechy-voiced battle-ax of a wife.

But today a professional woman overly devoted to her career might be a better example of the resistant wife. The two-income family puts extra tension on a marriage. The husband owes his wife some additional consideration around the house, even if her attitude about it is wrong.

The full-time homemaker is not immune to the feminist movement either. The homemaker can resist by idling away her time and not managing the household effectively.

Several years ago, my wife started feeling inadequate because she was "*just* a homemaker and mother." After some discussion, we realized she was being influenced in her thinking by the editorial bias of certain women's magazines. She promptly canceled her subscriptions.

The husband in the Love and Resist marriage should continue to love, irrespective of his wife's response. Since a husband's love is to be a decision and not a feeling, he can, through self-discipline, continue to nourish, cherish, and show consideration and respect, and not be harsh with his wife—but it's not easy.

The life of a man whose wife resists may be hard, but God will be glorified by his faithfulness to the Word of God. "A husband must not divorce his wife … Keeping God's commands is what counts. Each person should remain in the situation they were in when God called them" (1 Corinthians 7:11, 19–20).

The Love and Submit Marriage

I have known a handful of men whose marriages are really working well. After getting past the facade of wanting to appear like life is wonderful, most men will confess their marriage is not working like it's supposed to. It's the number one issue we see at our ministry—more than all the other problems *combined*. The Bible has few examples of marriages working right. Notable exceptions are Abraham and Sarah, and Joseph and Mary, two prominent examples characterized by love and submission.

How can we have a marriage that works? Here are a few ideas and cautions to help build a Love and Submit marriage.

Love Her as the Family Prophet, Priest, and King

Ephesians 5:25 offers *the principal instruction to married men*, "Husbands, love your wives, just as Christ loved the church and gave himself up for her." So if you want a biblical marriage, you need to understand how Christ loved the church.

Some men think Christ is Jesus' last name. Of course, Christ is not a name, but a title for Jesus that means "Messiah" or "anointed one." Jesus loved the church—His family—as its "Christ, or anointed one." Since husbands are to love their wives (and by extension their children, the fruit of their union) *in the same way as* the "anointed one" loves His family, they need to know exactly what Jesus was anointed to do.

In theology, Jesus, in his role as the Christ, occupies the classic threefold office of *prophet, priest,* and *king.* Because of Ephesians 5:25, you have been ordained as your family prophet, priest, and king. Let's explore these three roles.

1. The Role of a Prophet. A prophet represents God to people. In the Old Testament, a prophet would face the people and speak. Jesus is a prophet who spoke the Word of God to the people and is, in fact, the Word incarnate. A prophet speaks for God.

As a husband, you are anointed to be your family prophet. You represent God to your wife (and, by extension, to your family). When your wife reacts emotionally, you calm her with God's wisdom. You proclaim the gospel of faith to your family. You provide biblical instruction and training to your wife and children without becoming legalistic. You prepare family devotions and encourage private devotions. You are the arbiter of family values. You insist on regular church attendance. You are a *messenger* from God to your family.

2. The Role of a Priest. If a prophet represents God to people, then a priest represents people to God. In the Old Testament, a priest would turn his back to the people and mediate for them before God. Jesus is the High Priest who mediated between people and the Father by the sacrifice of His life. A priest mediates before God.

As a husband, you are anointed to be your family priest. You represent your wife and children to God. You spend time in prayer each day, remembering the needs and concerns of your wife. You pray for the salvation of your children. Like Job, you ask the Lord to forgive the sins of your children. You set the spiritual temperature in the home. You sacrifice your life for theirs. You are a *mediator* to God for your family.

3. *The Role of a King.* A king takes responsibility for the welfare of his people. He makes sure they get both justice and mercy. Jesus is a king from the line of David. A king leads, protects, and provides for his people.

As a husband, you are anointed to be your family king. You provide for the needs of your family. You work diligently to earn enough for food and shelter. You administer discipline with fairness. You quickly forgive and overlook offenses. You act in a manner worthy of receiving honor. You treat your wife with consideration and respect. You are careful not to be harsh with her. You are a *provider* for your family.

Time Together

Several years ago, my wife and I started a tradition of staying at the dinner table for twenty minutes or so after dinner. The kids raced off to practice guitar and do homework, and we would spend some time talking about each other's day. We've been doing this for decades. For the last few years, we adjourn to the couch after dinner where I rub her feet with lotion. It's not a law that we have to do it, so sometimes we don't, but we almost always spend this time together. This time investment tells her that I care. She knows I am for her, and the impact is that we are best friends. We can talk to each other about things we wouldn't talk over with anyone else — not in a million years.

Every marriage needs a balance between talking and listening. Carving out twenty minutes a day, whether over coffee in the morning or after dinner at night, will develop a *personal* relationship with each other. Harmony about family goals and problems comes from spending time fleshing out our differences about them. There can't be a meeting of the minds if the minds don't meet!

You may be thinking, *But you don't know my wife! She's the last person in the world I would want for a best friend. We have very little in common.* Think of your wife — your biblical role in her life. And think about what she was like when you first met. What attracted you to her? Since you are the spiritual leader, what responsibility do you need to take for any way you've gotten off track with each other? You may not be the easiest guy in the world to live with either! Give her the benefit of the doubt.

Why not run a thirty-day experiment? Spend twenty minutes each day talking with your wife. You can tell your wife about the experiment or simply do it and explain later!

Shared Responsibility

When I was in college, my roommate and I split the housekeeping duties. As the months rolled by, I got really steamed because I felt I was doing most of the work and my roommate was shirking. Finally, I couldn't take it anymore.

"Steve!" I exploded. "You are taking advantage of our relationship. I'm the only one who ever changes the empty roll of toilet paper. I always have to do the vacuuming, and you hardly ever wash the dishes."

"Me?" came his surprised yelp. "Why, you're the one who isn't pulling his fair share of the load. I'm the only one who ever mops the kitchen floor, and you have *never* taken out the garbage!"

We looked at each other in astonishment, and suddenly it dawned on both of us at the same time—we each remembered all the good things we did and forgot all the tasks we let slip through the cracks. We both inventoried the other's shortcomings and our own strengths. What an important lesson.

We decided if we were going to be successful roommates, we needed to make the relationship *90/10, both ways.* In other words, we realized if we both felt like we were giving 90 percent and only receiving 10 percent, then we would probably end up about fifty-fifty.

Abusing our mate's right to have help with family chores and duties can grate on a marriage. Marriages break down without cooperation. As one wife told her husband, "They named a street after you."

"Oh yeah. What's that?" he asked.

"One Way," she said.

Our marriages will work much better if we apply, by mutual agreement with our wives, the principle of *90/10, both ways*. Why? Because our human nature is to remember all the good things we did for her, and how she let us down.

HOW DO MARRIAGES GET IN TROUBLE?

Sometimes people marry for the wrong reasons. As one friend put it, "We were two ticks, both thinking the other one was a dog." More often, though, we marry with the best of intentions. But temptations start to work on us immediately.

My wife observes that most marriages begin to break down because the partners are *critical* of each other. When you are criticized, you naturally defend yourself in your mind. You begin to build up defensive walls around your self-image, with the unhappy result that you barricade yourself from your partner.

Power struggles over unyielded rights can doom a marriage. The presumed right to tell the other person what to do shows a lack of respect and sensitivity. We often tend to treat family members with a different measure of courtesy than we treat our friends or even total strangers. Since we don't *own* our partner, we should at least show her the same level of courtesy and respect we would show a stranger.

Another troubling problem is our preference for tasks. Men would rather work off an agenda or on a goal than struggle through the murky waters of building relationships. Working with like-minded men on a significant project appeals to a man a lot more than sitting up until midnight trying to express feelings!

Our self-centeredness is the root problem. When I married, I had an image of what marriage was supposed to be like. I pictured my wife serving my varied interests with doting affection, that my every wish would be her command. When it dawned on me that she wanted to be a teammate and not a slave, I became angry—both at her for not capitulating, and at myself for being so foolish.

SEX!

No temptation causes more problems for men than sex. Whether it's not enough, with someone else, pornography, or a troublesome secret thought life, our sexual drive is an Achilles' heel to every one of us. Just when we think we have our lust under control, temptation knocks again at the door of our passion.

One day I was standing in line to enter the White House for a briefing. To be totally honest, it wasn't actually the White House; it was the annex to the White House, although that's what they called it. I was standing in line with a friend, and we were talking about various matters. Somehow we started talking about lust, and I boasted, "That's a temptation the Lord has delivered me from; it's something I just don't struggle with anymore."

We went to our briefing. On the way out I decided to share a cab with some people. I was shoehorned into the cab next to a very lovely, warm lady. Our bodies were as close as a wet suit to bare skin. Every inch of my body was pressed against hers. I could feel her starting at my shoulder, running down my side, along the outside of my thigh, and next to my calf, all the way to my ankle. That was the longest twenty-minute cab ride of my life! Within moments of my thinking I had arrived, the Lord reminded me of how weak I am.

We must be committed to love our wife, and her alone, without reserve. Our culture does not prize sexual fidelity as one of its values—unless, of course, we get caught. But there certainly is no longer much cultural pressure to even pretend to be sexually pure.

For a marriage to survive today, a man and his wife must be at least as equally committed to the institution of marriage as they are committed to each other as individuals. If the institution of marriage itself is not a highly regarded value, what happens? Sooner or later, when one partner starts to feel unloving thoughts and wants to bail out, there is no moral glue to hold them together—no framework to motivate them to work through the problem.

MONEY

If sex is the impulsive marriage assassin, money is the killer that slowly strangles. Since money is the subject of the next section of this book, we will not expand in detail here, except to say getting a grip on how to handle our finances has as much potential to heal our relationships as virtually any other issue. No pressure on couples and families today exceeds financial pressure. Polls routinely show that families consider economic troubles the biggest problem they face. Money isn't important—until you don't have any! That's when our true colors often show.

COMMUNICATION

Because men and women are cognitively different in so many respects, communication between spouses frequently transmits on different wavelengths. The inevitable result of communication is misunderstanding. When we *are* talking, we have misunderstanding. How much more so, then, when we are not talking at all!

Do you remember the childhood game in which you would form a circle, and someone would whisper a phrase in the ear of the person next to them? Then each person would repeat the phrase to the person next to them, all the way around the circle, and the last person would repeat it out loud. Do you remember how different it would invariably be from the original? That's the misunderstanding that takes place when we *are* talking.

Albert Mehrabian, former professor of psychology at UCLA, suggested that only 7 percent of communication is the actual words. A remarkable 38 percent of the message is attributed to tone of voice, and 55 percent is credited to body language.[22] If you question this, as I did at first, consider this example.

How many different messages do you think we can communicate with these four words: "What do you want?" Let's suppose you had a hard day at the office. You're tired and frustrated, and someone cut you off on the way home. Then you had to stop in the driveway, get out, and move your son's bike and skateboard. Get the picture? What you want more than anything else in the world is about thirty minutes of peace and quiet.

So you greet everyone and promptly adjourn to your favorite chair with the newspaper. A few minutes later, your wife comes in to ask you a question. What's your response? Do you naturally set the paper down, gaze affectionately into her eyes, and say, "Hi, darling, what do you want?" Or is it more likely that you try to send her a signal by leaving your nose buried in the paper and ask in monotone disgust, "Yes, dear, what do you want?" Or is it possible that you might respond more abruptly—maybe even crumple the paper in affected anger—and bark, "What do you want?"

Same four words, yet three totally different messages. Why? Just picture in your mind the differences in tone of voice and body language in our example.

The inevitable result of communication is misunderstanding, because we assume the receiver picks up the same transmission we send. But the receiver always has a separate agenda and his or her own unique view of the world. Only through dialogue can we be certain we are being understood.

CONCLUSION

Many men are less than happily married. They don't *feel* like they are in love and don't understand the biblical definition of love. But it doesn't have to end that way. The Scriptures clarify the role of both husband and wife.

Four types of marriages are possible by combining the husband's response to his role with his wife's response to hers. He can either love or hate, and she can either submit or resist.

The Love and Submit marriage does not happen by contract, but by careful, daily administration of the biblical commands to love, cherish, nourish, respect, and provide for your wife, and to be considerate and not harsh toward her.

Are you less than happily married? Perhaps you are not unhappy, but you sense you are missing out on the best that marriage can offer. Have your wife read this chapter, and then spend some time together answering the sixteen questions below. Make a habit of talking about matters that matter.

QUESTIONS TO DISCUSS WITH YOUR SPOUSE

Spend twenty minutes together daily for thirty days — form a habit.

1. What are three to five things about me that you really like?
2. What are two things I do that you wish I would stop doing or change?
3. Where are you on your spiritual journey?
4. What do you think is the purpose of your life?
5. What is something we could do together in our spare time?
6. What is a trip you've always dreamed of taking?
7. What are your greatest regrets about your life?
8. What has been your biggest disappointment?
9. How do you feel about how the kids are turning (have turned) out?
10. If you could change any one thing about your life, what would it be?
11. If you had no one else to answer to, what would you like to be doing in five years? Ten years? In retirement?
12. What is one tangible way I can better express my love for you?

13. Where do you think you are, and where do you think I am, on this continuum?

Men: Love |————————————————| Hate

Women: Submit |————————————————| Resist

Discuss why your answers are different. Discuss each other's willingness to change.

14. Which of the four types of marriages do we have?

15. What practical steps could each of us take to have a Love and Submit marriage?

16. *Husband:* Read 1 Corinthians 13 to your wife out loud. Confess to her the areas where you have failed and ask her forgiveness. *Wife:* Do the same.

———————————— FOCUS QUESTIONS ————————————

1. How has the role of women changed over the past few decades? How have these changes been for the better? How have they been for the worse?

2. Read Ephesians 5:22–33. What is the biblical role of the wife? If our wives do submit to us, what implied responsibilities do we have?

3. What is the biblical role of the husband? Do you think it's important for a man to "feel" in love with his wife? Why?

4. What kind of love does the Bible command us to have for our wives? How is this different from the love we see portrayed on television and in movies?

5. Refer to Figure 9.4. If a marriage is not a Love and Submit marriage, which of the other three types is it most likely to be? Which of the four categories of marriages best

illustrates your marriage? What practical steps can you take to improve your marriage?

6. How much time do you spend with your wife on a daily basis? What do you think of the idea of spending twenty minutes a day together talking? Will you give it a try?

7. If both husband and wife each give 90 percent and expect 10 percent in return, their marriage will probably end up about fifty-fifty. Comment on this thought. What do you think of asking your wife to try out the concept of *90/10, both ways*?

CHAPTER 10

FRIENDS: RISKS AND REWARDS

Five years from now you will be pretty much the
same as you are today except for two things: the
books you read and the people you get close to.
Charles Jones

Jonathan said to David, "Whatever you
want me to do, I'll do for you."
1 Samuel 20:4

No one in their right mind would even dream of asking for the
kind of help Robert offered. In fact, I found his proposition
downright embarrassing.

A recession had brought the pressure of negative cash flow. Can
you think of any feeling gloomier than financial pressure? Robert and I had been friends for a dozen years. We just clicked. Our
mutual interest in business was a factor, but our personalities really
meshed too.

So it was natural for me to stop by and visit with Robert when my
business problems were bigger than my own ingenuity. He listened
patiently for a couple of hours. It was good for me to be able to sort
out my thinking.

Then Robert said a remarkable thing. Maybe I thought he would give me advice that would magically turn around the business. Perhaps I had been looking for some encouragement. But what he said floored me.

"I don't have any answers, but if the worst comes to pass," he said, "I've got enough money for the both of us to live on. Whatever I have is yours."

There was something about the way Robert said it that made me realize he wasn't just joking around. He really meant what he said. Of course, I could never take Robert up on his offer, but his act of true friendship reminded me of the God who owns the cattle on a thousand hills.

Suddenly the problems seemed minuscule. I knew God would provide for me. By being my friend, Robert had shown me how much God loved me, and I knew I would be all right.

THE PROBLEM

Do you have a close friend? I don't just mean someone to call for lunch, but I mean a genuinely *close* friend, a friend like you had in college or high school? The kind of friend you talked to about anything and everything. The kind of friend who just laughed when you said something really dumb. The kind of friend you could really let your hair down with. The kind of friend you knew would be there if you needed someone to talk to, or if you were in real trouble, or if you were hurting.

Whatever happened to those kinds of friends? Why don't men develop adult friendships that have those same transparent, vulnerable qualities as the friendships of our youth?

After we tear out the calendar pages of school days gone by, we get down to the tasks of establishing a career, choosing a life mate, starting a family, building a life, and accumulating things. During this "building" stage of life, not much time for friends is available—and the perceived need isn't that great. After all, a new wife and children meet many of our relationship needs.

But as time marches on, needs emerge that can only be met by other men—men who walk in the same shoes, men who share the same problems, men with similar life experiences—other Christian men. At some point, men realize they need genuine friends, but adult friendships are difficult to start and harder to keep.

The closest relationships most men end up with are those organized around their careers. All day long, men work on common tasks together, and those common goals create a level of fellowship and kindred spirit—whether that's hanging drywall or selling real estate. But work relationships rarely develop into personal interest, especially at any depth.

Most men have a friendship "deficit." Their balance sheets are empty when it comes to true friends. Most men don't know how to go about developing a true friend, or how to be one.

We may be surrounded by many acquaintances but lonely for someone to really talk to. We don't have someone to share our deepest dreams and fears with. We don't have anyone who is willing to just listen, to simply be a friend and listen, and not always have a quick solution.

Friends bring risks—rejection, betrayal, embarrassment, hurt feelings. But friends are worth the risk, if we can learn how to find them.

FRIENDS VERSUS ACQUAINTANCES

A successful businessman in our city was heard to say, "All you need in life are fifty friends. That's a party every week of the year!"

What he was talking about, of course, was not fifty *friends*, but fifty *acquaintances*. No man can maintain fifty friendships—to be a bona fide friend takes time and energy. None of us can keep up with more than a few genuine friends.

Once I boasted to an acquaintance, quite sincerely, that I had hundreds of friends. Without pause he said, "No, you don't. You may have met hundreds of people, but there's no way you can really know more than a handful of people. You'd be lucky if you had three real friends."

At first I was offended that he thought he knew so much about my situation. But as I reflected on what he said, I realized that I had a thousand acquaintances but, at that moment in time, *fewer* than three genuine friends. I've worked on this area of my life, and today I believe I have five real friends, including my wife.

We all have a "circle of friends," a group with whom we play golf, attend church, go to dinner, or share a common interest, like fishing or softball. Often, however, these are "well-patient" friends—that is, they are there for the good times.

What we are speaking about in this chapter is "sick-patient" friends—friends who will hang in there with us when we've lost our job, separated from our wife, found out our daughter is on drugs, or are just plain frustrated with our life.

Our circle of friends may be more than mere acquaintances, but they still don't know the "real me."

Are the men you consider friends really friends? Are they the kind of friends you can go to when you are in trouble, when you have really blown it? Or, as with the successful businessman, are your friends only there for the party? I think most men could recruit six pallbearers, but hardly anyone has a friend he can call at 2:00 a.m.

FRIENDS ARE HARD TO FIND

A prominent man like Don entertained a lot, so the cars in front of his house were not unusual. He gazed at the crowd gathered around his pool. "I wonder how many of these people would send me flowers if I was in an auto accident next week?"

"Wealth attracts many friends, but even the closest friend of the poor person deserts them" (Proverbs 19:4). How do we know if our friend is true-blue, or if he will turn out to be a fair-weather friend if we really have problems? Unless we get past talking about news, sports, and weather, we won't know until it may be too late.

Frankly, most men are ill-equipped to lead a discussion about the deeper part of life or feel awkward bringing it up for fear of offending someone. The Focus Questions at the end of each chapter in this book can be used to get past the shallow waters of small talk. But right now, let's take a pop quiz to see what kind of friends you have.

POP QUIZ

Perhaps you have several close friends, or maybe you have none. Or, more likely, you *know* many men, but you are not sure just how deep the waters run. Reflect on these questions, and see if you have gone far enough to develop some genuine friends.

1. When things go sour and you really feel lousy, do you have a friend you can tell?
   ☑ Yes ☐ No.

2. Do you have a friend you can express any honest thought to without fear of appearing foolish?
   ☑ Yes ☐ No

3. Do you have a friend who will let you talk through a problem *without* giving you advice? Someone who will just be a sounding board?
   ☑ Yes ☐ No

4. Will your friend risk your disapproval to suggest you may be getting off track in your priorities?
   ☐ Yes ☐ No

5. Do you have a friend who will take the risk to tell you that you are sinning? Or using poor judgment?
   ☐ Yes ☑ No

6. If you had a moral failure, do you *know* your friend would stand with you?

   ☑ Yes ☐ No

7. Is there a friend with whom you feel you are facing life together? A friend to talk over the struggles of life that are unique to men?

   ☑ Yes ☐ No

8. Do you have a friend you believe you can trust, with whom confidential thoughts will *stay* confidential?

   ☑ Yes ☐ No

9. When you are vulnerable and transparent with your friend, are you convinced he will not think less of you?

   ☐ Yes ☐ No

10. Do you meet with a friend weekly or biweekly for fellowship and prayer, and possibly for accountability?

    ☐ Yes ☑ No

If you were unable to answer yes to most of these questions, then let me urge you to consider the principles in this chapter and take the risk—develop a few close friendships. Wouldn't it be rewarding to retake this quiz in a year and score all yeses? Why do men struggle with developing true friendships?

TOO CLOSE FOR COMFORT

John knew he was leading a secret thought life, a life far different from the image he projected. He was never more aware than when he had lunch with his friend Bill. When Bill asked how things were going, John felt Bill somehow peered into his mind. The longer they were friends, the more "naked" his thoughts seemed.

In reality, John disguised himself completely and had Bill totally fooled. In time, he started to cancel out on lunches at the last minute, finally giving them up altogether. Bill was getting too close for comfort.

Men live with a paradox. We sincerely want to have close friends, yet we fear letting someone get *too* close. We worry that if someone *really* got to know us, they wouldn't like us. As someone starts to get too close, we find ourselves withdrawing—we change the subject, or figure out how to say good-bye.

We need approval, to be accepted by another person, but we fear the opposite—that we will be rejected. So we keep our distance. If we don't become vulnerable with someone, then we safely avoid the risk of rejection.

Few men have friends who really know the inner man. By keeping things at a distance—on a surface level (news, sports, and weather)—they don't have to feel the pressure of dealing with their weaknesses.

That is one of the problems with friendship. As we become closer to someone, we really *do* want to share our secrets with them. *We want to be known*, to have someone *care* about us and *help* when we are hurting. But we also find another force at work within us, urging us to keep our distance so we won't get burned. How do we get burned?

BETRAYED!

Julius Caesar trusted Marcus Junius Brutus implicitly. They had shared great ideas and their secrets together.

On the Ides of March, 44 BC, Caesar entered the Roman Senate house as usual, but on this day he was greeted by his assassins. He struggled to escape, clashing with the conspirators. Then he saw Brutus!—approaching with drawn dagger, ready to deliver a blow.

Stung by betrayal, Caesar abandoned his resistance, pulled his robe over his face, and uttered that famous, haunting interrogative, *"Et tu, Brute?"* or "You too, Brutus?" and went with no further protest to his death.

While few will ever know such stinging betrayal as Caesar, our friends can "stab" our trust to death.

Fred always greets me like an agitated porcupine; I come away pulling spikes out of my hide! I told my friend Jim in confidence how I struggled to like Fred. I just needed to talk it through with someone.

Two weeks later, a mutual friend said to me, "I know what you mean about Fred; I have the same struggle."

Betrayed! The consequences may not be catastrophic, but the trust level may be difficult to repair. Everyone, it seems, has at least one confidant — one *other* person they feel comfortable telling *your* secret.

The trouble, you can see, is if everyone has one other person they can tell, then soon the whole world knows! And nowhere is this more prevalent than in Christian circles. Lower-natured gossip often disguises itself as Christian concern: "We need to pray for [so and so]." Benjamin Franklin captured the idea when he said, "Three people can keep a secret, as long as two of them are dead."

Since everyone, and I do mean *everyone*, does have at least one other confidant, then the only way to avoid betrayal by a friend is to verbalize some ground rules. And if you learn that a friend has betrayed a confidence, you should try to save the friendship by a loving confrontation. If your friend is sorry (and he surely will be), then you have saved a friend. If not, it's no big loss.

Once, a depressed King David was being maligned by his enemies, who hoped for his death, slandered his reputation, and spread lies about him. But what really got to him was the treachery of his friend. He wrote:

If an enemy were insulting me,
    I could endure it;
if a foe were rising against me,
    I could hide.

But it is you, a man like myself,
>   my companion, my close friend,
with whom I once enjoyed sweet fellowship
>   at the house of God,
as we walked about
>   among the worshipers.

Psalm 55:12–14

Few types of emotional pain cut as deeply or wound as savagely as that of betrayal by a friend.

Trust, transparency, and vulnerability are the stuff of which true friendships are constructed. Often our fear of betrayal outweighs our willingness to risk trusting another man with our inner thoughts, so we choose to remain invulnerable. As the song goes, "And a rock feels no pain, and an island never cries."[23]

Of course, we do feel pain, and we do cry. That's why we need a friend.

MY FIRST ADULT FRIEND

Developing a friendship requires as much work, forethought, and effort to succeed as any worthwhile endeavor. Not long after becoming a follower of Christ I attended a men's retreat. One of the primary speakers, Tom Skinner, talked about relationships and the importance of getting close to someone to help each other develop into full spiritual maturity.

I thought about what was said and realized I wasn't in a relationship with another guy where we were pushing ourselves spiritually or thinking together about how to help change our city for Christ.

The next Sunday I asked a man thirty years my senior if he would like to meet weekly for fellowship, prayer, and accountability. Without reservation, he responded with an enthusiastic, "Yes!" We met every Wednesday for thirty-two years until he passed away.

I think many men have this same level of interest for a one-on-one friendship, but few take the initiative. If you want a real friend, you will probably need to be the one who takes the first step.

TAKING THE RISK

Personally, I have a propensity for close friends, and for many years I have taken the initiative to have several close friendships developing at the same time. But I must confess to more failures than successes.

It's not that the friendships failed. On the contrary, I enjoy a great circle of friends. Yet many of these friendships didn't reach their full potential. The veneer of personal vulnerability just couldn't be pierced, or if it was pierced, the relationship became too close for comfort.

When a man feels someone is getting too close for comfort, appointments inexplicably begin to conflict with the meeting time, or some similar reason to not meet develops. In my own case, I'm sure I'm at fault for any of my friendships that didn't reach their full potential, but at least I was willing to take the risk.

The price of friendship is personal vulnerability. If we stiff-arm our friend when he starts to get too close, he will understand the message and withdraw, unless he is particularly secure and committed to making the friendship work.

If our friend is committed, he will press us to be transparent. Then it's our move—we can peel back the mask or continue the stiff-arm. Of course, someone can violate the process of building relationships and come on too strong too quickly. But to work, transparency must eventually characterize a friendship. If someone gets too close for comfort, we have two choices: get real, or get too busy to meet.

FOUR GREAT REASONS FOR HAVING FRIENDS

Frankly, not many men are willing to take the risk. It sounds simple, but in practice it's complicated. The fragile male ego and the complicated dynamics of a relationship make for hard work and limited results. Is it worth it? Absolutely. Here are four of the benefits of having friends.

A Friend Is There When You Need Him

What is the purpose of a friend? Solomon, the wisest man who ever lived, wrote, "Two are better than one, because they have a good return for their labor: If either of them falls down, one can help the other up. But pity anyone who falls and has no one to help them up" (Ecclesiastes 4:9–10).

Moral failures, spiritual wilderness experiences, broken marriages, blows to our ego, career setbacks, sins—*everyone* falls down! Who will help us up? Our friend will help, if we have one, "but pity anyone who falls and has no one to help them up."

A friend can help us chisel the truth into our thinking. The battle for our minds intensifies as we become more spiritually mature—it never stops. A friend helps us defend ourselves against the enemies we can and cannot see. "Though one may be overpowered, two can defend themselves" (Ecclesiastes 4:12). No one can sneak up behind two men fighting back-to-back. Two men fighting back-to-back can cover all the angles.

A Friend Keeps Us on Track

The bank turned down the loan. It was the first loan I had ever applied for. Three years I had banked with them. Was I ever hot! I told everyone who would listen what a terrible deed those bankers had done to me.

A friend pulled me up short and said, "Pat, in life, if you like what you see, tell your friends. If you don't like what you see, tell only those folks." I realized what a fool I was to tell everyone except someone who could do something about it.

The executive vice president of the bank agreed to see me. I shared what my friend had said and told him I had come to set things right.

He made the loan. And then, for poetic justice, I struggled and had to make sacrifices to pay it back.

It frightens me how quickly I can go off on a tangent. I think most of us have the capacity to rationalize ourselves into believing our theories and ideas are always right. But just because we say something is so doesn't necessarily make it so. Worse still, our ego and pride always lie in wait for a moment of faintheartedness. A friend keeps us on track. "Wounds from a friend can be trusted, but an enemy multiplies kisses ... and the pleasantness of a friend springs from their heartfelt advice" (Proverbs 27:6, 9). We all need someone to do a "reality check" on us occasionally to make sure we are not kidding ourselves.

A Friend Helps Us Crystallize Our Thinking

"I just need someone to talk to," he said.

"Come on by," I replied.

For an hour and a half he went on and on. Then, without a moment's notice, he said, "Thank you. You have no idea how much this has meant to me," and he abruptly left. All I did was say hello and good-bye.

Think back to a time when you were deeply troubled about something; perhaps you are right now. You can't quite seem to think your problem through. Your spirit is troubled, and you are filled with anxiety as you try to sort out your thinking. *If only I had someone to talk to*, you wish. That's what friends are for!

Our minds play tricks on us, but a friend can help by acting as a sounding board. When we talk to a friend, we are forced to organize our thoughts into coherent sentences. Talking a matter through helps to crystallize our thinking in a way no other method of reasoning can do. There is a certain kind of *discipline* in speaking that doesn't exist in thinking. "As iron sharpens iron, so one person sharpens another" (Proverbs 27:17). Usually the right answer will make itself known when we "talk it out."

A Friend Will Listen

Other times we don't need a solution; we just need someone to feel our pain.

When Sid's voice came on the other end of the line, my hands began to tremble. As soon as I heard his tone of voice, I knew the deal was off. Somehow I knew it was useless to try to persuade him to change his mind; I would just become a pitiful beggar.

He continued to drone on, but my thoughts raced ahead—*cash flow, layoffs, all that wasted time, the shock of it. How will my company survive? I wonder if Patsy has left the house yet?*

The phone rang four times; my palms started to sweat. She always ate lunch with her sister on Mondays, and I guessed she had already left. A sea of anguish swept over me at the thought of not being able to talk to my best friend and wife, Patsy, right away. Then she answered—relief swept over me.

As only a friend will do, she canceled her plans so she could be with me. When we met at the restaurant parking lot, seeing my friend was like a warm ray of sunshine on a rainy day, consoling my downcast spirit.

She listened. That's all she needed to do.

What I wanted most of all was just someone to listen—to hear me without feeling the need to give me advice. Often what we need is not wise counsel, but wise empathy. Not words, just compassion.

Whom do you call when you get bad or sad news? Is there anyone who will care? Do you have such a friend? "A friend loves at all times, and a brother is born for a time of adversity" (Proverbs 17:17). "There is a friend who sticks closer than a brother" (Proverbs 18:24).

■ ■ ■

We've made true friendship look attractive in this chapter. And it is. Just like with anything worthwhile, however, friendship requires work—bona fide friendships must be developed.

To succeed past the cliché level of friendship requires an investment of time, trust, and vulnerability. The reward will be a genuine friend—someone about whom you can answer yes to the pop quiz questions we asked earlier.

FOCUS QUESTIONS

1. Most men do not have a close friend they meet with regularly.

   ❑ Agree ❑ Disagree. Explain your answer.

2. How many men do you know who have the kind of friend mentioned in the first question? Why do you think men find it difficult to establish and maintain close friendships?

3. Explain the difference between an *acquaintance* and a *friend*. Do you think it's possible to ever again have a friend like the friends of your youth?

4. Have you ever been stung by the betrayal of a close friend? How has the experience affected your other relationships?

5. Do you have anyone with whom you can be vulnerable? What would it take for you to be vulnerable with a friend?

6. Sometimes we need a friend to give us advice. Who gives you advice?

7. Sometimes we need a friend to be a sounding board. Who acts as a sounding board in your life?

8. Sometimes we need a friend who will just listen. Do you have a friend who will "feel" for you without giving you a big lecture?

PART 3

SOLVING OUR MONEY PROBLEMS

CHAPTER 11

MONEY: A BIBLICAL POINT OF VIEW

The problem with money is that it makes
you do things you don't want to do.
Wall Street, the movie

A faithful person will be richly blessed …
Proverbs 28:20

For several months Todd felt the pressure of his debts mounting. He loved the good life and had followed the advice of the magazine and TV ads. But his lifestyle put a strain on his family and weighed heavily on his mind.

His wife, Janelle, patiently supported him emotionally, but she, too, felt helpless. From out of nowhere, thoughts of divorce would pop into her mind, but she would immediately dismiss them. Still, she wondered if Todd would ever stop chasing the rainbow.

One particularly hot day, he took a long look at the swimming pools in the backyards of the neighbors around him. Todd contacted a pool contractor, who agreed to drop by after dinner to talk it over. Todd wondered how he could afford a new pool. "How are people supposed to make important financial decisions?" he queried to no one in particular.

THE PROBLEM

Recently I asked 150 men if they were having financial problems. Sixty percent of the men answered, "Yes." One man told me, "I don't have any problems money can't solve."

How would you rate your biblical IQ on money? Frankly, the Bible can be very confusing about money. Why? Since the Bible says so much about how to handle money and possessions, the subject is wide open for misunderstanding. Howard Dayton, financial author and founder of Compass—*finances God's way*, a financial training ministry, has counted about 500 verses in the Bible on prayer, but more than 2,350 verses on how to handle money and possessions. The entire Scriptures have to be combed to have a total grasp of what they say.

By winking at Scriptures we don't like and cherry-picking Scriptures we do like, we tend to create our own tidy little theology about God and money. The result is a personal perspective on money that often suits the desire of our private wish world, not one carefully chiseled by a search for truth.

The problem of money is summed up by Jesus: "No one can serve two masters. Either you will hate the one and love the other, or you will be devoted to the one and despise the other. You cannot serve both God and money" (Matthew 6:24). The word *serve* carries the meaning "to be a slave to, literally or figuratively, voluntarily or involuntarily."

It is not a question of *advisability*: "You *should not* serve both God and money." That would be a *priority* choice.

It is not a question of *accountability*: "You *must not* serve both God and money." That would be a *moral* choice.

Rather, it is a matter of *impossibility*: "You *cannot* serve both God and money." *There is no choice*; we each serve one, and only one, master. We are either a slave to God or a slave to money. Why did Jesus say we cannot serve both?

Frankly, this teaching is hard to understand and accept. I know I used to think to myself, *This principle must certainly apply only to weak people. I can see how it would apply to someone of less self-discipline and intelligence. But I am different. I think I can serve God just fine and still pursue my plans to acquire wealth.* But my best qualification to write on this subject is my own failure in handling money biblically.

How profound Solomon proved himself to be when he wrote, "Whoever loves money never has enough; whoever loves wealth is never satisfied with their income" (Ecclesiastes 5:10). Jesus knows the *need* for money we face; He knows the *pressure* we can be under to make money; and He knows its *allure* will pull us away from Him.

Money is intoxicating. It is an opiate that addicts as easily and as completely as the iron grip of alcohol or drugs. Its power to change us for the worse is close to that of Jesus Christ to change us for the better. Money possesses the power to rule our lives, not for good and forever, as Christ does, but rather to lure us, like a moth, too close to the flame until finally our wings are set ablaze.

Money enslaves men; it will work you till you die. And after it has conquered your poor soul, its haunting laughter can be heard howling through the chambers of hell. And then it seeks out another hapless, unsuspecting victim—an ambitious man like you who wants just a little bigger slice of the good life.

THE POWER OF MONEY

The wealthy Florida coastal town attracted upscale retirees from everywhere in the country. It seemed to Sandy like a perfect community for Cru's "I Found It" campaign. The program, you may recall, saturated communities nationwide with media coverage. The "I Found It" bumper stickers were everywhere! People who asked what had been found learned the answer: "new life in Jesus Christ."

Sandy, the local director, found a correlation between interest in the gospel message and the distance people lived from the ocean. The closer people lived to the water, the less interested they were. Conversely, the farther from the water they went, the greater the interest.

The wealthy people live in the condominiums closest to the water, while the service help, who work in the hotels along the coast, live in the mobile home parks farthest from the water.

Jesus said so much about money because it is the most insidious, beguiling, pervasive temptation. Money is not just a temptation for a moment of carnal pleasure; it's a temptation for us to be conquered by an inert, mindless master, one incapable of saving us from sin or satisfying the deep hunger of our soul for true peace, meaning, and purpose.

Jesus said that the Word of God sown "among the thorns refers to someone who hears the word, but the worries of this life and the deceitfulness of wealth choke the word, making it unfruitful" (Matthew 13:22). That's how it is over at the beach.

THE TEST OF A MAN'S TRUE CHARACTER

No test of a man's true character is more conclusive than how he spends his time and his money. If you want to know what is important to a man, you can ask him, and he will give you his best guess. He may think himself generous because he always drops change in the slot to help needy kids. But what is happening with the rest of his checkbook?

If we really want to know what is important to us, let's get out our calendars and our checkbooks; let's look at how we spend our time and our money, and then we will know what's really important to us. Because no test of our true character is more conclusive than how we use our time and our money.

OUT OF CONTROL

In chapter 1, "The Rat Race," I mentioned the shifting values of the generations from a meaningful life philosophy to one of making money. We have become a nation bewitched by bling.

Let me give an example. A friend and business colleague of mine — let's call him Jack — built his dream home at the peak of his earnings and the peak of the housing market. Over lunch, he told me his income plummeted to about 10 percent of what he had been making. He had burned through most of his savings, and the debt was eating him alive. He had to sell his dream home. He had tears in his eyes.

But then Jack went on to tell a remarkable story. He told me he and his wife had taken in two teenage girls after their mom died of cancer and their sister's husband kicked them out. Their father had bailed on them long ago. With no place to go, they called Jack's wife, who had just a week earlier offered to help if it came to that.

Jack and his wife had no idea what they were getting into. Everyone who works with homeless people knows that rule number one is *never invite them to move in with you.* But don't tell that to my friend Jack. They cared for those girls for ten months. By the end of that time, they had helped one girl get a full-ride scholarship to a great university. The other girl met three young Christian women who invited her to be their fourth roommate.

Jack and his wife epitomize the kind of Christians we all would love to be, don't they? Then he told me this: "Pat, I would have never in a million years helped those girls if I had still been flying high. I was out of control. I needed to be humbled. What's happening to me hurts, but I needed this."

The housing bubble that collapsed during 2007 and 2008 underscores the problem. Everyone was guilty — the banks, the builders, the borrowers. Driven by greed, they all wanted just a little more than they were entitled to — a bigger loan, a bigger profit, a bigger home. I'm sure that somewhere, someone is innocent. But the vast majority of people who bought houses they couldn't afford and the people who built, sold, and financed them knew exactly what they were doing.

Money, however, is not the measure of prosperity the Bible commends. Nor is it necessary to fret over whether or not God will provide for our needs. God, who owns everything, has *obligated* Himself to meet *all* the needs of the *faithful*: "My God will meet all your needs according to the riches of his glory in Christ Jesus" (Philippians 4:19). Our part? "Now it is required that those who have been given a trust must prove faithful" (1 Corinthians 4:2).

Since God has promised to meet all of our needs (as determined by Him, not us) if we are faithful and obedient to Him, then we can conclude that feeling out of control is self-inflicted pain. It results from serving money instead of God.

IS IT MONEY OR ME?

What is money? Money is morally neutral, just like a handgun or morphine. Put a pistol in the hand of a policeman and it's a tool of justice, but in the hand of a criminal it's an instrument of evil. Morphine in the wound of a soldier saves him, but it is death in the arm of a drug addict.

Money is simply a commodity, a medium of exchange, an inert means to other ends. We get money in four ways:

1. We exchange our labor for it.
2. We rent it to others for a return.
3. We hire others and earn a profit on their labor.
4. We take risks calculated to earn money.

Money, by itself, is uncomplicated. The problem, then, must be with men. Jesus said so much about money because He knew how much we would struggle with it—that it would be His main competitor for our affections.

We need money, lots of money, to meet our family needs. Money is not some ethereal felt need; money is a real need. When the first of the month rolls around and the mortgage payment isn't made, the pressure starts to mount. The mortgage company isn't looking for Jesus; they want cash! When the tenth of the month gives way to the twentieth, the stomach secretes an overdose of anxiety.

Whether rich or poor, everyone needs money. The more money we have, the more we need. Solomon wrote, "As goods increase, so do those who consume them" (Ecclesiastes 5:11). More money only brings more responsibilities. The poor sometimes have an advantage over the rich: they can still cling to the illusion that money will make them happy. Why do well-meaning Christians have such a wide diversity of opinions about how to handle their money?

THREE PERSPECTIVES OF PROSPERITY

The Bible is chock-full of teachings about money and possessions. Most of us, however, only have a partial understanding of God's money principles.

Figure 11.1 depicts a range of *theological perspectives* that are commonplace today. They are represented on a continuum, because an endless number of perspectives can be discovered if you talk to enough people. Everyone, it seems, has their unique opinions, many of which can be backed up by specific verses from the Bible.

The three prevailing perspectives are *poverty theology*, *prosperity theology* (sometimes championed as the *prosperity gospel*), and *stewardship theology*.

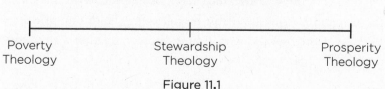

RANGE OF THEOLOGICAL
PERSPECTIVES OF PROSPERITY

Poverty
Theology

Stewardship
Theology

Prosperity
Theology

Figure 11.1

Difficulties arise because a case can be built for each of these three perspectives. The problem, however, is that God intended only *one theology*—not a menu of options to choose from, depending on individual tastes and preferences. How do different perspectives arise?

Most of us decide what we want to do, and then look for evidence to support the decision we have already made. That isn't very objective! We can call it cherry-picking the Bible—looking for verses we like and ignoring verses we would rather not be there.

We also kid, trick, and fool ourselves when we "wink" at Scripture. In other words, we see and understand, but our powerful self-will persuades us to simply ignore the truth.

To arrive at God's perspective, a man must be willing to look at the whole counsel of God—the whole Bible—and be willing to set aside his preconceived ideas. Figure 11.2 contrasts poverty, prosperity, and stewardship theology.

Poverty Theology

The disciple of poverty theology is disgusted with worldliness, best symbolized by man's obsession with money. He believes possessions are a curse and has rejected materialism in any and every form. A strong bias toward helping the poor exists, but he has few, if any, resources to actually help with the solution. A few guilty Christians with wealth may also fall into this category, especially if they inherited their money. As you can see in Figure 11.2, this view has considerable merit.

Prosperity Theology

The disciple of prosperity theology believes we have not because we ask not. They often have learned about tithing and have experienced the material blessings available by following the tithing principle. Because of their success with tithing, a preoccupation with money develops.

THREE PERSPECTIVES CONTRASTED

	Poverty	Prosperity	Stewardship
View of prosperity	Nonmaterialistic; disdain for possessions	Prosperity is the reward of the righteous	Possessions are a trust given in varying proportions
In a word, possessions are	a curse	a right	a privilege
Scriptural reference	Luke 18:18–22: sell, give to poor (rich young ruler)	Matthew 7:7–8: ask, seek, knock	Matthew 25:14–30: parable of bags of gold
Mitigation	Proverbs 21:20: "The wise store up choice food and olive oil, but fools gulp theirs down."	Proverbs 23:4: "Do not wear yourself out to get rich."	None
Needs met by	carefree attitude: don't worry; seek kingdom first (Matthew 6:25–34)	transaction: tithe for a blessing (Malachi 3:10)	faithful administration (Matthew 25:21, 23; 1 Corinthians 4:2)
Concept	rejecter	owner	steward
Attitude toward poor	we are	we owe	we care
Preoccupation	daily needs	money	wisdom
Attitude	carefree (Proverbs 3:5–6)	driven (Proverbs 10:17)	faithful (Luke 16:10–11)

Figure 11.2

The prosperity disciple soon begins to explain the lacking of others who don't experience God's financial blessings as a lack of faith. The other dimensions of a relationship with God become, somehow, less significant. Someone who is not doing well financially is looked on as not "reaching out and claiming their blessings." No room is allowed for God to call some people to be poor. Many disciples of prosperity theology live consumptive lifestyles.

Stewardship Theology

Stewards believe God owns and controls everything. Possessions are a privilege and not a right, and the steward indeed gives up his rights. He interprets Scripture as teaching that possessions are a trust given in varying proportions, depending on the innate, God-given abilities he has and his faithfulness and obedience to follow biblical principles. The steward believes prosperity results from faithfully administering his talents, as given by God at His sole discretion.

His preoccupation is not with accumulating wealth or renouncing it, but with being wise in the conduct of his affairs. His goal is to be like the man described in Psalm 112: "Good will come to those who are generous and lend freely, who conduct their affairs with justice ... They have freely scattered their gifts to the poor" (Psalm 112:5, 9).

■ ■ ■

Which one is the right choice? From the three descriptions we have just fashioned, you can see why confusion is possible. Depending on your upbringing, the influences on your life, and how you *want* to interpret the Bible, any of these three perspectives could seem unquestionably logical to you. But does that mean all three are correct? No, *God has only one perspective*, and it is the perspective of a steward. Closer examination reveals the perspectives of poverty theology and prosperity theology are rife with flaws.

LEAKS IN THE DIKE

The prosperity gospel doesn't hold water because it claims you can *give* to *get*. The theory is that you can create a binding *transaction* on God in which He is obligated to *bless* you. This view disregards your motives, whether or not you are living in sin, and God's plan for your life.

When I was a young businessman, I heard about the idea of pledging a tithe of a certain amount to God, and then, by faith, claiming the income level to support that amount. So I figured out a nice round six-figure income that I secretly desired, and I pledged to give God 10 percent of that amount.

I had been doing pretty well up to that point! All of a sudden, my income was clobbered. I had the worst year imaginable. I tried to buy God, and He chastened me severely and taught me a lesson I have never forgotten: "The blessing of the LORD brings wealth, without painful toil for it" (Proverbs 10:22). If you are experiencing trouble in your desire for wealth, you can be confident the Lord desires to teach you something.

Poverty theology is equally full of holes. The person who thinks one must be poor to be humble is mistaken. He doesn't understand God's mandate to be industrious and to make full use of his abilities, in whatever proportion they have been given. Since he has never had money or didn't have to earn it, he is categorically suspicious of anyone who has attained financial success. He believes true Christians should sell their possessions and give the proceeds to the poor.

One year we invited a prominent Christian speaker to town to speak at a leadership conference. We decided to host a luncheon for lawyers and judges the day before. I announced both the conference and the special luncheon at our church one Sunday.

After the service, I was accosted by a disciple of poverty theology. This man, who holds extensive postgraduate degrees, was earning his living as a substitute schoolteacher, barely making ends meet.

"I don't guess I will be able to come to your conference," came his sarcastic greeting.

"Oh, I am sorry to hear that!" I replied.

"Yeah, since I wouldn't be welcome at your elitist luncheon I am not interested in your message, whatever it is."

The message, at both the "elitist" luncheon and the conference, centered on the importance of building relationships between haves and have-nots, rich and poor, powerful and powerless. His presuppositions kept him from a significant blessing. "Desire without knowledge is not good—how much more will hasty feet miss the way" (Proverbs 19:2). God wants the message of reconciliation distributed to all classes and segments of society. The lawyers have as much right to and need for God's good news as any group.

THE BEST OF ALL THREE

Stewardship theology weaves the virtues of prosperity theology and poverty theology together with the rest of God's Word about money and possessions. In other words, much of poverty theology and prosperity theology is sound; error comes into play when one sees their perspectives as the total view. Stewardship theology would be impotent if it did not include the beautiful promises of God's blessings and the admonitions to care for the poor.

We could list hundreds of Scriptures to illustrate stewardship theology, but in the end all we would possess is a long list of rules and regulations. Being a steward is more of an attitude, a way of looking at life as a caretaker. It is an approach to our faith—it's looking not to our own interests but to the interests of others.

The shortcomings of poverty theology and prosperity theology are that they do not go far enough. When we host a dinner party, the preparations and cleanup are as important as enjoying our friends and the meal. We must include both *work* and *reward*.

Poverty theology exaggerates the role of sacrificial work, while the prosperity gospel overemphasizes financial reward. The steward leads a balanced life, enjoying God's abundance while always serving others in love.

Todd and Janelle were fortunate. As Christians, they woke up to their folly when Todd asked a caring friend for advice about whether or not to buy and finance that new pool. His friend challenged Todd about his material appetites. Todd responded. He decided to get out of the rat race—that unwinnable race that claims so many victims.

Todd started reading the book of Proverbs, and he was

overwhelmed about how much advice those thin, crinkly pages contained about money. Since there are thirty-one chapters in Proverbs, he decided to read the whole book through once a month—a chapter a day.

Most important of all, Todd purposed to stop playing games with God and committed to seek God first before the buck. He began to tithe and even went above a tithe when special needs came up in his church. Though paying off the balances of his cut-up credit cards came first, plans to start a savings account started to enter his mind.

The meaning of the word *steward* finally started to take shape in his thinking. Christians who disdained money turned him off, but he now recognized his own style had been to wrap his hand tightly around his money. A gesture came to mind of holding his money gently in the open palm of his hand—not too tightly, offering to take care of it while aware that God had entrusted it to him for a reason. The remorse for his financial unfaithfulness humbled Todd, and he asked the Lord to give him a fresh start and to show him how to be faithful.

Have you been trying to serve both God and money? Have you been cherry-picking or winking at what the Bible says about money? Ask God to forgive you for living by your own ideas, and ask Him to lead you to a proper perspective of money. Ask Him to increase your biblical IQ on money. When you become a faithful steward, God will guide you into an abundant life, and that's the gospel truth.

—————————— FOCUS QUESTIONS ——————————

1. Money is the path to contentment.

   ❏ Agree ☒ Disagree. Explain your answer.

2. Money represents different things to each of us. What are the reasons you want money (e.g., a symbol of achievement, a report card, a measure of self-worth, an improved

standard of living, provision for your family, greed, ambition, fear, or financial independence)?

3. Do you want to be rich? What do you think "rich" would do for you? For your family? For God?

4. Read Matthew 6:24. What is the greatest risk of putting money first in your life?

5. Each of us has some possession or net worth goal, often unstated to anyone, which symbolizes having arrived. What is yours? Would you be willing to say to God, "Your will be done with regard to this goal/ambition"?

6. What are the pressures on you to make and spend money? Read Ephesians 6:10 – 18. How can you overcome these pressures?

7. Does God want Christians to have money? Is prosperity an acceptable goal for the Christian?

8. What is your perspective of money? Do you see it as a right you have, a necessary evil, a trust for which you are accountable, or in some other way? Read 1 Corinthians 4:2.

CHAPTER 12

THE FOUR PILLARS OF FINANCIAL STRENGTH

Entrepreneur's credo: A dollar borrowed is a dollar
earned, a dollar refinanced is a dollar saved,
and a dollar paid back is gone forever!
Ted Miller

Whoever gathers money little by little makes it grow.
Proverbs 13:11

Todd and Janelle started looking for ideas to make them financially responsible. In this chapter we'll look at four ideas that, if we try nothing else, will revolutionize our lives and help us become faithful stewards.

1. EARNING: LITTLE BY LITTLE

Devon asked the members of his Bible study group to pray for his business. The slow season was extending into spring, and he needed to start selling some boats or go out of business. The tension in his face and voice communicated the gravity of his request.

"What has to happen for things to turn around?" someone asked.

"I need to sell five boats this month or I won't make it." The group prayed faithfully. At the end of the month Devon gave a report to the group. "You will never believe what happened!" he exclaimed. "We didn't sell a single boat this month. But we sold enough batteries, skis, ropes, anchors, and other accessories to give us a pretty good month. And now the boat shoppers are starting to come into the showroom.

"I can't believe how God works! He answered our prayers, but in a way totally different than I expected. He did it little by little!"

Brian's goal was to own enough rental property to give him a comfortable annual income. He planned to buy houses that would throw off cash of $50 to $200 each per month.

I distinctly remember thinking how unambitious that sounded. My ambition was to make it big by selling large properties and knocking down huge commissions that would make his rent checks look like chump change. Five years later, I was still a slave to closing that elusive big deal, while Brian earned all of his income while he slept.

Without actually knowing it, Devon and Brian had implemented a scriptural principle: "Whoever gathers money little by little makes it grow" (Proverbs 13:11).

This principle runs counterculture. In the rat race, the quick money is the way to go, but as these tortoise-and-hare experiences show, slow and steady wins. And it's more dependable too.

2. SAVING: LITTLE BY LITTLE AS WELL

The "little by little" principle applies not only to earning but also to saving. "The wise store up choice food and olive oil, but fools gulp theirs down" (Proverbs 21:20). Contentment will be a stranger in a home that saves no reserves for emergencies and financial security.

When we spend up to the limits of our income (and beyond), we just dare our car to break down or the water heater to leak and ruin the carpet. The Bible even teaches that if a man doesn't provide for his family, he denies the faith and is worse than an unbeliever (1 Timothy 5:8).

As I pointed out in chapter 7, men in their fifties often realize they were so busy taking care of their company's affairs that they never took time to put their own financial house in order. And then they must try to do in ten years what they should have done in forty—the normal career length. That puts them under a lot of pressure to make high-risk investments. And inevitably a few investments then go sour, which only adds to the stress of trying to provide for retirement. How should we go about building a "nest egg" for our retirement?

The Nest Egg Principle

You can pick the annual retirement income you want. That's right. Pick any income level you want, and then follow this simple plan: Each year of your forty-year career save 10 percent of your desired annual retirement income and put it into a qualified retirement plan, and you can extend your targeted income in perpetuity.

How does this work? Here's an example:

Desired Annual Income at Retirement	$40,000
Amount to Save Each Year	$4,000
Required Average Annual Earnings Rate	6.2%
Number of Years	40

Here are the results at retirement:

The Nest Egg (Capital Accumulated)	$651,000
Yield Required to Produce Desired Income	6.2%
Annual Retirement Income	$40,000

Note: Tax and inflation consequences are not considered. Part or all of the money saved can be sheltered through proper tax planning (e.g., in my insurance policies, the cash value increases accumulate on a tax-deferred basis), and retirement income can be protected through lower tax rates and tax-exempt income instruments (e.g., municipal bonds).

If you're getting a late start, you can catch up by saving more, earning a higher interest rate, or some of each. Here are the required interest rates you would have to earn for shorter periods of time to produce the same income:

Time Periods:	30 years	20 years	10 years
Yield Needed	8.3%	12.8%	27.0%
Capital Accumulated	$479,000	$316,000	$147,000

As you can see, the requirement to earn a higher yield goes up disproportionately as the window of time narrows. That's because the money is not available to compound over a large number of years. Obviously, the opportunity to make double-digit returns requires high risk and would be difficult to achieve.

Keep in mind any desired income level can be extended by saving 10 percent of that amount for forty years at 6.2 percent. If you are behind, try saving a larger percentage of your income. Since this treatment barely scratches the surface, ask a competent financial adviser to help you determine where you are today and what you need to do to retire successfully. Ask them to help you "back into" a specific program to accumulate a nest egg, little by little, which will provide you and your wife the security of a predictable retirement income.

I believe a permanent insurance program should be the foundation of every investment strategy. Excellent yields are attainable if you stick with the top few mutual companies.

The Nest Egg Principle is as encouraging for the young man as it is discouraging for the older man who has not practiced the principle of gathering money little by little. If you can't take advantage of the Nest Egg Principle because you've waited too long, be sure to teach your children and grandchildren about the nest egg. Start by having them save 10 percent of their allowance and summer job earnings.

Teach them the habit of saving. Very few financial pointers will ever be as helpful.

The Nest Egg Principle captures the essence of the biblical view of money. Christianity is a way of life—a different way of life. This principle personifies the character qualities of that different way of life—quietness, diligence, industry, prudence, patience—little by little.

3. SHARING: WHERE TO STORE YOUR MONEY

Because of a good economy, we began to earn more money than needed to live in the manner to which we were accustomed. We lived in a neighborhood where our children were happy, secure, and settled. My wife liked the convenient location and the neighbors. One of my daughter's very best friends lived two doors down. No dogs barked in the middle of the night, and no expressway drowned out the conversation when we grilled in the backyard.

Since we were making enough money to live in a bigger, more expensive house, I began to make plans to move. That's what people do when they can afford to, isn't it? We can generally slot people's income level by the house they live in, because most people keep trading up to the most expensive one their income will allow. People with a $25,000 income live in homes that $25,000 of income can afford; people with a $50,000 income live in homes that $50,000 of income can afford; people with a $150,000 income live in homes that $150,000 of income can afford, and so on.

Yet we loved our neighborhood. And we knew that people and relationships were more important than possessions. But the social pressure to buy the bigger house preoccupied my mind. The image of having money and making sure everyone else knew it pulled like a tug-of-war against the Christian worldview.

One day I noticed I was the only family member pressing for

the move. That got me thinking. Finally I yielded my ambition to move to the bigger house and allowed God to work. We decided to redecorate instead.

Over the years we began to give shape and form to the belief that God wanted us to put a cap on our standard of living. And however He blessed us over and above that standard, He wanted us to help fulfill His purposes.

This decision evolved. We didn't actually sit down and write it out on a piece of paper. Rather, over time, by our lifestyle and actions, we inbred it into values. Then one day we said it out loud, and that settled the issue.

So now we live by a predetermined standard of living. And everything God entrusts to us above what we need to live on and save for retirement, we give to help build His kingdom. The sense of usefulness and the impact we are having leave us with a deep confidence that we are truly significant, not for our own self-gratification, but in a way that will last forever.

In Matthew 6:19–21, Jesus says:

> "Do not store up for yourselves treasures on earth, where moths and vermin destroy, and where thieves break in and steal. But store up for yourselves treasures in heaven, where moths and vermin do not destroy, and where thieves do not break in and steal. For where your treasure is, there your heart will be also."

If we want to live more for God, one way is to give more of our resources to God. The more money we give to God's work, the more our hearts will be fixed on Him. The opposite is just as true: Don't give money to God's work, and your heart will not be fixed on Him.

What is the right way to give money to the Lord? Each of us should give to the Lord an amount of every dollar earned in proportion to the way God has blessed him, with a minimum of 10 percent. This 10 percent minimum is the same thing as a tithe. Jesus clearly affirmed tithing. He said:

"Woe to you, teachers of the law and Pharisees, you hypo-
crites! You give a tenth of your spices—mint, dill and cumin.
But you have neglected the more important matters of the
law—justice, mercy and faithfulness. You should have practiced the latter, without neglecting the former."

Matthew 23:23

This money should be set aside as it is earned. Those of us who
own our business or work in sales may deduct normal business
expenses from the top line before calculating the 10 percent minimum. Since I receive health insurance separate from my paycheck, I
also tithe the dollar value of those benefits.

This money is to be used in the work of the church. The church
is both the congregation you belong to and the larger work of the
body of Christ worldwide. Each local church has its own recom-
mendations, and you should follow them if they agree with your conscience. Many worthwhile organizations without church affiliations
exist that should be supported as God directs you through prayer.

Your giving should be done in secret to guard against any temptation to become proud. If you cannot give offerings that exceed
10 percent and do it cheerfully, don't. But it's a blessing if you can.
Develop regularity to your giving. God doesn't need endowments.
Systematic giving is good discipline.

You should give your gifts as an offering to God, and not to
men. Don't seek the praise or approval of men, and don't look for a
blessing from specific people or churches or organizations to whom
you give. God will bless you for your cheerful giving, although the
blessings may be spiritual more than material.

The highest form of giving is called sacrificial giving. You might
think of it as giving until it hurts. Most people give out of their
abundance—they don't really miss it when it's gone. To give more
than the comfortable-to-part-with amount is the most dedicated

form of giving, which is merely sending it ahead to be stored where moth and rust do not destroy. That's the best place to store money.

4. AVOIDING DEBT: STOP PRETENDING

Why do men go into debt? Consumerism, the economic theory that a progressively greater consumption of goods is beneficial, depends on a constant sparking of our desires to buy things—anything and everything. The goal is more consumption. The strategy is to keep the image of the beautiful, wrinkle-free life ever before us, unconsciously marketing to our hidden needs for love, approval, companionship, relief from anxieties, and significance.

There are two ways to acquire and accumulate: *income* and *debt* (see chapter 1, "The Rat Race," Figure 1.2). If the lure of the Madison Avenue lifestyle is larger than our income (personal productivity), then we can finance our way to prosperity (debt).

Debt beckons like a sweet siren song luring a mariner to destruction against rocky shoals. Her lyrics deceive us into thinking that borrowing can help us achieve the beautiful, wrinkle-free life. When possessions are the measure of a man, more than his skill and contributions to society, then he feels pressure to go into debt to aid in his search for significance.

Debt is the opposite of savings. Why? *Men either earn interest or pay interest.* Just as our savings earn a wage, debt has the associated expense of interest. Charles Lamb said, "The human species, according to the best theory I can form of it, is composed of two distinct races, the men who borrow, and the men who lend."[24] Which are you?

The trouble with debt is that you have to pay it back! It's easy enough to run up debt, but difficult to raise the money to pay it off. Debt is an obligation to repay the money we borrowed to acquire a possession or experience for which funds were not available, but credit was.

Debt enables men to pretend to be somebody else. Proverbs 12:9

counsels, "Better to be a nobody and yet have a servant than pretend to be somebody and have no food." And Proverbs 13:7 reads, "One person pretends to be rich, yet has nothing; another pretends to be poor, yet has great wealth."

Debt is a symptom of a consumptive lifestyle—not always, but usually. Like a mirage, debt beguiles us to believe it will satisfy our thirsts.

But debt is also addictive; once we find out how to get things with it, we drink up more and more of it as if it were sweet wine. The taste of the things debt enables us to buy delights our palate. But the frustration of how to repay the debt produces an acid that eats at the lining of our gut like the torch of a welder cutting steel.

The real problem, you see, is that long after the novelty has worn off, long after the vacation is over, we have to pay the money back. Debt lets us pretend to be somebody we are not, at least for a while. But the facade doesn't fool the bill collectors.

The Bible has no prohibition against going into debt. Yet most of the Scriptures that do relate to debt are cautionary or deal with solving the problems debt creates. While there is no specific prohibition, debt is discouraged: "The borrower is slave to the lender" (Proverbs 22:7). Savings, the opposite of debt, is encouraged, and debt is discouraged.

Quarterback Tim Tebow's father, Bob, a family man with five children, visited the Philippine Islands. While there, he sensed God leading him to return and share Christ with the peasants in the hill country.

One day several of his friends received a letter that simply read, "God has called me to the Philippines to share Christ with the people there. By the time you get this letter, we will be in Seattle, where we plan to sell our car. Here is a list of the things I'm going to need. Please take care of it."

Four years later, Bob returned for a furlough and visited our Bible study group. In his first four years, he had introduced ten thousand people to a saving faith in Jesus Christ and started twenty-seven churches! He has since shared the good news with millions. Picture the loss for the kingdom of God if Bob had been unable to go—if his debts would have forced him to say, "No, I want to go, but I can't."

If God called you to a ministry, could you go? Or would your debts prevent you from going? Second Timothy 2:4 reads, "No one serving as a soldier gets entangled in civilian affairs, but rather tries to please his commanding officer." Debt epitomizes entanglement in the affairs of this world.

I believe there are contemporary as well as biblical reasons to avoid debt. These last few decades have been tumultuous— deregulation, tax reform, bursting bubbles, stock market crashes, Wall Street corruption, out-of-control federal spending, a staggering federal deficit, dependency on foreign debt, and a constantly changing economy.

Financial author Howard Dayton first alerted me to the fact that the United States had no foreign debt before 1985. Since then, the U.S. Treasury has borrowed more than five trillion dollars from foreign entities.[25] America was a net lender nation up until 1984, but we have steadily increased our foreign debt to an unconscionable level and become a net debtor nation.

In Deuteronomy we are told that a country that is obedient will lend to many nations but borrow from none. But if a nation is disobedient, the aliens among them will rise higher and higher and will lend to them, but that nation will not lend back (see Deuteronomy 15:4–6; 28:43–46).

We were on the verge of becoming that nation when I first wrote this book in 1989. What a difference twenty-five years can make— we just keep sinking deeper and deeper into foreign debt. America's precarious dependence on the continued goodwill of other countries is ample reason alone to steer clear of debt.

Give these ideas a try: Earn little by little, save 10 percent, share 10 percent or more, and steer clear of debt. How simple! And how easy to scoff at. However, if we follow these principles we are virtually guaranteed a promotion to a new job — the job of faithful steward.

FOCUS QUESTIONS

1. The Nest Egg Principle shows how simple it would be for all people to retire in financial security. Why do most people end up financially strapped?

2. How much money is enough for you? Why? Would you be willing to put a cap on your standard of living? Read Ecclesiastes 5:10 – 12.

3. Most men have too much debt.

   ❏ Agree ❏ Disagree. Explain your answer.

4. Read Deuteronomy 28:1 – 2, 12, 15, 43 – 46. America became a debtor nation for the first time in our history in 1985 and has continued to steadily amass a huge foreign debt. Proverbs tells us, "The borrower is slave to the lender." Do you think there is a correlation between our disobedience to God's Word and our growing debtor status? What are the risks we face as a nation because of this change of status?

5. As an individual, are you a borrower or a lender? Do you think the Scriptures in the previous question apply to individuals? Why, or why not? If yes, how?

6. Read Proverbs 12:9 and 13:7. Have you used debt to supplement your personal income and pretended to be somebody you are not? What is wrong with using debt in this way?

7. What action steps would you be willing to take this week that will help put you in the position of saving 10 percent, sharing 10 percent, and getting out of debt?

PART 4

SOLVING OUR TIME PROBLEMS

CHAPTER 13

DECISIONS: HOW TO MAKE THE RIGHT CHOICE

Once — many, many years ago — I thought I made
a wrong decision. Of course, it turned out that
I had been right all along. But I was wrong
to have thought that I was wrong.
John Foster Dulles

Elijah went before the people and said, "How long
will you waver between two opinions? If the LORD
is God, follow him; but if Baal is God, follow him."
But the people said nothing.
1 Kings 18:21

In my thirties, I became convicted about the way I spent my evenings. Precious time vegetated away while I watched television, not to mention the wrong thoughts it stimulated!

Frankly, though, because I'm a morning person, I was just too tired to do much else. To at least partially redeem the time, I rode a stationary exercise bicycle in front of the TV, but even that was still boring. I desired to spend more time with the Lord, but I was married to the television.

The best time of the day for me is not evening but the wee hours of the morning. One evening the big idea finally hit me: Why not go to bed one hour earlier! That would accomplish several objectives. I could exercise in the morning when rested and, by using an optional reading stand, read the Bible at the same time.

Best of all, I could go to bed when I was really tired. The trade: an hour of television for extra time with the Lord. Not much thought required for that. And, finally, I could eliminate a source of temptation in my thought life.

As ingenious and productive as the idea seemed, I just couldn't quite make the decision to change. I knew it was the right idea, but twelve years of inertia encumbered me. After the idea came to me, months and months went by, but nothing happened until one day, finally, I *decided* to make the change.

THE PROBLEM

We all do exactly what we decide to do; we are the sum of our decisions. Even not making a decision is a decision in itself. If your daughter's school play starts at 11:30 a.m. and at 11:35 a.m. you are still on the phone to the home office, you have made your decision.

Decision making determines *who* and *what* we are more than any other aspect of our lives. These decisions can come to pass in an instant, or we may agonize over them for weeks, months, or even years.

As important and pervasive as our decision making is, the process remains mysterious and artful. *Bass & Stodgill's Handbook of Leadership* cites more than 7,500 research studies and monographs on executive leadership and decision making. Yet its editor was unable to find a common set of factors, traits, or processes that identified the qualities of effective leadership.[26]

Former National Security Advisor Zbigniew Brzezinski once revealed, "Seen from the outside, decisions may often seem clear and concisely formulated ... But one learns that so much of what happens ... is the product of chaotic conditions and a great deal of personal struggle and ambiguity."[27]

And more succinctly, the chief executive officer of a Fortune 500 company put it this way: "I'll be darned if I understand how we make some of our most important decisions around here."[28]

If the most highly trained decision makers have this degree of difficulty making good decisions, should we expect our decision making to be any easier? Does a set of principles exist that, if we follow, will overshadow this overwhelming evidence?

Many men, unable or unwilling to make wise decisions, ruin their lives and fill them with heartache, strife, and pain. Business problems, marriage problems, children problems, priority problems, moral problems, ethical problems, spiritual problems, time problems, stress problems, health problems, money problems—virtually all of our problems can be traced to a poor decision, a decision made by a process that is barely understood.

THE PRIORITY/MORAL DISTINCTION

Aside from minor decisions, like which way to drive home from work, decisions tend to be *priority* decisions or *moral* decisions. Priority decisions are choices between *right and right*. In other words, two or more choices can be made, either of which would be morally right. They represent our choices about how to allocate our time and money.

Deciding whether to take your wife out to dinner or play ball in the city league that night is a priority decision. Working on Saturday morning or spending the time with family is a priority choice. Investing in the stock market or staying liquid is a choice between two acceptable alternatives. The only imperative in making priority decisions is to be wise—to choose between good, better, and best. We will devote the next chapter to searching out God's priorities for men.

Moral decisions, on the other hand, are choices between *right and wrong*—there is the morally correct choice and the morally wrong choice. To make the wrong choice is sin. The decision whether or not to report overcharges to a customer is a moral choice. Whether or not to engage in mental adultery with a young beauty at the office is a moral decision.

The power to make correct moral decisions results from a man's desire to have integrity and the enabling power of God. We will devote an entire section of this book to integrity issues.

Decisions that have *both* moral and priority implications are not merely decisions about how to spend time and money, but carry with them the full weight of God's principles. The purchase of a new car is a simple priority decision when transportation is your consideration when purchasing. But the decision to purchase a luxury car we covet that robs money away from higher priorities, like savings pledged to college tuition or tithing, takes on the added dimension of a moral issue—a choice between right and wrong.

HOW TO NOT MAKE
THE WRONG DECISION

Since effective decision making seems so puzzling, and because the consequences of making the wrong choice can be so devastating, knowing how to not make the wrong decision carries as much weight as knowing how to make the right one. In fact, *the best insurance for making the right decision is to know how to not make the wrong decision.*

Peter Drucker, in a *Harvard Business Review* article, "Getting Things Done: How to Make People Decisions," writes:

Executives spend more time on managing people and making people decisions than on anything else—and they should. No other decisions are so long lasting in their consequences or so difficult to unmake. And yet, by and large, executives make poor promotion and staffing decisions. By all accounts, their batting average is no better than .333: at most one-third of such decisions turn out right; one-third are minimally effective; and one-third are outright failures.[29]

I learned in my PhD studies that a full two-thirds of all organizational change initiatives fail outright, whether public or private, profit or not for profit. Here's the bottom line: most decisions fail.

So how can we improve our batting average on our own decision making? Since the research shows that making good decisions is not only hard, but a mystery, let's concentrate on how to avoid making the wrong decision.

History provides examples of hundreds of crucial decision makers, some good and some bad, who have changed the course of human history—men like Martin Luther, the apostle Paul, and Abraham Lincoln, and others like Hitler, Stalin, and Mussolini. Or more recently, Martin Luther King Jr. versus Osama bin Laden. But no decisions come close to the significance of Jesus' three decisions when tempted by Satan in the desert just before He started His public ministry. Jesus gives us a model of how to not make the wrong decisions.

THE MAGNITUDE OF JESUS' DECISIONS

He had fasted forty days and He was hungry. Satan approached Jesus with defeating Him on his mind. If he could persuade Jesus to change sides, he would win the greatest negotiation in history.

Imagine the consequences. If, when tempted, Jesus had made the wrong decisions, then He would have ended up just another sinner like us. No one would believe He is God. He would not be an innocent Lamb to die as a sacrifice for our sins, and today we would still be waiting for the Messiah.

But Jesus did make the right decisions, and, as a result, "We do not have a high priest who is unable to empathize with our weaknesses, but we have one who has been tempted in every way, just as we are—yet he did not sin" (Hebrews 4:15).

HOW JESUS DECIDED

The first decision Jesus had to make, whether or not to turn stones into food, was a decision about whether or not to rebel against God's plan for His life (see Matthew 4:1–3).

Satan probably wondered if Jesus would be an easy mark. His first temptation of Jesus was the tried-and-true ruse he had pulled on Adam and Eve—he tried to entice Jesus with food. Satan probably thought to himself, "Why not? It has worked before."

Jesus' response gives us *the first principle of effective decision making*. He answered, "It is written: 'Man shall not live on bread alone, but on every word that comes from the mouth of God'" (Matthew 4:4). Our first step in making good decisions by not making wrong decisions is *to live by the Word of God*.

The second decision, to jump off the roof of the temple, was the decision whether or not to test God. We, too, must decide whether or not to put God in a position in which He must save us from our own foolish decisions. When I was in high school, I was arrested as a minor and held for being intoxicated. My father had to come to the city jail and sign for me. I put him a position where he had to rescue me. I don't need to go into detail about how angry he was!

In the same way, we're not to test God by putting ourselves in foolish positions that require Him to save us. Satan tempted Jesus to make a decision in which the odds for success were slim—unless God intervened. Satan even quoted Scripture to Jesus to entice Him. As Shakespeare said, "The devil can cite Scripture for his purposes."

But Jesus answered Satan, "It is *also* written: 'Do not put the Lord your God to the test'" (Matthew 4:7, italics added).

In the same way, the devil tempts us to wink at and cherry-pick the Bible for our own wrong priorities and immoral purposes. *The second principle of effective decision making is to not put God to a test.* Don't put yourself in a position that requires a miracle!

I imagine that for those first two temptations Satan disguised himself as a friend, maneuvering himself into a position of trust. But when his first two temptations failed, he decided to go for it all.

The third decision Jesus made, whether or not to worship Satan, was the decision to renounce the Fatherhood of God and serve other gods. How often we men jump the tracks and serve other gods— money, position, power. As a teenager I renounced the fatherhood of my own dad, quit school, and joined the Army. I abandoned the authority structure of my home and pursued my own plans.

At first we might conclude this was an easy decision for Jesus to make, but probably not. Satan, the deceiver, is too crafty to knock on the front door wearing a red suit and carrying a three-pronged spear. Surely he tried to disguise himself in some way.

But Jesus didn't disappoint us. He called Satan by name and said, "Away from me, Satan! For it is written: 'Worship the Lord your God, and serve him only'" (Matthew 4:10). *The third principle of effective decision making is to always worship God and serve Him only* in your decisions.

These three principles of decision making will not guarantee that we will always make the right decision, but they will give us the highest probability of not making the wrong decision. They are *risk management* principles, ideas to keep us close to God's plan and purpose for our lives. Here they are again:

1. Make decisions according to the *Word of God*; if your decision contradicts Scripture, it's a bad decision.

2. Avoid foolish decisions that *test God*; don't put yourself in a position that requires a miracle to bail you out.

3. Avoid decisions that reduce your *worship and service to God*; don't get caught up in the rat race and chase phony gods.

Jesus referred to the Word of God each time He faced a difficult decision. He knew the inner strength of a man wasn't enough—we need a citadel of truth to give us a moral backbone. A man who lives by the Word of God will make the right choices and prosper in all his ways.

CONSEQUENCES

Every decision we make has *consequences*. The consequences always include, as a minimum, *spiritual* and *financial* dimensions. Christ's announcement that a man "cannot serve both God and money" contemplates the spiritual and financial aspects of every decision we make. While we can't *serve* both, both have *consequences* in every decision.

Every decision is at least a spiritual decision. The underlying premise of the Christian life presupposes that *all* of life is spiritual, so it follows that every decision results in a spiritual consequence.

■ ■ ■

A man received an unsolicited job offer that required him to work fifty hours a week instead of the forty he currently worked. He didn't need the money, but took the offer anyway.

Something in his schedule had to fall by the wayside, and he stopped reading the Bible and coaching his son's Little League team. With the facts presented, it's clear in this example that this man made the wrong choice.

But taking the job could easily have been the right decision under a different set of conditions (to keep his wife from having to work, for example). In this case, though, we can still see the potential negative impact this decision will have on his spiritual and family life. How we spend our time and money brand us and shape who we are.

We can also say without hesitation, *every decision is at least a financial decision.* A financial consequence flows from every decision we make.

If you are in sales, the decision to coach your son's Little League team will reduce your selling time in the field and, obviously, your income. When you follow Christ in your business practices, you will always try to do the right thing. And it always costs more to do the right thing, right? If you seek to follow His Word, your saving habits and charitable generosity will often change sharply, and those decisions have financial consequences.

FORGIVEN BUT STILL IN JAIL

One of our greatest hopes and promises is that our sins are forgiven. God patiently waits for us to confess and renounce our sins, and then He grants us all the rights of a co-heir with Christ.

However, a huge difference exists between receiving *forgiveness* and receiving a *pardon.* If a man robbed a convenience store, and later became a Christian and confessed his sin, he is still *guilty.* His *verdict* may be influenced by his contrition, and he can be sure he is *forgiven* by God, but he must still bear the *consequences*—he still goes to jail.

One of the most pathetic moments in human history involved King David, a man after God's own heart, from whose lineage Christ was born. David committed adultery with Bathsheba. If that wasn't enough, he arranged for the death of her husband, Uriah.

Bathsheba became pregnant and bore him a son. But God, angered by David's sin, confronted him through the prophet Nathan. David repented and exclaimed, "I have sinned against the LORD."

Nathan replied, "The LORD has taken away your sin. You are

not going to die. But because by doing this you have shown utter contempt for the LORD, the son born to you will die" (2 Samuel 12:13–14).

David, in a grief-stricken moment, "pleaded with God for the child. He fasted and spent the nights lying in sackcloth on the ground. The elders of his household stood beside him to get him up from the ground, but he refused, and he would not eat any food with them" (2 Samuel 12:16–17). Nevertheless, the baby died.

We can choose our way, but we cannot choose the result. Forgiveness, yes. But every decision has its consequences. We really are the sum of our decisions.

LIFE IN THE FAST LANE

Jim spent eight years in prison for murder. He was a drug dealer. In prison, Jim found a second chance in Christ. Now a minister, Jim often speaks to high school students about the decision to take drugs.

"Don't let anyone kid you," he tells them. "Drugs are fun; drugs make you feel good; and getting high is fun. You know the beginning of drugs, and it's fun. But I know the end of drugs." And then Jim tells them about the decisions that nearly ruined his life forever.

While most of us will never self-destruct in the way Jim did, we all face the choice of doing things that look fun but will result in a life of pain — divorce, financial disaster, disease, and relationship problems. Why are we so foolish to think we will either escape the consequences or somehow be uniquely equipped to handle what comes? Adulterers get divorced, drug users become addicted, dishonest men lose their jobs, smokers get cancer. It doesn't happen every time, but it's the rule — it's cause and effect.

The big question for most of us is, "Is life in the fast lane where God wants me to be?" We need to start by acknowledging that the rat race is an unwinnable race.

Men in the twenty-first century are worn-out, fatigued, and

overcommitted. Do you find it hard to keep up with all your responsibilities? The man with a full résumé always pays a price to get it. Everyone has the same 168 hours a week to work with, so something has to suffer when we are an elder, a businessman, a civic leader, and a sportsman. The family usually pays the price. Every man has some priority that competes with putting God first in his life. What's yours? When we run in the rat race, precious little time remains for God and our family. Wouldn't you like to get out of the rat race? Prayerfully ask God to help you make the right choices, to improve your decision-making scorecard. Look at what is written in Scripture about the rat race (Galatians 5:7, 9, for example). Decide to get out of the fast lane.

If you were speeding down the inside lane of a busy interstate highway at eighty miles an hour and decided to get off the road, you wouldn't swerve sharply without warning. First, you would notice the road was crowded — that you had a lot of company in the fast lane. You would turn on your blinker and start to work your way over. Even then you would have to wait for an exit ramp.

If you will decide to get out of the fast lane, God will help you — just like He helped Jesus make the right choices. He is not so much interested in your *position* as He is in your *attitude,* not so much in where you *are* as in where you are *going.* When we make the decision to get out of the fast lane, He will bless the direction in which we are moving. He will empower us to make the adjustment, to find an exit. It's really the decision to be a biblical Christian instead of a cultural Christian.

We all do exactly what we decide in our minds to do. We can decide with or without God's help, but He promises to always help us if we will trust in Him. "It is God who works in you to will and to act in order to fulfill his good purpose" (Philippians 2:13). Jesus paid the ultimate price — bearing our sins in His death — so that the power of God would be available to help us make the right decisions.

———————— FOCUS QUESTIONS ————————

1. What is your personal batting average on making good decisions on the big issues?

2. Describe one very good decision you have made. What factors in making your decision contributed to its success?

3. Describe one lousy decision you have made. What caused you to make this decision? What consequences have you had to bear because of it? Would you make a different decision if you had it to do over again?

4. Men are the sum of the decisions they make. What are some ways in which you have observed other men ruining their lives by the decisions they make?

5. Read 1 Timothy 6:6 – 10. Why do you think it is so hard for men to live by God's principles?

6. A *priority* decision is a decision between right and _____.

   A *moral* decision is a decision between right and _____.

7. What are the three principles Jesus applied when tempted to make the wrong decisions?

8. Every decision is at least a spiritual decision.

   ❑ Agree ❑ Disagree. Why, or why not?

9. Every decision is at least a financial decision.

   ❑ Agree ❑ Disagree. Why, or why not?

CHAPTER 14

PRIORITIES: HOW TO DECIDE WHAT'S IMPORTANT

The constant desire to have still more things
and a still better life and the struggle to obtain
them imprint many Western faces with worry
and even depression, though it is customary
to conceal such feelings.
Aleksandr Solzhenitsyn

"Teacher, which is the greatest
commandment in the Law?"
Jesus replied: "'Love the Lord your God
with all your heart and with all your soul
and with all your mind.' This is the first
and greatest commandment."
Matthew 22:36 – 38

Almost everyone has gone grocery shopping on an empty stomach and without a shopping list. Everything that tastes good looks especially attractive, and the shopping cart ends up filled with too many snack foods and not enough nutrition.

When the cashier rings up the final total and announces the bill, you are in a state of shock at the cost of your unplanned shopping spree. The worst part may not be the cost, but explaining to your wife how you spent so much money and still didn't get what the family needed!

The object of grocery shopping is to purchase a nutritionally balanced diet for the family. Shopping without a list risks spending your time and money on the wrong food.

Life's many options can be like the well-stocked shelves of a grocery store. To have any control over our lives whatsoever, we must decide in advance what we will give ourselves to.

The object of setting priorities is to allocate limited amounts of time and money where God directs us. But too often we choose our priorities with the same foresight as our trip to the grocery store, and the things we give priority to are simply not what our family needs or God wants.

THE PROBLEM

According to the dictionary, a priority is something that we give precedence to by assigning a degree of urgency or importance to it.

Most men have not settled the issue of what their priorities should be. Among those who do know, too few live according to those priorities.

The possible choices of what our priorities could be are like those well-stocked shelves at the grocery store. Unless we know exactly what we are looking for, we will load ourselves down with snack foods that don't provide us with the nutrition of a balanced "priorities" diet.

We need look no further than our own neighborhood on a Saturday morning to see how many different priorities men have set for themselves. One man gets up early, while another sleeps until ten o'clock. One man plays golf every week, and another watches his son's soccer game.

One man does yard work, but his neighbor goes into the office to catch up on paperwork. Another washes his car and cleans the garage, while his neighbor shoots baskets with several of the kids on the block. One relaxes with the paper; another reads his Bible. One man takes his family out to breakfast; another eats breakfast in bed.

Perhaps no other time of the week reveals more about us than how we spend Saturday morning. We discharge our work Monday through Friday, and Sunday is the Lord's Day, but Saturday is the day we decide for ourselves.

Saturday is like the discretionary income in our paycheck. Most of our paycheck goes to essentials, but the amount left over can be spent as we want. How do you spend your Saturdays? Does the way you spend this discretionary time reflect the priorities you would like to be remembered for?

ESTABLISHING WHAT IS IMPORTANT

What is important to God? The answer reveals what our priorities ought to be, and priorities help us narrow our focus. What are God's priorities for a man's life? Has God already made out a "shopping list" for us? As we explore God's priorities, keep these four angles in view:

1. Who and what does God want me to *be* and to *do*?
2. How does God want me to use my *time* and my *money*?
3. What *character* and *conduct* traits does God desire in me?
4. What *relationships* and *tasks* does God want me to emphasize?

Simply stated, God wants us to live by biblical priorities, to be biblical Christians. At the risk of stating the obvious, secular values lead to secular priorities, and biblical values lead to biblical priorities. So in our self-examination, let's ask ourselves if our value system follows the Christian worldview or not.

When we say yes to the Christian worldview, we must adopt biblical priorities. They will be a flashlight in a dark world, illuminating the way for how we spend our time and money. They will be a method for us to determine what we give precedence to.

Gertrude Stein, the American writer, owned two Picassos. She always used to tell her friend, "If the house were on fire and I could only take one picture, it would be those two." Choosing between two or more competing priorities is tough work, but it's where we see in a tangible way how our interior life has progressed.

Most men are more task-oriented than relationship-oriented, so, consequently, they do better on tasks than relationships. That being the case, let's look at relationship priorities first, the area where we are usually weakest.

OUR TOP PRIORITY

If the Bible is clear on anything, it is clear on the subject of our top priority.

One day an expert in the law of God tested Christ with a question: "Teacher, which is the greatest commandment in the Law?" Jesus replied by quoting from the scroll we know as the book of Deuteronomy. He said, "Love the Lord your God with all your heart and with all your soul and with all your mind" (Matthew 22:36–37).

If we penetrate the full scope of this great commandment, if we absorb the weightiness of its importance, if we saturate our minds with the Word of God, and if we devote every ounce of our strength to loving God, then our lives will take on a new dimension. A softness will begin to appear and, as the book of Zephaniah puts it, "He will take great delight in you; in his love he will ... rejoice over you with singing" (Zephaniah 3:17). Our relationships will begin to thaw out. The beginning of the day will bring excitement, not dread. We will hear the birds singing again, like we did when we were younger. And in the smells and sounds we will be warmed by the presence of God, and we will be cooled from the heat of our anguish by the breeze of the Holy Spirit against our soul.

This is the essence of our being. Of course, we are not going to sit around all day and merely think loving thoughts. Rather, we are going to set our hands to the task God has given or will give us, at the same time remembering that our most important work is to love Him. Whatever task He gives us provides an opportunity to demonstrate our love and gratitude for Him in a tangible way.

To know God is to love Him. A man who understands how deeply God longs for a personal relationship with him will be overwhelmed by how God took the initiative in his life. God wrote the greatest "love note" ever written:

> For God so loved the world that he gave his one and only Son, that whoever believes in him shall not perish but have eternal life.
>
> John 3:16

IMPLEMENTATION

How can we demonstrate our love for God? The most practical way is to obey Him. If you or I had twenty-four hours to live, what would we want to tell our loved ones? Of course we would want to share with them the greatest treasures, the deepest secrets, the most important of our thoughts. John, in chapters 13 through 17, records Jesus' remarks to His disciples during the last twenty-four hours of His life after He was betrayed. Certainly, then, they represent some of His most important ideas.

John 14:15 reads, "If you love me, keep my commands." Verse 21 reads, "Whoever has my commands and keeps them is the one who loves me." And verse 23: "Anyone who loves me will obey my teaching." To obey Him is to love Him. How do we obey God?

Bible Study. One practical way to demonstrate our love is to obey

His instruction to study the Word, and to do so daily. Start with fifteen minutes or so. Pick a regular time and place, like you did for high school homework. I started with fifteen minutes, which soon became thirty, then forty-five, and then an hour. It's hard to get too much!

Prayer. The Bible tells us to "pray continually" (1 Thessalonians 5:17). What does that mean? We all carry on a running dialogue each day. Who do you talk to during the day? Do you talk to yourself, or do you talk to God? When you are mulling over a problem, include God as your conversation mate.

Also, set aside some time right before or after your Bible study for prayer. For one week, record how much time you spend each day in Bible study and prayer. I think you will be amazed at what you discover!

Worship. I don't think a man can say he loves God very much if he doesn't attend church regularly. The Bible instructs us to worship God in His house on a regular basis. Do you remember how you used to "hang out" at your wife's place when you were still dating? They couldn't have kept you away with mortar fire! That's what love does.

Jesus established the church. He loves the church and gave Himself up for her. While the people of God, not a building, are the church, the institutionalized church is the historic vehicle for the people of God to come together. The physical church, a facility, has been part of spiritual life since ancient times. Before buildings (synagogues), there were tents. King David's last act was a building fund drive for a new temple for God. The reason for coming together is to build a community of people who hold each other up—and pick each other up when necessary.

Join a church where Christ is honored and the Bible is held in high regard.

Sharing. Everything costs money. That's one of life's little realities we can't escape! The wheels of Christianity grind at an enormous cost. God planned that we would pay for this cost by each contributing back to His work 10 percent or more of the money we earn.

People need the Lord. The spreading of the gospel and making disciples is the main work of the church. "How, then, can they call on the one they have not believed in? And how can they believe in the one of whom they have not heard? And how can they hear without someone preaching to them? And how can anyone preach unless they are sent?" (Romans 10:14–15). We might add, "And how can anyone be sent unless we pay for them to be sent?"

The man in the mirror can do nothing better than look intently into the Word of God that gives freedom and discover the principles, precepts, and guidelines offered. Read and meditate on the Word, pray (talk) with Him constantly, and worship Him with your praise, time, and money.

PRIORITY NUMBER TWO

At the same time Christ answered the expert in the law about the greatest commandment, He also cited another commandment, one found in Leviticus, which He noted as the second most important: "Love your neighbor as yourself" (Matthew 22:39).

Our second highest priority also revolves around relationships — loving others. Scripture instructs us about every relationship imaginable. The highest among these "others," if we are married, is our spouse. A wife is a gift from God, and in the eyes of God a man and his wife are as one (see Genesis 2:24).

Our children depend on us for their needs in the same way we look to our heavenly Father for ours. Our relationship with our own parents is so highly thought of by God that He made it one of the Ten Commandments: *Honor your father and mother.*

The gleanings of the Bible speak as much to how we relate with others as any subject. The Scriptures offer guidelines for family, friends, enemies, strangers, the poor, employers, and employees, so we devoted several chapters to our relationships with our wives, children, and others.

Our relationship priorities distill to these two great truths: *Love God and love others*. If we could change ourselves in these two areas alone, we would have demonstrated more of the gospel of Christ than any generation before us.

Too often we see the speck in the eye of the other person, but don't pay enough attention to our own need for change. Leo Tolstoy put it well when he said, "Everybody thinks of changing humanity, and nobody thinks of changing himself."[30] Our relationship priorities are the best place to start a change. Now let's look at a priority that is often treated like an orphan in our fast-paced world.

REST

Are you tired? I don't mean just physically tired, but emotionally and mentally tired? I don't know about you, but everywhere I go these days I see tired men. Just plain exhausted.

Two kinds of tired make their way into my life. Sometimes when I go home, I'm "good tired." You know the feeling. You spent yourself in a worthy cause. You're tired—but you feel great!

Theodore Roosevelt described "good tired" this way:

> It is not the critic who counts; not the man who points out how the strong man stumbled, or where the doer of deeds could have done them better. The credit belongs to the man who is actually in the arena; whose face is marred by dust and sweat and blood; who strives valiantly; who errs, who comes short again and again ... who knows great enthusiasms, the great devotions; who spends himself in a worthy cause; who at the best knows in the end the triumph of high achievement, and who at the worst, if he fails, at least fails while daring greatly, so that his place will never be with those cold and timid souls who neither know victory nor defeat.[31]

Don't you just love that kind of talk? That gets me fired up! That's good tired.

But that's not the kind of tired most men are these days; most men are just worn-out tired. One of the greatest Christian fallacies is that we are not doing enough for the Lord. You've heard men say it: "I just wish I was doing more for the Lord." It's not that we are not doing enough, but that we are doing too much of the wrong things.

As a young Christian, I didn't have a clue about God's priorities for my life. I lacked the self-confidence to say no because I honestly didn't know where the boundaries were. So I said yes to everything, and I wore myself out. Some people do too much out of guilt, but mine was out of ignorance of biblical priorities. I only knew enough to be dangerous.

One fall I went to a men's retreat just to get a break from it all. Tom Skinner, the primary speaker, stunned me—totally and completely—with his teachings about biblical priorities. I was so impressed that we invited Tom to come to Orlando to share his understanding of the Scriptures with some tired, worn-out friends. Tears of relief flowed from several of the Christian "workaholics" who attended.

Jesus did *not* say, "Come to me, all you who are weary and bur- dened, *and I will give you more work to do.*" He said, "Come to me, all you who are weary and burdened, and *I will give you rest.* Take my yoke upon you and learn from me, for I am gentle and humble in heart, and *you will find rest for your souls*" (Matthew 11:28–29, italics added). Our emphasis always seems to be on doing. But God is interested in our rest. It is a priority with Him and, therefore, us.

Some of us worry so hard that we get no rest—even when we're taking time off. The rest Jesus offers isn't just for the physically tired, but for the emotionally and mentally tired too. "The sleep of a laborer is sweet, whether they eat little or much, but as for the rich, their abundance permits them no sleep" (Ecclesiastes 5:12). This "worry tired" may be the most tired of all.

We have spent extra paragraphs on this priority because it's over-looked yet needs our attention. Isaiah gave special attention to worn-out, tired men:

He gives strength to the weary
   and increases the power of the weak.
Even youths grow tired and weary,
   and young men stumble and fall;
but those who hope in the LORD
   will renew their strength.
They will soar on wings like eagles;
   they will run and not grow weary,
   they will walk and not be faint.

Isaiah 40:29–31

WORK

Men need a forum in which to find their significance and make their contribution. That forum is work. Our propensity for work finds its origins at the very beginning of creation when God prescribed work as the manner in which we would occupy our days.

The purpose of work is to glorify God with the abilities He has given us. By pursuing excellence and by settling for nothing less than our personal best, we demonstrate to a world weary of Christian "talky-talk" that Christ can make a difference in a man's life here and now.

Paul places such a high emphasis on work that he says a man who doesn't work (if he is able) shouldn't be allowed to eat (see 2 Thessalonians 3:10)! Paul himself often earned income as a tentmaker. That's all we'll say about vocation here since we devoted an earlier chapter, "The Secret of Job Contentment," to our work life.

GOOD WORKS

To have a faith without any good works is no faith at all. Our faith, not our good works, allows us to enter into relationship with God, but "we are God's handiwork, created in Christ Jesus to do good works, which God prepared *in advance* for us to do" (Ephesians 2:10, italics added).

In other words, God didn't give us salvation for our benefit alone. Rather, He has a will, a purpose, and a plan for every man that includes some good work He had in mind for us before we even knew Him.

The areas in which God wants our help in building His church (family) fall into the category of "disciple making." Becoming and making disciples is the chief work of a Christian (see Matthew 28:18 – 20). Being a disciple includes three parts:

1. A disciple is called to live in Christ. This includes salvation, abiding in Him, and introducing others to Him (see John 1:12; 8:31-32; Acts 1:8).

2. A disciple is equipped to live like Christ. This includes spiritual growth and transformation, and helping others learn about and become like Him (see 2 Timothy 3:16 – 17).

3. A disciple is sent to live for Christ. This includes serving others, bearing much fruit, loving others, and caring for the poor and needy (see Matthew 25:37 – 40; John 13:34 – 35; 15:8; Galatians 2:10).

Making disciples is God's agenda. We often try to make it more complicated, but these are the three tasks God wants us to help Him with.

Different men can contribute to these three areas in different ways, depending on their temporal and spiritual gifts. Each of us must make an honest assessment of how we are endowed in intelligence, wisdom, acquired competencies, and innate abilities.

The spiritual gifts we most frequently think of are serving others, teaching, encouraging, contributing to the needs of others, leadership (including administration), showing mercy, and preaching. Four passages of Scripture give us an inventory of the different spiritual gifts God gives to men:

- Romans 12:4–8
- 1 Corinthians 12:1–12
- Ephesians 4:11–12
- 1 Peter 4:10–11

Why not look these up and answer the question, "What are my gifts?"

About our task priorities, we can see that God wants us to work and provide for ourselves and our families, while at the same time working on His three agenda items (calling, equipping, sending), using the different temporal and spiritual gifts He gives us.

To summarize, five overarching areas of importance to God form the foundation on which we are to prioritize our lives:

1. To love God
2. To love others
3. To rest
4. To work
5. To do good works

Let's say you have been charged with the crime of being a biblical Christian. Would there be enough evidence to convict you? Or would the jury come back with the verdict "cultural Christian"? To be a biblical Christian is to have these five priorities in balance.

This all sounds so simple, but we know there is fierce competition with biblical priorities.

THE COMPETITION WITH GOD'S PRIORITIES

Trying to keep up with all of our responsibilities, like an old farmer said, is like trying to put two tons of fertilizer in a one-ton truck! What competition do we face when we try to live by God's priorities?

The world system, far different than the spiritual life, competes directly with biblical priorities. We are to be aliens and strangers here, pilgrims who are just passing through:

> Do not love the world or anything in the world. If anyone loves the world, love for the Father is not in them. For everything in the world — the lust of the flesh, the lust of the eyes, and the pride of life — comes not from the Father but from the world. The world and its desires pass away, but whoever does the will of God lives forever.
>
> 1 John 2:15 – 17

The slave master "money" indentures men to a bankrupt set of priorities. No slave master has ever been more cruel or ruthless than money. "No one can serve two masters ... You cannot serve both God and money" (Matthew 6:24).

For example, consider Joe, an acquaintance of mine. He wanted to be rich. He also wanted to be a Christian. Bible study interfered with selling time, and church came at a time when he needed to recover from the exhaustion of the week. In the end, being rich was more important, and he walked away from God. "Some people, eager for money, have wandered from the faith and pierced themselves with many griefs" (1 Timothy 6:10).

This competition, *the world* and *money*, must be part of our lives. However, we must be their masters, and they must be our slaves.

God knows we face choices more numerous than our time and money resources. That's why He has so clearly outlined His agenda to us and has shown us what our priorities should be. Men frequently pine for direction from God, saying, "If I only knew God's will for my life." We need look no further than the Bible. The Bible is God's will — it has the answers.

—————————— FOCUS QUESTIONS ——————————

1. How do your dreams and hopes for your children reflect your own priorities? Do they reveal any weak spots or blind spots in your thinking?

2. Read Matthew 22:36 – 38. What is, and should be, the significance of this command on the way we prioritize the use of our *time* and *money*? Give an example.

3. Read John 14:15, 21, 23. What is the relationship between *obedience* and *loving God*? Give an example in which you obeyed in some unpleasant situation out of love for God?

4. What is one area of your relationship with God in which you are not doing all that you should (e.g., Bible study, prayer, worship, sharing)? What is something practical you are willing to do to improve your relationship with Him?

5. Read John 15:12 – 14. Who is someone you would be willing to die for, and why?

6. Read Genesis 2:15. Is vocation a holy pursuit? In what ways can our vocation contribute to God's agenda?

7. What "good work" do you think God may be calling you to do?

8. Is rest a priority with you, or do you feel guilty when you relax? Read Matthew 11:28 – 30. What is Christ's position on rest?

9. How does "the world" compete in your life with biblical priorities? Give an example.

10. How does "money" compete in your life with biblical priorities? Give an example.

CHAPTER 15

TIME MANAGEMENT: DOING GOD'S WILL

One of the greatest reasons people cannot
mobilize themselves is that they try to accomplish
great things. Most worthwhile achievements
are the result of many little things done
in a single direction.
Nido Quebin

There is a time for everything, and a season
for every activity under heaven.
Ecclesiastes 3:1

Ask any informed Christian to list the ten greatest Christian leaders of the last one hundred years and Bill Bright, who with his wife, Vonette, founded Cru (Campus Crusade for Christ), is guaranteed to make their list.

In any group of Christians, ask, "Has your life been influenced by the ministry of Cru?" and anywhere from 20 percent to 80 percent of the hands will shoot up. In one seminary, 75 percent of the students became Christians through Campus Crusade.

My wife, Patsy, and I became the host couple in Orlando for Executive Ministries, one of the forty or so ministries under the Cru umbrella. We had never met Dr. Bright but were excited to learn he would be attending our national conference. I was eager to meet him!

In his opening conference remarks, Dr. Bright made an unforgettable statement, which I jotted down verbatim: "I try to prioritize everything I do in light of the Great Commission."

I pictured him preaching to groups of hundreds — even thousands — and I visualized him sharing the gospel with important heads of state. And surely he fired the enthusiasm of his twenty-five thousand staff members with rousing challenges.

One of Patsy's best friends from college lived in the city where we held our conference. She was a Christian, but her husband, Tom, had walked away from the Lord many years before, and their marriage had enough gas left to go about two more weeks. We asked them if they would be our guests at our closing banquet, and they said yes.

During the banquet, Nancy DeMoss told Dr. Bright about our friend Tom. However, there were about one hundred well-heeled people who all wanted to say hello to Dr. Bright that night after his address. I didn't think I had any chance whatsoever of introducing Tom to Dr. Bright. These people who were waiting had bucks! And, as you can imagine, the ministry always needed more funds. So I naturally assumed Dr. Bright would visit with potential financial supporters when the dinner broke up. Wrong. He made a beeline for Tom.

For the next hour and fifteen minutes he shared and listened to Tom and helped him commit his life to Christ. By the time they finished talking, only six of us were left in the room — Bill and Vonette, Tom and his wife, and Patsy and me. So much for making valuable contacts.

When Bill Bright said he tried to prioritize everything he did in light of the Great Commission, I had no idea he meant one person at a time. Many times after that, I saw him leave the crowd to minister to some individual.

One person at a time, Dr. Bright managed his time as strategically as any living person. He didn't become a great leader by doing great things, but by doing many little things in a single direction. I'm certain if he had set out to be great, he would have fallen flat on his face, like many of us do. He didn't set out to be great — he set out to be faithful.

THE PROBLEM

The problem of time management showed up on a written survey I conducted as the number one problem men are concerned about. In our rat-race world, we frequently just can't find enough time to accomplish all the things we should do and would like to do. Where do we find the time to meet all of our responsibilities?

Yet if any one characteristic in our "multiple choice" culture is common to all men, it is that we all have the same amount of time to work with. Bill Bright, Rick Warren, Martin Luther, Abraham Lincoln, me, you — we all have the same 168 hours to work with each week. Since each of us is gifted with the same number of hours, other factors must explain why we get different results.

The time management problem is less a *tips and techniques* problem than it is a *strategic* problem. The issue is not so much memorizing twenty clever ideas to help accomplish every item on our to-do list, though tips and techniques are helpful. Rather, the issue is gaining a clear understanding of God's *purpose* for our lives, living by biblical *priorities*, and making *plans* that reflect God's will for our lives.

In this chapter we want to examine the strategic aspects of time management. We won't delve into such tips as not handling email twice or controlling interruptions. Many excellent books and seminars are available to help with day-to-day time management. What we want to talk about is the larger perspective of how to discern what we give our time to in the first place—how we convert our priorities into a plan of action.

We want to look at some issues that need to be resolved *before* we mobilize ourselves into action. Too often we get ahead of God and make decisions without consulting Him.

FROM PURPOSE … TO TIME MANAGEMENT

Bill Bright used to close his letters, "Yours for fulfilling the Great Commission in this generation." I imagine that comes as close to a Written Life Purpose Statement as we'll ever find (see Matthew 28:19–20). Since Dr. Bright knew his life purpose, he had a clear grid through which he could filter competing priorities and demands on his time.

A couple traveling through the countryside was lost. They spotted an old man on the side of the road and asked, "Where are we at?"

"Where are you going?" came his reply.

"We don't know," they said.

"Then it doesn't matter."

When we don't have a sense of where we are going, where we are now isn't that important. Only when we know our purpose—where we are going—can we make heads or tails out of how to use our time.

Follow this progression: Our purpose helps us prioritize. Our priorities form solid ground to stand on when we make plans and set goals. Time management is no more and no less than strategically "engineering" a progression from purpose to priorities to plans and goals.

God always provides enough time to accomplish His plans. We each have all the time we need to do everything God wants us to do. We just need to use it more productively. We need to stop always going for the "long bomb" and run more dependable short yardage plays. We need to block and tackle better. If we do, we will have all the time we need. If we don't, we'll have to punt. "Little things done in a single direction" — that's the way.

TIME IN PERSPECTIVE

No period of time is longer than the forty-eight-hour wait for the biopsy results on a lump removed from your wife's breast. No period of time is shorter than the renewal date on a ninety-day note. Sometimes time passes too slowly, but sometimes much too fast.

The dictionary defines time as a nonspatial continuum in which events occur in apparently *irreversible succession* from the past through the present to the future.

In other words, time marches on. Once you have missed your plane — you've missed it. This irreversibility factor is what grabs us. If we could only repeat our lives and right our wrongs. If we could only retrieve the angry word, or the lie, or the misspent time with our kids. Grown and gone. In an irreversible succession. The dictionary defines management as the act, manner, or practice of managing, supervising, or controlling. Since time spent is irreversible, how do we control and supervise time to make the most of it? It may be irreversible, but it doesn't have to be a mere chain reaction. We can influence time. How do we get in step with the way God wants us to use our time?

DISCERNING GOD'S WILL

I wonder if your experience in figuring out what God wants you to do is anything like mine. I seem to go through five stages before I am marching in step with God's will:

1. I tell God what I am going to do.
2. God responds.
3. I *beg* God to let me do it anyway!
4. Finally I humble myself and listen.
5. God tells me what *He* is going to do.

Step One: I Tell God What I Am Going to Do

> To humans belong the plans of the heart ...
>
> Proverbs 16:1

I don't know about you, but there are many situations I don't like to bother God with unless I have to. I know He has a lot on His mind—wars in the Middle East, droughts in North America, famines in Africa, earthquakes in Central America. Rather than take up His valuable time, I frequently make plans without consulting God, intending to bring Him in on them later. It's "plan, then pray."

Once we decided to open an office in Tampa. Only later did I mention this to the Lord. Instead of asking His advice, I told Him what I was going to do, "Oh, by the way, we have decided to open a branch office in Tampa. Please bless us."

Step Two: God Responds

> ... but from the LORD comes the proper answer of the tongue.
>
> Proverbs 16:1

A few months later, the earth collided with the moon, and our new Tampa operation was in deep weeds. The anchor tenant in our building became insolvent, and our office there was spending money like it grew on trees. Only then did it dawn on me that I had run ahead of God and my plan didn't have His stamp of approval. "Many are the plans in a person's heart, but it is the LORD's purpose that prevails" (Proverbs 19:21).

Step Three: I Beg God to Let Me Do It Anyway!

> All a person's ways seem pure to them, but motives are weighed by the LORD.
>
> Proverbs 16:2

Even though God had responded and made it entirely clear that I had run ahead of Him, my financial, emotional, and time investments were now pretty substantial. So I pleaded my case before God in prayer, begging Him to change His mind and allow us to succeed in Tampa.

Sometimes He does change His mind (or so it seems to us) and let us have our own way, even though a great lesson inevitably still lies ahead for us. Other times, as in the case of our Tampa office, He brings His often painful discipline into our lives, and we struggle for survival. Still other times, He puts the brakes on our plans right then and there, and the issue is settled.

Step Four: Finally I Humble Myself and Listen

> Commit to the LORD whatever you do, and he will establish your plans.
>
> Proverbs 16:3

After I have pleaded and realized I am unable to persuade God to do it my way, I usually like to go off and pout for a while. When will I ever learn that a pity party never really puts things in perspective?

Sooner or later I come to my senses and still myself before the powerful God who wants to guide the use of my time. He is slow to anger, abounding in love—how grateful I am for His patience with me.

The encouragement of the psalmist comes to mind: "I remain confident of this: I will see the goodness of the LORD in the land of the living. Wait for the LORD; be strong and take heart and wait for the LORD" (Psalm 27:13–14). Even when we have blown it, He will come to our rescue when we listen and wait patiently for Him to act. There may be consequences to bear, but He rescues us.

Step Five: God Tells Me What He Is Going to Do

The LORD works out everything to its proper end.

Proverbs 16:4

When we have listened for God's leading for a time, perhaps a long time, a sense of His desire for our lives starts to take shape in our minds. He sometimes leaves us alone with our thoughts, perhaps for years, causing us to trust in Him and Him alone. Peter reminds us:

> But do not forget this one thing, dear friends: With the Lord a day is like a thousand years, and a thousand years are like a day. The Lord is not slow in keeping his promise, as some understand slowness. Instead he is patient with you, not wanting anyone to perish, but everyone to come to repentance.
>
> 2 Peter 3:8–9

We had to shut down our Tampa office at a major, major financial loss. Even though God forgives, we must still bear the consequences of our decisions.

Through this experience I put God in charge of my life in a new and deeper way. My former plans for my life became despised memories; I detest that I ever had my own ambitions. I pray, *God, I crucify those plans, and I purpose to not make any more plans for myself. However I spend my time from this day forward will only be how You direct me, and only after a period of patient listening. Amen.*

I graduated from "plan, then pray" to "pray, then plan."

Discerning God's will is the cornerstone we must lay before we mobilize ourselves and take that first step.

THE MOST EFFECTIVE TIME MANAGEMENT STRATEGY

Nothing wastes more time for the Christian than pursuing his own independent will. Nothing wastes more time than having to undo what we shouldn't have done in the first place. When we make plans apart from God that end up having to be withdrawn, we lose. We lose in time, money, and relationships.

The most effective time management strategy is to eliminate the first three steps we just described. Instead of wasting limited time making plans without God's direction and approval, we can make our plans by *first* listening for His voice. When we don't hear His voice, we should wait patiently for Him to act—His timing is always perfect. This is *strategic* time management, not mere *tactics*.

Instead of arguing for God to bless the scheme we put into motion (which He has stalled), we can humble ourselves and listen for His instruction before we ever start.

When a goal, plan, or idea begins to form, that's the time to consult with God. We should pray over our plans before our minds are made up.

A *made-up mind is almost impossible to change.* Before we take any action, we should pray and seek the counsel of godly men. This is the most strategic way to manage our time.

EFFICIENCY VERSUS EFFECTIVENESS

The three junior executives were as different as earth, wind, and fire.

The first rarely checked with his boss. He set his own priorities but frequently had to redo work or, worse, found out he had completed a project no one cared about. His skills were sloppy, and his boss usually found errors in his calculations, which had to be redone. He was both *inefficient*—the work he did was wrong—and *ineffective*—he worked on the wrong projects.

The second junior executive was a planner. He mapped out his plans and kept his boss informed through emails. He never asked if he was on the right track or if his boss had any suggestions, but at least he kept his boss informed. He was very *efficient*—he did good work. But he was *ineffective* because he often wasn't working on the right projects.

The third junior executive was wise indeed. After a project took shape in his mind, he would present his idea to his boss. Then he would listen carefully for the voice of experience. Adjustments would be made, and sometimes project ideas would be abandoned altogether. When he finally tackled his work, he breezed through his task like the movement on a fine Swiss watch. He was *efficient* (he did the job right), and he was *effective* (he did the right job).

Efficiency is doing the job right. Effectiveness is doing the right job right. It's not enough to do the job right if it's the wrong job. Just like the third junior executive, the most effective time managers are those who consult with "the boss" to confirm they are doing the right job. There is no cigar for doing the wrong job right.

In our spiritual pilgrimage, we may execute all the spiritual disciplines efficiently—such as Bible reading, prayer, church attendance, tithing—but if we don't translate them into our daily living, then we doom ourselves to an ineffective spiritual life. We should continually remind ourselves of Socrates' refrain: "The unexamined life is not worth living."

We must see our spiritual life as the first link in everything we do, not as some independent activity we perform that is unrelated to the details of daily living. To be effective with our time requires us to bridge the spiritual life to our life at home and in the workplace, to see the totality of what we do as a singular life.

Our motto should be "one life, one way." When we live as if all of life is spiritual—which it surely is—we translate the will of God into the minutiae of our lives, where it belongs. Wisdom (which God promises to every man who asks for it) is the prerequisite of effective time management, not hard work.

HARD WORK

One of the biggest disappointments in the management of our time is the theory that hard work is the road to success. While it is certainly true that no success will come to a lazy man, it is not conversely true that hard work assures a man success.

The blessing of God determines a man's lot in life. The station in life we each achieve results from God doing His part and us doing our part. Our part is to be faithful — to be diligent, industrious, and creative. God's part is to provide the increase as He sees fit.

We plant the seed and till the soil, but God sends the rain and the sun and makes the seeds grow. We don't know if our hard work will make us wealthy or not. Why, we can't even predict what will happen ten minutes from now! These matters are in the providence of a sovereign God. Solomon wrote:

> Sow your seed in the morning,
>> and at evening let your hands not be idle,
> for you do not know which will succeed,
>> whether this or that,
>> or whether both will do equally well.
>
> Ecclesiastes 11:6

Since God chooses how He will bless us, why wear ourselves out to get rich? The best time management strategy of all is to not be so serious about ourselves and the importance of our contribution to our success. True enough, we should work hard, but "do not wear yourself out to get rich; do not trust your own cleverness. Cast but a glance at riches, and they are gone, for they will surely sprout wings and fly off to the sky like an eagle" (Proverbs 23:4 – 5).

■ ■ ■

A gift store owner arrived at his store at 7:00 a.m. Monday through Saturday. He was there until 9:30 p.m. every night — thirty minutes after closing. To make more money, he didn't hire part-time help for the evening shift. Still, after fifteen years, he lived from week to week, with few reserves to fall back on if business went bad. Because he worked so hard and still didn't seem to get ahead, he was bitter. His customers sensed his tension and hostility, and so repeat business was slow.

The owner of an insurance agency refused to work nights and weekends. His theory was, "If it can't be done before 6:00 p.m., then I don't need the money." Since his home life was balanced, he was warm and concerned about his customers. They always felt they were important to him. He found time to play golf once a week and contributed to community life through involvement with the local university.

Hard work is a virtue—it has dignity—when it's part of a balanced schedule. The effective time manager finds time for all of the priorities God has for the Christian.

THINGS THAT LAST

There is a thin, delicate line that represents the threshold between this world and the next—physical death. Part of effective time management is understanding the significance of crossing that line. Men who do not know Jesus Christ have a far different destiny on the other side of that line than those of us who do.

The cardinal time management question is this: Are you doing anything with your time that has the potential to last forever? In your busy-ness have you carved out time for good works that contribute to forever? Or are you so consumed with supporting a lifestyle or pursuing other personal ambitions that everything you are doing will be left behind?

In *How to Win Friends and Influence People*, Dale Carnegie wrote about too many of us: "His toothache means more to him than a famine in China that kills a million people. A boil on his neck interests him more than forty earthquakes in Africa."[32]

The only part of life that crosses the threshold between this world and the next is the human soul. So if we want to make a contribution to forever, then we should become more interested in the other person and spend time helping them "break the code" on how to gain eternal life. This should start in our home and spread to every arena of our lives, not as a rote activity, but fired by the intensity of our own gratitude toward God.

Have you ever noticed how a man who has stopped smoking tries to convert everyone he meets into a nonsmoker? Have you ever noticed how someone who has enjoyed an elegant dining experience tells everyone he meets about his discovery? Frankly, most men seem more interested in converting others to nonsmoking and their favorite restaurant than to eternal life.

Often we don't share our faith in Christ with others because we fear we will offend them and they will dislike us. The fact of the matter is that half the people in the world aren't going to like you anyway, so they might as well not like you for the right reasons! If one hundred people dislike you but one person becomes a Christian, would that be worth the effort? The truth is that ninety-nine out of a hundred people will want to answer and discuss the question, "Where are you on your spiritual journey?" My own experience is that virtually every man wants to discuss this important question. All you have to do is ask.

When planning the use of your time, be sure to include time for things that have the potential to last forever.

THE ROAD TO GREATNESS

Don't you marvel at the accomplishments of some men? How do they get so much out of their time? The apostle Paul was such a man.

But Paul didn't do great things. He did small, obedient things that, when totaled, were found to be great. But even then, he wasn't considered great in his own generation. When he arrived in Rome

244 | SOLVING OUR TIME PROBLEMS

near the end of his career, no one had heard much about him (see Acts 28:21–22). His many small contributions were only seen as great in retrospect.

Often, in the presence of great men, we will find those around them arguing and disagreeing, whether we're talking about Paul, Martin Luther King Jr., or Jesus Himself. Jesus said a prophet is without honor in his hometown (see Matthew 13:57). Yet long after they are gone, the wisdom of what such a man said and did reverberates through the minds of his followers.

The book of Acts portrays a travelogue of Paul's life. Once he traveled to Corinth. When he first arrived, he divided his time between making tents and speaking in the synagogue on the Sabbath. Later, friends joined him there, and he was able to devote all of his time to preaching. When the Jews became abusive, he started preaching exclusively among the Gentiles. He just kept plugging away.

Paul stayed in Corinth for a year and a half, and then he moved on to Ephesus, Caesarea, Antioch, Galatia, and Phrygia, strengthening the disciples wherever he went. His life is a study in doing the little things right. His was no glamorous life. He had no international organization, just a few friends who stood beside him. He understood that God always includes enough time to accomplish His plans.

CONCLUSION

Our purpose, our priorities, our plans and goals—these determine how we spend our time. In turn, like Paul or Dr. Bill Bright, how we spend our time determines who and what we are. The critical step is to start listening before we decide, because a made-up mind is almost impossible to change.

Doing the job right is not enough; we need to do the *right* job right! That's where time management gets strategic. Hard work alone is not enough; we have to create a life-sustaining balance among all our priorities. And we can't possibly be called effective, strategic time managers unless we devote some time to things that have the potential to last forever.

Let's all decide to manage our time by God's priorities, to make our decisions under the premise that all of life is spiritual. When we become a pliable piece of clay in the Potter's hands, He will mold and shape us into effective time managers, and show us His will for our lives.

FOCUS QUESTIONS

1. "One of the greatest reasons people cannot mobilize them-selves is that they try to accomplish great things. Most worthwhile achievements are the result of many little things done in a single direction" (Nido Quebin). Can you give an example in which you have tackled a project so big that you never could get it off the ground? What factors kept you from success? What is the best way to make progress?

2. Read Ecclesiastes 3:1–8. So many of us are pushing hard all the time. Life seems to be a struggle. It's as though we are trying to put two tons of fertilizer into a one-ton truck. According to this passage, we can see that a sovereign God is in control of an ordered world. Do we or do we not have enough time to do everything God wants us to do? How should we approach our days if God is, in fact, in control?

3. Identify an area where you have been pushing too hard. What changes could you make to acknowledge and better enjoy God's plan for your life?

4. Read Proverbs 16:2. In what ways do you deceive yourself into thinking that God owes you a positive answer on plans that you have hatched without His counsel?

5. Read Proverbs 16:3. What do you think it means to "com-mit to the LORD whatever you do, and he will establish your plans"?

PART 5

SOLVING OUR TEMPERAMENT PROBLEMS

CHAPTER 16

PRIDE

I am the greatest. Not only do I knock 'em out;
I pick the round!
Muhammad Ali

God opposes the proud but shows favor
to the humble.
James 4:6

I wonder if your experience with waitresses is anything like mine. When I go out for breakfast, I'm usually in a good mood — morning is my time of day.

Nothing gets a day off to a worse start than a surly waitress. You know the kind I mean. Without a trace of a smile she slams the coffee cup down and splashes coffee on the wrist of your white shirt. Watch out! Here comes the silverware! *Clunk*.

You ordered your eggs over light, but they come out charbroiled. By now you have confirmed that waitresses resent men and are bitter about their station in life. You think, "With an attitude like that, no wonder she's a waitress."

Over the years we begin to look down on waitresses. Notice how many men treat waitresses the next time you're out, and then watch how they treat their colleagues.

THE PROBLEM

Men want and need to feel good about themselves. What could be more natural and more beneficial than to feel good about yourself—to have a good self-image? But when does being proud of our position or accomplishments become a sin? Is anything wrong when our chest swells in pride at the home run our son hits?

Pride is a sin of comparison in which we compare our strengths to the other fellow's weaknesses. In order to make ourselves feel better we put other people down, sometimes verbally and sometimes just mentally. The easiest way to look down on others is to pick out people of less stature and accomplishment. And it's particularly easy to pick out other people's weaknesses to compare to our strengths.

The subtle sin of pride beguiles every Christian man. The most invisible of sins, pride seeps into the Christian life like water oozes into the moat around a sand castle on the beach. It requires no effort on our part to get in, but all of our strength to keep out.

Is there more than one type of pride?

TWO TYPES OF PRIDE

The Bible describes two types of pride. The first, *Pride Type 1*, is found in Galatians 6:4: "Each one should test their own actions. Then they can take pride in themselves alone, without comparing themselves to someone else." The key to a proper type of pride is to not compare ourselves to others.

Rather than testing our self-worth by comparison to others, we are encouraged to practice self-examination. The Bible stands as the yardstick we measure ourselves against. And when we score well, we congratulate ourselves, but not at the expense of someone else.

Pride Type 2 is a spurious feeling of superiority that stalks Christians. Because Christians who walk closely with God lead lives more righteous than some, it's easy to look down on others of less spirituality. C. S. Lewis once said, "A proud man is always looking down on things and people: and, of course, as long as you are looking down, you cannot see something that is above you."[33]

Jesus told a parable to just such people, men "who were confident of their own righteousness and looked down on everyone else" (Luke 18:9). A religious leader prayed to God and thanked Him that he was not like all other men—robbers, evildoers, adulterers, and a nearby tax collector—but that he was a good man. The tax collector, who usually associated with prostitutes, gluttons, and drunkards, prayed also. But he would not even look upward and pleaded for God to have mercy on him because he knew he was a sinner.

Jesus concluded the parable with these words: "I tell you that this man, rather than the other, went home justified before God. For all those who exalt themselves will be humbled, and those who humble themselves will be exalted" (Luke 18:14). By comparing himself to the tax collector, the religious leader elevated himself at another's expense, comparing himself to a weak man rather than a strong God.

Why didn't he compare himself to Moses, Abraham, or King David? When you and I compare ourselves pridefully to other men, why do we pick out the man who isn't as loving a husband, or the fellow who travels too much and doesn't spend as much time with the kids as we do, or the colleague who doesn't have the same mental bandwidth that we have?

We pick out the weaknesses in others because *pride is a sin of comparison in which I compare my strengths to another man's weaknesses.*

TWO TYPES OF HUMILITY

Just as there are two types of pride, there are two types of humility. In Romans 12:3, we confirm the definition of the right type of pride—Pride Type 1—and learn how to define the right type of humility—Humility Type 1.

For by the grace given me I say to every one of you: Do not think of yourself more highly than you ought, but rather think of yourself with sober judgment, in accordance with the faith God has distributed to each of you.

Humility Type 1 is simply not thinking of yourself "more highly than you ought." This affirms the cliché, "Humility is not thinking little of yourself; rather it's simply not thinking of yourself." A humble man does not look down on others. He can be both proud and humble at the same time—proud of himself without comparison to others and humble by not thinking of himself more highly than he ought.

At the same time, many men suffer from a wrong kind of humility. *Humility Type 2* is the opposite of Pride Type 2. If I compare my weaknesses to your strengths, I will end up with a negative self-image. Self-depreciation is a grueling, harmful poison to the spirit and mind. As harmful as it is to think more highly of yourself than you ought, thinking too lowly of yourself will sentence you to a life of mediocrity.

KEEPING THE RIGHT BALANCE

A gymnast who performs on the balance beam must move confidently across the beam, yet at the same time exercise caution not to fall off to one side or the other.

We each walk a pride/humility balance beam. We must confidently move across the balance beam with the right combination of Pride Type 1 and Humility Type 1. Still, we must always exercise caution to not fall off one side into Pride Type 2 or the other side into Humility Type 2.

If we begin to think of ourselves more highly than we ought, we slip and fall off the beam into Pride Type 2. Or if we begin to think self-defeating thoughts, we slip off the other side of the beam into Humility Type 2.

Figure 16.1 illustrates the balance beam we walk to keep pride and humility in proper perspective. Pride and humility are not mutually exclusive. Rather, as Figure 16.1 shows, we are to have Pride Type 1 and Humility Type 1 simultaneously. We don't look down on others, but we have tested our actions and take pride without comparing ourselves to others. We don't think of ourselves more highly than we ought, but we soberly think well of ourselves according to our faith.

MY OWN FOOLISH PRIDE

My greatest desire during my first year after college, working in the business world, was to own an American Express card. That small, green card seemed to me a proxy for success that would announce to the world that I was somebody.

But I didn't have the credit, so in order to get a card I had to find someone to cosign the account. I was so hungry for the image that I asked my father-in-law to cosign for me (which he did). They stamp the year you first became a "member" on the face of the card, and that grows more important with each passing year. Once I saw some men at dinner compare dates, with the most long-standing member winning the right to puff up in smugness.

PRIDE/HUMILITY BALANCE BEAM

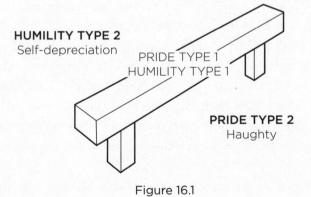

Figure 16.1

If you were to call the vice president of marketing at American Express and ask them to define their product, what do you think they would say? Do you think they would tell you, "That's easy. Our product is a plastic card that you can use to acquire just about anything in the world you desire, just about anywhere in the world you want."

No, if you called the vice president of marketing at American Express and asked them to define their product, they would tell you the product is *prestige*. Every move the American Express Company makes is intended to enhance the notion that to own an American Express card is to have "prestige."

My own compulsion to obtain that little green card resulted from an intense desire for prestige. To gain an American Express card is to gain prestige.

When the American Express Gold Card became popular, I didn't want one. Since the Gold Card signified the holder had a $5,000 line of credit, I reasoned it would be a step back in prestige for me to have one. Why? By then I already had a much larger line of credit with my bank, and I didn't want anyone to think I only had a $5,000 line.

But when the Platinum Card came out, well, that was a different story! To qualify for the Platinum Card, you had to spend a minimum of $10,000 on your existing card in the previous twelve months. Now that's prestige! By obtaining the Platinum Card, you could send the high-status message to everyone.

One small problem — I had spent nowhere near that kind of money on my Green Card. So even before the Platinum Card officially debuted, I began to put everything on my Green Card — airplane tickets, hotel charges, purchases of clothes, shoes, and luggage. I was amazed at how many places take American Express. Of course, this is exactly what the American Express Company had in mind.

Their goal is to generate more sales volume per card. One way to accomplish such a goal is to offer more prestige for spending more money. The cost for the Platinum level of prestige was more than seven times the annual fee for the Green Card.

One day I realized my reason for having an American Express Platinum Card was not for the extra benefits and conveniences that it offers—which are considerable—but to make me feel more important than men who didn't have one.

In my mind I had rationalized the necessity of the Platinum Card because I traveled and entertained so much. In reality, I was merely letting myself be pressed into the mold of this world. I happily carry a Green Card again (better a little prestige than none at all).

TOO MUCH OF A GOOD THING

God blessed my business career with abundance, prosperity, and honor. As I mused with a friend about why God blessed me so, when other men of far greater talent struggled, he responded, "God is blessing you because He trusts you." I have treasured those words.

But somewhere along the way, my heart grew proud—not in arrogance, but in a subtle way of looking down on others, commending myself for superior accomplishment. I became smug over my worldly success.

One day God decided to get my attention. He realized my trustworthiness was slipping. He decided to faithfully discipline me with a test that eventually lasted seven years. He put my business on its back, but it was the best education and the most spiritually rewarding time of my life. I wouldn't want to have to repeat it, but I wouldn't trade it for anything. It was God sparing me from a life of foolish pride.

All men tend to become satisfied and forget who God is and what He has done for us. Moses cautioned the Israelites that when they had become satisfied, they should praise the Lord their God and be careful not to forget Him:

"Otherwise, when you eat and are satisfied, when you build fine houses and settle down, and when your herds and flocks grow large and your silver and gold increase and all you have is multiplied, then your heart will become proud and you will forget the LORD your God."

Deuteronomy 8:12–14

NO PERMISSIVE PARENT OR TYRANT

Another cause of Pride Type 2 is an absence of the fear of God. The fear of God, which we'll talk about in the next chapter, is a difficult concept to get hold of. The fear of the Lord is to hate evil, to be consumed with reverence for God. God is love, but He is also holy and just. A man is to worship God with reverence and awe, for our "God is a consuming fire" (Hebrews 12:29).

A just God is worthy of our reverential fear. If He were not just, then He could be either a *permissive parent* or a *tyrant*. We have no fear of a permissive parent, because we know we can always talk him out of the spanking.

To fear an oppressive tyrant is to fear injustice—getting what we *don't* deserve. But the fear of God is the reverence we give to God Almighty because He has the power and authority to give us what we *do* deserve. The fear of God keeps a man humble; the absence of the fear of God leads to Pride Type 2.

King David wrote, "I have a message from God in my heart concerning the sinfulness of the wicked: There is no fear of God before their eyes. In their own eyes they flatter themselves too much to detect or hate their sin" (Psalm 36:1–2).

The man who does not fear God becomes so proud that he cannot detect his own sinfulness.

THE FRAGILE MALE EGO

Do you use your wife's hairspray? Of course not! So how did the Madison Avenue pin-stripers get men to use hairspray? They put it in black cans.

Black is the macho color. The Mafia drive black cars; dark suits project a strong image; and black leather jackets are the classic icon of the tough guy. So if you want to get men to do something that is traditionally done only by women, appeal to the macho in the male ego — make the can black.

When you have a moment, compare the ingredients in your black can of hairspray with the contents of the white can your wife uses. There is, of course, no difference inside the can, only in the packaging. The packaging is designed to allow the male ego to continue to feel strong and powerful, like a proud lion. Much of what we do is to preserve the image we have of ourselves. This hairspray example simply points out how easily we deceive ourselves, and how much effort we put into making ourselves feel important.

OUR GREATEST STRENGTH IS OUR GREATEST WEAKNESS

At the office I am very analytical and logical. My precise, incisive way of looking at problems has been one of my greatest strengths.

One day I walked into the house, only to be greeted by my wife's long face.

"What's the matter, honey?" I asked.

She unfolded a typical neighborhood spat that all kids go through. But these were not just any kids — these were our kids, and the day had been particularly hard on her. Her nerves were totally frazzled. I listened carefully and then counseled her with three easy steps to patch things up.

At that point I figured out I had said the wrong thing, because she broke into tears. She didn't really want me to solve her problem; she wasn't interested in my keen analytical powers. She just wanted someone to listen.

Sometimes our greatest strength can be our greatest weakness. What is strength at work can be weakness at home. In the same way, when we become confident in our own Christian walk, that strength can become a weakness if we compare ourselves to others.

Pride Type 2 is even more of a temptation to Christians than to nonbelievers. Because of our pursuit of moral living, we can look and see how our morality really *is* superior to those around us. The more self-righteous we become, the greater the potential for us to become proud. God prefers a humble sinner to a proud religious man.

NO RUNTS, NO PECKING ORDERS

My daughter had two hamsters, one of which was the runt of his litter. She knew he was the runt, which is why she picked him out. Women are like that, aren't they?

Every litter has a runt. He's the little guy who has to work extra hard for his share of the food. The rule is survival of the fittest.

As a teenager I tried to raise chickens to make spending money. The venture was meant to be a commercial enterprise, but it turned out to be more for education than profit.

Those chickens made their own chicken coop rules. The boss chicken could peck on anybody he wanted to peck on. Then there was a number two chicken. She could peck on anyone except number one. The number three chicken could peck on everyone except number one and number two. The poor chicken at the end of the pecking order was flat out of luck—truly henpecked!

We organize our society into pecking orders and runts. But God doesn't have any runts. Christ came to usher in a new order—to love our neighbors as ourselves—without thinking of people in a pecking order.

Remember the waitress at the beginning of this chapter? Talk to your waitress sometime. It can be a hard life. The younger ones are often divorced and lonely, supporting young children on what's lunch money to many men. The older ones often work because their husbands died and made no provision for them. Both young and old *must* work and—because some of us think we're better than they are—not always under pleasant circumstances. No wonder some of them are a little surly. So should we peck away at them? Instead, shouldn't we make an effort to cheer them up and let them know there are Christians who care about them? Or, to get really practical, maybe double our normal tip.

THE PRICE OF JUDGING OTHERS

One symptom of pride is a dead giveaway: the constant critiquing of others. Nowhere is this more prevalent than in the Christian community. Men are constantly judging other men's spiritual condition on the basis of outward appearances. Men constantly editorialize about why some people are successful and others are not. There is no end of putting down Christian men who are not successful by worldly standards, and no end of being suspicious of those who are.

Jesus said:

> "Do not judge, or you too will be judged. For in the same way you judge others, you will be judged, and with the measure you use, it will be measured to you.
>
> "Why do you look at the speck of sawdust in your brother's eye and pay no attention to the plank in your own eye?"
>
> Matthew 7:1 – 3

When I am harsh in judging others, others will be harsh with me. How does this principle work? Everyone has met a special man at some time. He is gracious in his speech and never speaks ill of anyone. You can just tell his heart is pure. In fact, you can never remember him losing his temper. How do you speak of him to others? Don't you give him a big buildup? He is gracious, and people are gracious in return.

We also each know men who are abrasive and irritating. They are always demeaning others through innuendo and ethnic slurs. You suspect they always work off hidden agendas. You wouldn't trust them if your life depended on it. When you have the chance to give an opinion about such a man, don't you give a bad report? This is how it works: "One who loves a pure heart and who speaks with grace will have the king for a friend" (Proverbs 22:11). If you are gracious and humble with people, they will speak well of you to others. If you are arrogant and have a critical spirit toward others, they will pass up no opportunity to tell others how they *really* feel about you.

PRIDE: A SIN OF TRANSITION

Pride is the first of the seven cardinal sins (see Proverbs 6:16–19) and a fountainhead of other sins. Through the passageway of pride, men pass into the sins of a hard heart. Pride is the patriarch of man's sin.

Once I was given a bit of advice, unsolicited, from a man not as commercially successful as I was. He counseled me not to build a particular building. I ignored his advice, thinking myself wiser. Within months I was in the grip of a gigantic fight for survival. The building wasn't leasing up fast enough, and the mortgage payments were eating us alive. My pride had led me to an error in judgment— failing to seek counsel. "Plans fail for lack of counsel, but with many advisers they succeed" (Proverbs 15:22).

Pride can lead to discord, jealousy, conceit, haughtiness, boasting, fits of rage, envy, arrogance, an independent spirit, hatred, self-righteousness, a judgmental attitude, and a sanctimonious attitude.

THE SIN OF A BLIND MAN

Jesus called the Pharisees "blind guides" (Matthew 23:16). There is no group in the Bible to whom Jesus was more opposed than the Pharisees. He despised their hypocrisy; He found their proud hearts repugnant. No sin more conclusively violated the new command He gave—to love one another—than the pride of the blind guides.

Are you blind to the needs of other people? Do you see the anger of men as a cry for help, or as a provocation for a counterattack? Do you differentiate between classes of people with a pecking order you have devised? With God there is no favoritism, and we are to show no partiality. Christ's example to us was humility, and we are to have His same attitude. God opposes the proud but shows favor to the humble. We are not to be proud, but willing to associate with people of low position, and we are not to be conceited.

Pride Type 2 is the pathway to hard times. A man's pride brings him low. Before a man's downfall, his heart is proud. Pride goes before destruction, and a haughty spirit before a fall. Disgrace is the by-product of pride. The Lord detests all men who are proud; they will not go unpunished.

Pride Type 2 defies detection. It cloaks itself with shadows. We are blind to pride because it is hard to see in the dim light of the shadows. When we lose our temper with our wives or dwell on women in our secret thought life, those are high-awareness sins. Pride, though, is more subtle.

Frankly, all of us are guilty of pride and should ask God to make us humble so we will not suffer pride's consequences—disgrace, destruction, downfall, and opposition of our plans by God. This may sound unpleasant, but only radical surgery will remove this soul-destroying disease from our hearts.

But let's also never forget that, as with any moral imperative, none of us can actually be this kind of man through our own strength. Seriously, is there anything in your personal history that even remotely suggests you can pull this off?

However, Jesus was this kind of man, and by prayerfully depending on Him to live in and through us by faith, we can conquer our pride. In fact, wouldn't you agree that's the only way it's ever going to happen?

——————— FOCUS QUESTIONS ———————

1. Is it wrong to enjoy recognition, to let your chest swell up in pride when you are complimented? Don't we all need to be encouraged?

2. Do you think the sin of pride is easy or hard to self-diagnose? Why?

3. Read Romans 12:3. In the context of this verse, what is one way to define wrongful pride?

4. Read Galatians 6:4. Describe the kind of pride commended in this verse.

5. How have you been wronged by someone's pride (arrogance, critical spirit) recently? How do you think that person developed such an attitude?

   Possible Answers:
   - Became satisfied and forgot who God is (Deuteronomy 8:10–14, 17–19).
   - Did not possess the fear of God (Psalm 36:1; Mark 5:39–40).
   - Sincerely thought God wasn't needed (James 4:13–17).
   - Other answers: _____

6. Read Proverbs 3:34; 16:5, 18; 18:12; Luke 18:14. What is the destiny of a proud man?

7. Describe an area of your life — work, wife, kids — in which pride is hurting you. How? What can you do about it?

CHAPTER 17

FEAR

The only thing we have to fear is fear itself.
Franklin Delano Roosevelt

"Take courage! It is I. Don't be afraid."
Jesus, Matthew 14:27

You may be surprised to learn that Franklin Delano Roosevelt was born an aristocrat. His wealthy, influential parents wisely raised him, however, to believe the privileged must shoulder a greater responsibility to help the less fortunate.

Although shy as a teenager, Roosevelt blossomed when he enrolled at Harvard University, where he contributed to campus life by becoming involved in sports and the school newspaper.

Roosevelt was already a distinguished public servant, having served as a state senator and assistant secretary of the Navy, when tragedy struck—he fell ill to a severe case of polio. The dark days that followed left him in twisted physical pain. But a determined Roosevelt, whose career many observers thought was over, summoned the depths of his personal courage and regained the use of his hands and learned to walk with braces. During his convalescence, a fear of fire tormented Roosevelt—that he would be trapped in a burning building. His life already devastated, who would blame him if he spent the rest of his days wallowing in self-pity? Instead, he struggled to overcome his disability and conquer his fears.

Eight short years later he became governor of the state of New York.

And just eleven years after he was stricken and paralyzed, after enduring countless months of severe pain, after being urged to retire, Franklin Delano Roosevelt — man of fear, man of courage — was sworn in as the thirty-second president of the United States of America.

When he took his oath of office, the country was in the depths of the Great Depression. One in four men was unemployed; many men had no money to buy food for their families; and many had lost their homes. The great nation had been driven to its knees; God had humbled America.

Like Roosevelt's legs, the country was crippled in fear. Who better could symbolize the paralysis people felt? Men everywhere felt the ruthless clutch of dread and wondered if they were next. Imagine one out of every four men in your neighborhood unemployed. The men on either side of you have been foreclosed. You have lost all or most of your savings through a stock market collapse. A lot of us today can relate, having been through our own private Great Depression, and it's terrifying. Where do you turn?

Against that kind of backdrop, Franklin Delano Roosevelt scuffled to the microphone and delivered one of the twentieth century's most riveting inaugural addresses: "The only thing we have to fear is fear itself."

THE PROBLEM

What are you afraid of? What makes you worry? Is it the job jitters? Do you think a pink slip may be in the wind? Maybe you work under the constant tension of a boss who is always trying to outsource and downsize. Perhaps you have just learned you have a disabling illness, and you don't know how you will support your family. Death might look better to you than life.

Some of you have a business deal that is hanging on by a frayed thread. You've been working on it for months. If it falls through, you will have to severely alter your lifestyle—you may lose everything. The thought of having to start over makes your hands tremble.

You may have a son or daughter on drugs. Embarrassed and frightened, you don't know where to turn for help. You may be worried you're about to lose an important account that will devastate your cash flow. Maybe people intimidate you, and your relationships are filled with anxiety.

Some men sense no direction for their lives, and they fear God has abandoned them. Some fear an uncertain future. Some do not have an assurance that when they die, they will actually be in the presence of God.

Most of us are consumed by the problems this very day is bringing to our doorsteps. You're thinking, *I don't have any problem with eternal life and salvation and all of that—it's these next twenty-four hours that I'm worried about.*

Every man struggles with the emotion of fear. Fear of failure, fear of rejection, fear of sudden disaster, fear of men—fears of all sorts elbow their way into our stream of conscious thought. Yet most of us are conditioned to deny we even have these fears. While some fears are constructive—many heroes are born by their reaction to a life threat—most fears handicap men. And while fear itself is certainly not sinful, if it leads to not believing God, it can *become* sinful.

For most of us, how fear affects us is taking place through a process we barely comprehend. So let's spend this chapter exploring and understanding what fear is all about, and how to cope with it.

Fear and courage are opposites. The dictionary defines courage as the state of mind that enables one to face hardship or disaster with confidence and resolution. Fear is the agitated state of mind that cripples us from looking any further than the hardship itself.

The Bible repeatedly encourages us to not be afraid. When Jesus speaks, He often begins, "Don't be afraid!" We are told that God has not made us timid or fearful but gives us power, love, and self-discipline (see 2 Timothy 1:7). We are even told that the man who fears has not been made perfect (complete) in love (see 1 John 4:18). If everywhere in the Scriptures we are encouraged to not be afraid, why do we constantly struggle with all types of fears?

WHY AM I AFRAID?

To be afraid is to not *fully* trust God. He instructs us to not be afraid, promising that if we cast our anxiety on Him, He will take care of us (see 1 Peter 5:7). Now, if we don't take Him at His Word on this, then we have not fully trusted Him. Fear and lack of trust go hand in hand; where you find one, you will find the other. So if we are to understand why we *do* fear, we must understand why we *don't* trust God.

Like sore thumbs, three reasons stick out why we choose to be afraid rather than trust God.

I've Been Lied to All of My Life

I remember being suspicious that my high school girlfriend had gone out on a date with another guy. When I confronted her, she vehemently denied it. Later I picked a fight with the senior (I was a mere junior) who I suspected was the "other" knight in shining armor. My fears were confirmed, and it cost me a bloody nose.

We're all liars, aren't we? You are a liar. I am a liar. My wife is a liar. My parents lie. My business colleagues lie. My children lie. All of our lives we have been lied to.

Do you know any sin more prevalent than the little white lie? The white lie easily wins first prize for the most frequently occurring verbal sin. One researcher found that when two strangers engaged in conversations, 60 percent of his participants lied, on average, three times in the short span of ten minutes.[34] One source found that adults admit to telling thirteen white lies each week. That in itself is probably a white lie. I'm sure the number is actually much higher, but who wants to confess to being a liar? *Everyone* tells white lies.

Since we have been lied to all of our lives by everyone we know, should we be surprised that when we read the Bible, we can hardly believe it is true? Even though the Bible says to "not be afraid" and trust God, we wonder, at least occasionally, if it is really true because we have been lied to all of our lives.

There Is No Such Thing as a Free Lunch

The Bible promises that if we trust God with our lives, He will meet all of our needs and direct all of our paths. The message intrigues us: If we will confess our weaknesses and sins, God will not only forgive us but also cleanse us from all of our unrighteousness. In other words, *God will give us everything we have ever wanted, in exchange for everything we have ever wanted to get rid of.*

Most men find this hard to swallow the first time they hear it. It sounds very much like a free lunch, and we all know very well that there is no such thing as a free lunch! Nevertheless, God offers us a "free lunch," paid in full by Someone else.

If we confess our sins and follow Him, He will give us everything we have ever wanted: love, joy, peace, patience, kindness, goodness, faithfulness, gentleness, and self-control—all our New Year's resolutions. For this free lunch, all we have to do is allow Him to blot out the memory of everything we have ever done that is wrong.

Is it any wonder that so many men find the gospel hard to understand? The gospel really is unique. Jesus Christ came because men were unable to keep God's laws. But because God is just, someone had to receive punishment for our sins, so Jesus substituted Himself for us. It was *our* sins—yours and mine—for which Christ died. It wasn't *His* sins, but *our* sins! That's what Scripture means when it says, "Very rarely will anyone die for a righteous person, though for a good person someone might possibly dare to die. But God demonstrates his own love for us in this: While we were still sinners, Christ died for us" (Romans 5:7–8).

Men find trusting God difficult because our experience tells us there is no free lunch. Instead of taking Him at His Word, we keep looking for the angle, the loophole. *Where's the catch?* we wonder. The end result is that we don't trust God fully, and that sets fear loose to roam the hallways of our minds.

We Really Are Guilty

The third reason we don't trust God revolves around our moral guilt. Our moral guilt is what convicts us that we are sinners. We know we have been guilty of moral depravity in our thought lives, our speech, and our actions. We find our sins contemptible; we despise our unrighteousness; we grieve over our incurable and wicked hearts.

We really are guilty, and we know it. We really do deserve God's punishment and wrath. We really should be afraid of God, who has the power to give us what we justly deserve. But in God's hard-to-fathom love, He has withheld His punishment from us and brought it on the Lord Jesus instead.

You may find trusting God difficult because you know you really *are* guilty, and you simply can't believe that God would be so gracious that He would actually forgive you and remove the guilt you feel for your sins. Yet, that is *exactly* what He does.

When men do not accept God's forgiveness for their moral guilt, they have not been "made perfect in love," and the fear of their guilt remains with them. But "perfect love [Jesus Christ] drives out fear, because fear has to do with punishment. The one who fears is not made perfect in love [Jesus Christ]" (1 John 4:18). God has withheld His punishment, so we don't have to fear—so that we can trust in Him.

So then, many men find trusting God difficult because we have been lied to all of our lives; we don't believe in getting a free lunch; and we have difficulty accepting God's forgiveness. And men who don't trust God often find themselves stuck in the *Cycle of Fear*.

THE CYCLE OF FEAR

One day Jesus needed some time alone, so He instructed His disciples to get into their boat and go ahead of Him to the other side of the lake. The clear skies shone brightly, and they set sail. Sometime during the evening hours a storm came up, and the boat was buffeted by the waves and wind (see Matthew 14:22–31).

About that time, Jesus came walking toward them—walking on the water. They were terrified at the sight of Him, thinking He was a ghost! Fear gripped them.

Immediately Jesus said, *"Take courage! It is I. Don't be afraid."*

I can imagine Jesus may have had more to say to them, but just then Peter blurted out, "Lord, if it's you, tell me to come to you on the water." If they were close enough to see each other and talk, why make such a nonsensical request? Wouldn't it have been better to say, "Lord, please come into the boat and save us!"

Jesus probably saw an illustration in the making, because instead of suggesting a wiser plan, He told Peter, *"Come."*

Then a remarkable thing happened. Peter got out of the boat and began to walk on the water. We always think of Jesus walking on the water, but Peter, a man like us, also walked on water. That must have really taken some faith.

But just as Peter was on his way to becoming a hero and media celebrity, the Cycle of Fear began: *"He saw the wind."* Reality set in. Suddenly he realized the crazy thing he was doing—he was walking on water! He saw the wind and realized he was in the middle of a fierce storm.

How many times have each of us started out on a project— maybe a new job—with great faith, only to find ourselves in the middle of a fierce storm? Maybe we set sail when the skies shone brightly, maybe we sensed the Lord sent us on our mission, but then the storm came. We looked around and we "saw the wind." The first step in the Cycle of Fear is *reality*—we see the wind.

Then Peter was no longer interested in the original goal of being like Jesus. No, instead he saw the wind, and *"he was afraid."* The second step of the Cycle of Fear is our *response*. When reality sets in, we respond in fear. We may have had big plans to raise godly kids. Or we dreamed about the glory of owning our own business. But when we are forced to face reality, and the kids go off the rails or sales are not enough to cover the costs, our response is to be afraid.

Once fear seized Peter, he found himself "beginning to sink." His faith had kept him afloat, but when he chose fear over continuing his faith, *he began to sink*. The third step in the Cycle of Fear is the *result*. As we respond to reality, we often begin to sink. Our faith kept us afloat, but when the winds came up and buffeted our career or business or family, we soon saw that our faith was too little. We saw the wind; we became afraid; and we started to sink in the swirling waters of our problems.

Now, Peter was no fool. When he began to sink, he had the presence of mind to call out for help (which is more than some of us do). He cried out, *"Lord, save me!"* This simple prayer is the fourth step in the Cycle of Fear—the *return*. Peter returned to his source. His faith was not enough to keep him afloat, so he wisely acknowledged he needed help and returned to his source of power, Jesus, calling out to him, "Lord, save me!" When you are beginning to sink in the deep waters of your fears and problems, do you remember to return to your source?

Have you ever noticed that when someone is in dire straits, they never call on anyone but God? Have you ever heard a greedy businessman fall on hard times and say, "Money, please save me!" Even the purported atheist, when his life is threatened, cries out, "Oh, my God!"

How did Jesus respond to Peter's brief prayer, "Lord, save me"? He could have been filled with disgust, which would probably have been my response. I was thinking as I read the story, "You idiot! Were you born stupid, or were you just having a stupid attack?"

I might let him take on a few gulps of water just to teach him a thing or two. But Jesus' response was quite nonjudgmental. Instead of a sanctimonious rebuke, Jesus gives us the fifth and final step of the Cycle of Fear, the *rescue.*

Immediately, without hesitation, Jesus reached out His hand and caught Peter. The wonderful news about the Cycle of Fear with which we each struggle is that no matter how much wind we see, no matter how big the storm, no matter how afraid we become, no matter how deep we are sinking, when we return to Jesus, He will rescue us.

He doesn't promise to save your business, or get your son off drugs, or bring your wife to Christ, or keep you from losing your job, but He does promise to save you. Rescue by Jesus is the great promise we have if we will only call out to Him when we are afraid.

Everyone struggles with the Cycle of Fear. No once-for-all cure exists. But you can decrease the amount of time you spend in this cycle by following this charge from Jesus: *"Take courage! It is I. Don't be afraid."* Let's learn how to obey Jesus and move from *the Cliff of Fear* to *the Cliff of Courage.*

FROM CLIFF TO CLIFF

In the story of Peter walking on the water, Jesus expressed great patience and saved Peter from the Cycle of Fear. But can a man move past the Cycle of Fear and overcome his fears?

We often find ourselves standing on a Cliff of Fear peering across a wide, deep chasm to a Cliff of Courage where we wished we could stand. But how do we get there? Figure 17.1 illustrates the dilemma. Jesus gives us the answer.

Right after Jesus saved Peter, he said, *"You of little faith. Why did you doubt?"* Faith is how we traverse from the one cliff to the other. We cross from the Cliff of Fear to the Cliff of Courage on *the Bridge of Faith.* Figure 17.2 shows how faith bridges the gorge between fear and courage.

WHAT IS FAITH?

"Faith is confidence in what we hope for and assurance about what we do not see" (Hebrews 11:1). *Faith is always oriented toward the future.* We don't need courage to face what we already know. It is an uncertain future that gives birth to doubts and fears.

We don't know the details of what will happen in the future, but we do know God will take care of our needs and unite us with Himself forever. That's what faith is. An old saying sums it up, "We don't know what the future holds, but we know who holds the future."

THE CLIFFS OF FEAR AND COURAGE

Figure 17.1

Jesus is the pioneer and perfecter of our faith (see Hebrews 12:2). As we fix our eyes on Him, He increases and perfects our faith. Many times I heard Dr. Bill Bright say, "Faith is like a muscle. The more you exercise it, the bigger it grows."

So when we find ourselves standing on the Cliff of Fear, peering across the wide expanse toward the Cliff of Courage, let's remember that faith in Jesus and the certain future He controls is our bridge across.

GODLY FEAR VERSUS SECULAR FEAR

One of the most misunderstood principles of the Bible is the fear of God. What is the difference between the fear of God and secular fear (the other fears) with which we struggle?

Often the fear of God is dismissed as a translation problem. It is suggested that the fear of God is merely reverent thinking about Him. Actually, the fear of God involves an understanding of who God really is and a hatred of everything that is not of God. Proverbs 8:13 reads, "To fear the LORD is to hate evil." To effectively hate evil, a man must be able to differentiate between good and evil.

THE CLIFFS OF FEAR AND COURAGE

Figure 17.2

We fear men for a very practical reason: *Men have the power to give us what we don't deserve or to withhold from us what we do deserve.* Men have the capacity to do the wrong thing.

I remember my first really big deal. The commission was six figures—was I excited! At the closing, the buyer ranted and raved and threatened not to close unless I took a cut in commission. A neophyte, I crumbled at the thought of no closing and settled for one-sixth of the earned fee. We have good cause to fear men — they can deal out injustice to us.

We should fear God for an equally practical reason: *God has the power to give us what we deserve.* God does *not* have the capacity to do the wrong thing.

What we deserve is punishment for our sins. But God chose to withhold His punishment and instead sent Jesus to die a substitutionary death in our place for our sins. Whew! Now, *that's* hard to get your arms around. God is just, unlike men, and He demands that evil be punished. But, thank God, He developed a plan for us to escape His wrath — Jesus Christ. And because of our faith in Christ, we now deserve eternal life, which God has freely given us.

Do we know whom to be afraid of? We fear men, but they have no genuine power over us. We become concerned that they will cheat us in a business deal, withhold the pay raise, fire us, or rob our house. But God has genuine power. He has the power of life and death; He has the power to judge our sins; He has prepared an eternal home for us; He promised that "in all things God works for the good of those who love him, who have been called according to his purpose" (Romans 8:28); and He says we will be "*more* than conquerors" (Romans 8:37, italics added). Now, let me ask you, Whom are we better off fearing — God or man? "Fear of man will prove to be a snare, but whoever trusts in the LORD is kept safe" (Proverbs 29:25).

John Witherspoon wisely wrote, "It is only the fear of God that can deliver us from the fear of man."[35] We are much better off fearing God, who can give us what we do deserve, than fearing men, who — though they can give us what we don't deserve or withhold what we do deserve — are unable to harm us in any permanent way.

WAS JESUS EVER AFRAID?

No. Emphatically. Absolutely. Never. Not once.

The fact that Jesus was never afraid offers us hope. He was *tempted* to fear, but He never succumbed. If ever a situation merited fear, it was Jesus at the Mount of Olives on the night He was betrayed by Judas (see Luke 22:39–46).

Jesus knew His fate — His destiny. All of His life pointed to the inevitability of that night. So He withdrew with His disciples to their usual place on the Mount of Olives. Jesus knew the temptation to become afraid that would beset Him. He said to His disciples, "Pray that you will not fall into temptation."

Then Jesus withdrew a stone's throw and prayed His well-known prayer: "Father, if you are willing, take this cup from me; yet not my will, but yours be done." To ask God to change His mind is our first clue to the torturous condition of Christ. He was sitting on death row. He knew that tomorrow He would die. He was being tempted to fear.

Just then, God sent an angel to strengthen Him. Have you ever been in the clutches of fear and asked God to deliver you from the temptation to give in and become afraid? When we ask Him, He will always strengthen us, just as He did Jesus. In 1 Corinthians 10:13, we find the promise, "When you are tempted, he will also provide a way out so that you can endure it."

At this point, the agony of Jesus reached its peak, because He began to sweat drops of blood. This medically documented phenomenon, *hematidrosis*, only occurs in rare instances of extreme anxiety.

UNBUNDLING OUR EMOTIONS

At this point, it will be helpful for us to *unbundle our emotions* and differentiate between *fear* and other emotions of *anxiety* and *dread*.

The Bible describes Jesus' condition as one of *agonia*, which translates as "agony" or "anguish" as the result of a struggle. According to *Strong's Exhaustive Concordance of the Bible,* this is the only time *agonia* is used in the Bible. I think we can say conclusively that Jesus underwent the most terrifying temptation ever encountered, yet He neither feared nor sinned by not believing His Father.

Since Jesus had been strengthened, He was standing on the Cliff of Courage. His *circumstances* did not change, but His *attitude* did. God did not remove the source of agony, but He did strengthen Jesus so that He did not become afraid. Agony—yes. Fear—no. That's our hope.

Jesus told the disciples, "Pray that you will not fall into temptation." Because Jesus overcame this temptation, we have His power to overcome it too.

FOUR STEPS TO OVERCOME FEAR

When we have an anxiety attack, let's try to unbundle our emotions and eliminate fear. Step 1 is to feel our way through the fog to the Bridge of Faith. Step 2 is to crawl across to the Cliff of Courage. Step 3 is to submit our circumstances and attitude to God and His will. Step 4 is to wait patiently for God to act.

We can unbundle our emotions and eliminate fear. We may not be able to change our circumstances, but we can restrict our emotions to the agony and anguish of the situation.

Remember this:

> No temptation [fear] has overtaken you except what is common to mankind. And God is faithful; he will not let you be tempted beyond what you can bear. But when you are tempted, he will also provide a way out so that you can endure it.
>
> 1 Corinthians 10:13

Every opportunity to fear is also an opportunity to trust God and move from the Cliff of Fear across the Bridge of Faith to the Cliff of

Courage. Sooner or later, we all "see the wind." We all become afraid and begin to sink. Those are the opportunities we have to trust God, and call out to Him, "Lord, save me!"

---------------- FOCUS QUESTIONS ----------------

1. All men struggle with the emotion of fear.

   ❏ Agree ❏ Disagree. Explain your answer.

2. Why is it so hard to have faith, to not be afraid, and to trust God?

3. What are you currently struggling with that has you afraid? How can you overcome your fear? (See "Cycle of Fear.")

   Cycle of Fear:

   - Reality — We see the wind.
   - Response — We become afraid.
   - Result — We begin to sink.
   - Return — "Lord, save me!"
   - Recovery — Jesus reaches out His hand.

4. Why can't we overcome our fear in one fell swoop? Why do we have to wrestle with it day by day? Read Matthew 6:34.

5. Courage and fear are opposites (see Matthew 14:27). What makes you feel courageous? What is the biblical way to courage? (Read Mark 4:40 and refer to Figure 17.2).

6. Describe the difference between secular fear (fear of man) and godly fear. Read Proverbs 8:13; 1 Peter 3:10 – 14.

7. When you have done everything you can do and things still don't seem to be working out, how are you to respond? Read 1 Peter 4:12 – 19; 5:6 – 7, 10.

CHAPTER 18

ANGER

"I lose my temper, but it's all over in a minute,"
said the student. "So is the hydrogen bomb,"
I replied. "But think of the damage it produces!"
George Sweeting

My dear brothers and sisters, take note of this:
Everyone should be quick to listen, slow to speak
and slow to become angry, because human
anger does not produce the righteousness
that God desires.
James 1:19 - 20

Daniel and his wife, Kristin, were driving home from a welcomed night out for dinner. The Baltimore streets were crowded with traffic. As Daniel slowed for a traffic light, a cab driver swerved his steed into the narrow space in front of Daniel's car.

Daniel leaned on the horn and began to yell expletives at the cabby. But the light turned green, and the driver took off. Daniel decided to teach the cabby a lesson and began to chase him down the street, honking and screaming and waving his hands out the window.

Finally, the cab driver caught a red light, and Daniel pulled alongside the passenger door of the cab. He ranted and raved, but the cab's window was rolled up. After thirty seconds or so, the cab driver leaned over, rolled down his window, and dryly asked Daniel, "What do you want me to do, buddy—drop dead?"

What is something that really makes you angry? One day I was walking out of a large mall where we occasionally shop and saw a man tongue-lashing his seven-year-old son. His timid wife, holding an infant child, looked on—her demure face frozen in apprehension. Suddenly, without warning, the father wound up and slugged his son in the face.

The boy began to cry; the mother became hysterical; and I flushed with the rage of injustice until I thought the veins in my neck would burst. Nothing makes me angrier than to see a father strike his child with a closed fist.

THE PROBLEM

How did you answer the question—What makes you angry? I wonder if, like me, you thought of an instance when righteous anger boiled inside you, or if your mind reflected on a time you were angry because you couldn't have your own way.

Occasionally we become angry for a righteous cause, but 99 percent of the time we become angry because we are *selfish* and *impatient*. I gave a self-serving example of my own anger, but I assure you that 99 percent of the illustrations I could have used would not flatter me very much.

Anger lurks behind the closed doors of most of our homes. Personally, I have never lost my temper at the office—I would never want my colleagues to think I couldn't control myself. Because the gospel is true, I have become more patient with each passing year, but I have to admit, when we had children in the home, rarely a week went by without the sparks of family life providing good tinder for a roaring fire of anger.

We put on a good show at work and our social gatherings, but *how you are behind the closed doors of your own private castle is how you really are.* At the end of a long, hard day at work, when you pull up the drawbridge to your own private castle, your family gets to live with the *real you.*

Anger destroys the quality of our personal lives, our marriages, and our health. Angry words are like irretrievable arrows released from an archer's bow. Once released, traveling through the air toward their target, they cannot be withdrawn; their damage cannot be undone. Like the arrows of the archer, our angry words pierce like a jagged blade, ripping at the heart of their target.

When anger pierces the soul of the home, the lifeblood of the family starts to drain away. You may notice that a secretary seems to find you attractive. You reflect on how your wife no longer appreciates you. It never occurs to you that if that secretary knew the *real you*—the angry you who lives secretly behind the closed doors of your home—she would find you about as desirable as a flat tire.

This chapter is addressed to the *real you* who lives behind closed doors. That's the man I'd like to talk to, and that includes me.

THREE ANGRY MEN

Freddie Flash has a short fuse. It doesn't take much to set him off. Because he has such a low flash point, he loses his temper too often. His anger problem is a *frequency* problem. Some of his friends have been heard to say, "Freddie is mad at the world."

Minor irritations blow way out of proportion with Freddie. He is an angry man looking for a place to be angry, exploding at the slightest provocation, though his anger subsides just as quickly. He thinks the harm he does is inconsequential. It hasn't dawned on him that it's not the single occurrence but the frequency that has branded him as someone to avoid. Freddie has an angry spirit.

Cary Control doesn't become angry every day. But boy oh boy, when Cary's long fuse finally burns down, the dynamite explodes! He loses control and strikes out with a verbal tirade that makes his wife's knees wobble and his children flinch in terror. His anger problem is an *intensity* problem.

When first married, he would strike his wife, though he tried to pull up at the moment of contact. He would immediately break down in tears and plead for forgiveness.

Cary's bitterness about his station in life consumes his every waking moment, and sometimes the pressures of life just overwhelm him. The intensity of his anger frightens him, but he just can't seem to keep the lid on it all the time—sometimes he just has to let off steam. Cary is sitting on a volcano of anger.

Gary Grudge never has an outburst of anger. Instead, Gary seethes with anger and plots his revenge. His counterattacks are designed to discredit the man he hates. Gary often wakes up in the middle of the night, a cold sweat reminding him of the one who has done him wrong. His anger problem is a problem of *duration*.

As a grudge holder, Gary feels the toxic juices of anger burn on the lining of his stomach wall like rust remover on an old, corroded hinge. He feeds his ulcer the right foods, but his high blood pressure and colitis require a doctor's prescription. Gary just can't bring himself to forgive and let go.

Freddie Flash, Cary Control, and Gary Grudge show us the three main symptoms of our anger: *a low flash point* (a frequency problem), *losing control* (an intensity problem), and *holding a grudge* (a duration problem). If these are the *symptoms* of our anger, what are the underlying *sources* of our anger?

WHAT MAKES US ANGRY THAT SHOULDN'T

Seven sources of anger stir up our sinful nature and hamper our effort to live by the Spirit. In a life fully surrendered to the lordship of Jesus Christ, these seven reasons for anger are opportunities to either become angry or to trust God with yet another area of our lives.

1. Violation of Rights. Everyone believes they have certain rights. On a physical level, we each feel we have certain "space" rights. Psychologists tell us we consider an eighteen-inch zone in front of our face as private. One reaction to the invasion of this space is to fester in anger.

2. Disappointment with One's Station in Life. Many men become bitter with anger when they begin to suspect that their "oyster" doesn't have the pearl they wanted. Many of us need to accept our lot in life as from the Lord, provided we have been faithful with our abilities.

For other men, Proverbs 19:3 sets the record straight: "A person's own folly leads to their ruin, yet their heart rages against the LORD." Fewer slots exist at the top than men trying to fill them. If we are not content with what we have, the issue is not getting more but learning to be content with our circumstances.

3. Blocked Goals. Setting and achieving realistic goals can be a great source of personal satisfaction. Everyone sets goals, though some are not consciously aware of the process. When we are blocked from achieving our goals, for good cause or not, we frequently respond in anger.

Psalm 37:5–8 gives the best formula for setting goals and how to respond—and not respond—when they're blocked:

Commit your way to the LORD;
    trust in him and he will do this:
He will make your righteous reward shine like the dawn,
    your vindication like the noonday sun.
Be still before the LORD
    and wait patiently for him;
do not fret when people succeed in their ways,
    when they carry out their wicked schemes.
Refrain from anger and turn from wrath;
    do not fret—it leads only to evil.

4. Irritations. Life's little irritations often seem to weigh more heavily on us than our true dilemmas. "She squeezes the toothpaste from the top, but I squeeze it from the bottom." "Billy! How many times do I have to tell you? Don't bounce that ball in the house!"

Nothing is more irritating to me than a sticky shirt on a hot summer day. You know what I mean—those days when you climb into a car that's as hot as an oven. Within moments, sweat drips down your face, and your T-shirt gets soaked in a couple of minutes. When you arrive at your destination, you climb out of the car, but your shirt doesn't—it's stuck to your car seat.

Ecclesiastes 7:9 urges us, "Do not be quickly provoked in your spirit, for anger resides in the lap of fools." In other words, don't have a "spirit" of anger.

5. *Feeling Misunderstood.* As I mentioned earlier, many years ago I heard Dr. Henry Brandt say something that made an indelible impression on me: "Other people don't create your spirit; they only reveal it." When my feelings get hurt, and anger begins its predictable rise inside me, I have to confess that the other person isn't making me angry; they only reveal the anger that was already there, lurking just below the surface of my conscious thoughts.

We often think people don't understand us—our feelings, our attitudes, our abilities, our potential. They probably don't. But holding a pity party and becoming angry doesn't help us resolve the misunderstanding.

Benjamin Franklin commented, "Anger is never without a reason, but seldom with a good one."

6. *Unrealistic Expectations.* I expect strangers to let me down. But when my Christian friends let me down, sometimes it upsets me. The problem occurs when I set unrealistically high expectations for my friends and family. For some of us, our families would have to be perfect to live up to some of our expectations.

We frequently don't build enough slack into what we expect from our loved ones. But everyone trips, including ourselves, and we need to build some slack into our expectations. "Get rid of all bitterness, rage and anger, brawling and slander, along with every form of malice. Be kind and compassionate to one another, forgiving each other, just as in Christ God forgave you" (Ephesians 4:31–32).

7. *Pathological/Psychological.* Occasionally a man will have a problem with anger because of an illness or emotional disorder. A man abused as a child has a higher statistical probability of having the same anger problem as his own father.

A man whose frequent and intense eruptions of anger permanently alienate family members, or worse, cause a man to strike family members during his angry outbursts, should seek professional counseling—right now, today.

Frankly, most of our anger ends up as sin. The seven reasons for anger we've just reviewed have two characteristics in common: *selfishness* and *impatience.* We are happy as a clam when people agree with us, let us have our own way, and give us what we want. But they don't always see it our way, and our selfishness and impatience often lead to angry outbursts.

Surely, though, there are times when anger is appropriate.

IS ANGER EVER JUSTIFIED?

What usually makes us angry are things like our mother-in-law calling as the family is sitting down to dinner, an associate who is habitually late, or the subcompact that dives into the space in front of us as we slow down for a red light.

The things that usually don't make us angry, but should, are racial prejudice, abortion, declining moral values, and other injustices.

When we observe *a miscarriage of justice* against another, a controlled, focused anger—righteous indignation—can work for a positive result. Anger at injustice, when the stench of prejudice and bigotry rises to our nostrils, will consume righteous men with a passion to correct the evils they see. The greatness of our country rests on the bedrock of our hatred of injustice.

Betrayal by a friend when done with malice is fair cause for anger.

A secret told in confidence that is betrayed seems reason enough to become angry. Or an untrue rumor that threatens our reputation seems just cause to make our anger burn.

Even so, our focus should be on avoiding anger. "Fools give vent to their rage, but the wise bring calm in the end" (Proverbs 29:11). We should keep our anger under control and be patient. "Better a patient person than a warrior, one with self-control than one who takes a city" (Proverbs 16:32).

Every one of us feels the biting sting of betrayal from time to time, but instead of responding in anger we can rely on a remarkable promise.

THE PROMISE FOR THE UNDESERVED CURSE

I would like to share a wonderful secret with you. Actually, it's no secret — it's in the Bible. But few men know about this choice morsel. You never again have to worry about an unjust rumor, because here is *The Promise for the Undeserved Curse.*

The first time I started to spread my wings to fly higher in business, the pellets started to whistle by my ears. "He will never be able to get the financing for that office building." "He doesn't have the expertise to make it fly." "I heard he is having cash flow problems." People can be vicious.

I learned a quick lesson: *The visible target is the one that gets shot at.* You can disappear in the middle of the flock, or you can set yourself apart for excellence and become a target.

As the undeserved rumors and snide remarks started to make their way back to me, I was devastated. I was trying to rise above the quagmire of mediocrity, but there were all these shotguns aimed at me.

One morning, as I lamented to the Lord over this unfair criticism, He kindly guided me to a proverb that has changed my life. No longer do I concern myself with what others might say about me. Instead, I simply recall the promise of God to each of us who is wrongly maligned: "Like a fluttering sparrow or a darting swallow, an undeserved curse does not come to rest" (Proverbs 26:2).

In some mysterious way, by the power of God's Holy Spirit, an undeserved curse goes in one ear of the hearer and out the other. God miraculously helps the hearer discern what is true and not true.

You can probably remember hearing some juicy gossip about a man you know, and, even though you heard it, you discerned that it just wasn't so. Even though it went in one ear, you let it go out the other.

What's the most vicious rumor mill of all? The Christian grapevine, which sometimes has the dual function of a "prayer chain." Here is how it works: I hear a juicy piece of gossip about Tom. He has been seen at lunch with another woman. I am much too respectable to pass on such unverified gossip. However, at lunch with Ed the next day I discreetly inquire if he knows anything about Tom for which we should be in prayer. Ed looks surprised, and then he becomes suspicious.

He asks if there is something going on with which he might help. I say, "Well, I probably shouldn't say anything, *but* I just heard Tom is *having an affair* (note the change from "seen at lunch" to "having an affair"). We had better be in prayer for him."

That evening Ed and his wife have dinner with the Thompsons. In a matter-of-fact way, Ed mentions during dessert that Tom is in need of prayer.

"Oh, why is that, Ed?"

"Well, I heard that Tom is thinking about leaving Jane. He has been keeping a girlfriend in an apartment downtown. Let's ask the Lord to intervene."

Is it any wonder Tom is seething with the anger of betrayal? The worst part is that the woman he took to lunch, a buyer for one of his customers, didn't give him the order. But Tom doesn't need to worry. The promise for the undeserved curse will soon straighten everything out.

WHAT HAPPENS WHEN WE BECOME ANGRY

When my son was eight years old, he got into the habit of spilling his chocolate milk. One night at dinner he knocked over a full sixteen-ounce glass, which splattered everywhere. In a huff, I stormed into the bedroom like a pouty little child and refused to return to the dinner table.

"A quick-tempered person does foolish things" (Proverbs 14:17). When we become angry, we run the risk of becoming very foolish. Of course, this most often happens at home, behind closed doors, where the drawbridge has been drawn up for the night.

Our anger has its own consequences. "A hot-tempered person must pay the penalty; rescue them, and you will have to do it again" (Proverbs 19:19). Our company once had an executive who became angry at the slightest provocation. He had terrorized the secretarial staff, and the other executives hated him.

I continued to forgive and forget, until finally word came back to me about the impact of his anger. He had alienated most of the leasing brokers in town—people we heavily relied on to help lease our buildings. The straw that broke the camel's back came when I learned he was chewing out tenants who were calling in routine maintenance requests.

One morning I asked this executive to come to my office and said, "Fred, I love you—I really do. But the business portion of our relationship has come to its natural conclusion. You're fired."

A hot-tempered man must pay the penalty. A hot-tempered man who is rescued will have to be rescued again.

When we act like Gary Grudge, we become the prisoner of the

one we hate. Dr. S. I. McMillen, in his book *None of These Diseases*, eloquently captures the fate of the grudge holder:

> The moment I start hating a man, I become his slave. I can't enjoy my work anymore because he even controls my thoughts. My resentments produce too many stress hormones in my body and I become fatigued after only a few hours of work. The work I formerly enjoyed is now drudgery. Even vacations cease to give me pleasure. It may be a luxurious car that I drive along a lake fringed with the autumnal beauty of maple, oak, and birch. As far as my experience of pleasure is concerned, I might as well be driving a wagon in mud and rain.
>
> The man I hate hounds me wherever I go, I can't escape his tyrannical grasp on my mind. When the waiter serves me porter-house steak with French fries, asparagus, crisp salad, and straw-berry shortcake smothered with ice cream, it might as well be stale bread and water. My teeth chew the food and I swallow it, but the man I hate will not permit me to enjoy it . . .
>
> The man I hate may be many miles from my bedroom, but, more cruel than any slave driver, he whips my thoughts into such a frenzy that my innerspring mattress becomes a rack of torture.[36]

Another result of our anger concerns our health. Fully 75 to 90 percent "of all doctor's office visits are for stress-related ailments and complaints."[37] The secretions of anger from the adrenal, thyroid, and pituitary glands release their toxins into our bloodstream. Our anger (and our fear) causes heart attacks, strokes, arteriosclerosis, high blood pressure, ulcers, and scores of other killer diseases.

WHEN IS ANGER A SIN?

Usually. Anger usually works its way into sin. "My dear brothers and sisters, take note of this: Everyone should be quick to listen, slow to speak and slow to become angry, because human anger does not pro-duce the righteousness that God desires" (James 1:19 – 20). When we are patient, there is peace, but when we are angry, we spark the anger of others. Before we know what happened, our remark about the other guy's ugly tattoo escalates to accusations about our mother's heritage.

The best guideline for anger is found in Ephesians 4:26–27: " 'In your anger do not sin': Do not let the sun go down while you are still angry, and do not give the devil a foothold." Three bits of wisdom reside in this passage. First, control yourself and don't sin in your anger. Second, never go to bed angry. We should get down on our knees, forgive, and ask forgiveness. Third, when we are angry, our self-control is at risk. The devil may see a crack in the door and find a foothold. Never let the sun go down and remain angry. That's when anger becomes sin.

RESPONDING TO THE ANGER TEMPTATION

Here are some scriptural guidelines on how to respond to the temptation to sin in your anger.

- *Keep Control.* "Fools give vent to their rage, but the wise bring calm in the end" (Proverbs 29:11).
- *Overlook Offenses.* "A person's wisdom yields patience; it is to one's glory to overlook an offense" (Proverbs 19:11).
- *Avoid Angry People.* "Do not make friends with a hot-tempered person, do not associate with one easily angered, or you may learn their ways and get yourself ensnared" (Proverbs 22:24–25).
- *Appease Anger.* "A gentle answer turns away wrath, but a harsh word stirs up anger" (Proverbs 15:1).

CONCLUSION

Men usually become angry out of selfishness and impatience rather than out of outrage over injustice toward others. Freddie Flash has a short fuse; his anger is a frequency problem. Cary Control doesn't become angry every day, but when he does—watch out! He loses control; his anger is an intensity problem. Gary Grudge plots his angry revenge. If you cross him—you pay; his anger is a duration problem.

Men become angry when they shouldn't for the seven reasons we described earlier. The only time our anger is justified is when, under control, we constructively respond to an injustice or a betrayal.

The Promise for the Undeserved Curse, Proverbs 26:2, protects us from the unfair rumors and gossip that try their best to malign our good character.

When a man becomes angry, he runs the risk of doing foolish things. A hot-tempered man must pay the penalty for his anger. Often that penalty is imposed on a man's health.

Are you an angry man? Have you been kidding yourself that you are a pretty nice guy because everyone at work loves you? Remember, how you are behind the closed doors of your private castle is how you really are. That's the man, who along with me, should reread this chapter.

If you are an angry man who would like to overcome your sin of anger, the first thing to understand is that you can't do it on your own. If you attempt to conquer your anger by human effort or will, you'll fail. But Jesus *in* you can and will give you the power to succeed—usually over time—if you make Him part of your quest. So what should you do next, practically speaking?

First, invite Jesus to guide you every step of the way and give you His power and strength. Second, isolate the reasons for your anger from the list of seven sources of anger in the beginning of the chapter. Ask God to reveal the depth of your sin in the area of anger. Third, ask Him to forgive you for your sin of anger and to change you into an unselfish, patient man.

Fourth, the next time you feel your blood beginning to boil, ask yourself, "Am I becoming angry for a *selfish* reason? Am I becoming angry because I am *impatient*?" If you are, *delay saying or doing anything*.

Finally, go to those whom you have hurt with your anger and ask their forgiveness. (By the way, if you're not saying, "I'm sorry," for *something* several times a day, you're probably deluding yourself.) If you have wounded them deeply, they may not respond right away. That's all right. As you change, they will respond to the new you. What could be more exciting than the prospect of restoring your home from a torture chamber to a castle?

————————— FOCUS QUESTIONS —————————

1. It's okay for men to get angry.

   ❏ Agree ❏ Disagree. Explain your answer.

2. Read Ephesians 4:26 – 27. When does anger become sin?

3. What is a pet peeve of yours that really ticks you off? Do you think your anger is a proper response?

4. When does anger have benefits that exceed the costs? (Hint: Do a traditional business "cost/benefit" analysis.)

5. Read Proverbs 22:24 – 25. What is the risk of associating with angry people?

6. Review how to respond to the temptation to become angry:

   • as per Proverbs 29:11
   • as per Proverbs 19:11
   • as per Proverbs 15:1

7. Is God an angry God? Read Psalm 30:5; 78:38 – 39; 103:8; Jonah 4:2; 2 Peter 3:9. Based on what these verses tell us about God, what should our attitude be?

8. According to Galatians 5:16 – 17, how would you describe the two forces at work within you? How can a man walk by the Spirit?

CHAPTER 19

THE DESIRE TO BE INDEPENDENT

I am the master of my fate;
I am the captain of my soul.
William Ernest Henley

LORD, I know that people's lives are not their own;
it is not for them to direct their steps.
Jeremiah 10:23

Brad wobbled a few feet away from his dad to explore. Suddenly he realized he had crossed the room and, panic-stricken, he turned and raced back, threw his arms around his dad's knee, and squeezed tight!

In a while, his bravery returned, and he teetered and tottered into the next room. Things were pretty quiet for a minute or two, until suddenly Brad burst through the doorway and bolted at full speed toward his dad, threw his arms around him, and almost knocked him down.

Brad was two years old then and already beginning to assert his desire to be independent. But his early independence coexisted with an absolute trust that his dad would always take care of him. In the same way, as children of our Father in heaven, we can choose to trust Him—or live in rebellion against Him.

THE PROBLEM

We are raised to be independent. From their earliest homilies, Mom and Dad taught us to be independent with our lives and to make our own place. Most men are taught to pull themselves up by their own bootstraps. "Life is what you make of it," we're told.

We learn early that we can author our own destiny; we can be the captain of our soul, the master of our own fate—or so it seems.

Men want to control their own lives. Even if we were not taught to seek independence, which most of us were, our own human nature would pull us in that direction. We want the freedom to chart our own course. We want the power to shape the events of our lives. These are the hallmarks of our desire to be independent. But in our effort to be self-reliant, we often break ranks with God and go our own independent way.

There is an abrupt difference between taking *responsibility* for our lives and trying to live *independently* from God. We are to take responsibility for our lives—no one will go to work in our place; no one will pay our bills. The difference is this: Responsibility recognizes *our part* and *God's part*. Our part is to trust God and faithfully fulfill our duties. God's part is to provide for all of our needs and well-being. Independence rebels against the influence of God, thinking it can meet its own needs.

The independent man thinks, *I want to do what I want to do, when I want to do it, wherever I want to do it, with whomever I want to do it. I want to be in control. I want to satisfy my ambitions. I don't want to be dependent on anyone. People let me down. God will let me down. I can make it on my own.*

If I can be independent, then I will not need to rely on anyone else. I will not have to trust anyone else, and I will be able to avoid the pain of being disappointed and disillusioned.

If I can be independent, then I can be in control of my own life; I will have the power, whether through money or influence, to get my own way; I will have the freedom to come and go as I please.

This desire to be independent, more often than not, disguises itself. To all external appearances, our mate and friends think we are on the right track, but we often practice a passive sort of self-reliance. Not open rebellion, but we don't really seek the counsel of God and often shun His advice — we do our own thing.

The opposite of desiring to be independent from God is to trust Him. The man who does not trust God trusts in himself and the philosophies of this world, which is the epitome of independence.

THE HUMAN POTENTIAL MOVEMENT

I was very active in the human potential movement, both before and after I became a Christian. Every book that expounded the merits of "willing your way to success" was in my library. "What the mind can conceive and believe it can achieve," went the reasoning.

In fact, I believe that, in many ways, my life is a product of the human potential movement. It would be difficult indeed to be in the marketplace and not be at least partially influenced to believe "you can have it all." We Christians don't have any special inoculation against the desire to be independent.

It's true. By the power of our might and the strength of our own hands, we *can* achieve many worldly successes. The problem is, however, that God doesn't want us to trust in ourselves; He wants us to trust in Him.

TRUST IN MAN AND TRUST IN GOD CONTRASTED

Jeremiah, the weeping prophet, records a vivid description that contrasts the fate of the one who trusts in man (the independent man) and the man who trusts in the Lord (the dependent man).

The Independent Man

This is what the LORD says:

Cursed is the one who trusts in man,
> who draws strength from mere flesh
> and whose heart turns away from the LORD.
That person will be like a bush in the wastelands;
> they will not see prosperity when it comes.
They will dwell in the parched places of the desert,
> in a salt land where no one lives.

Jeremiah 17:5–6

The man who depends on his own strength or trusts in the value system of this world will be miserable. The kind of man God speaks of in this passage is not some wicked sort of evil fellow. Rather, the Bible describes a valiant man—someone who is a winner by all external appearances. But inside he has turned his heart away from the Lord. And what is the fate of the self-reliant man? Like a bush that bears no seed, he tumbles along, producing no fruit, headed nowhere.

The independent man is never able to satisfy his thirst for significance and purpose. Couldn't his "wasteland" be a state of mind just as easily as a place? We all know men who live in opulence, yet the creases in their faces betray that they live in a parched land.

Recently, I passed by a distinguished elderly gentleman as I was walking out of a convenience store. I couldn't help but notice what a soft, gentle face he had. It occurred to me that every man's face tells a story about his life. Some men have soft faces, like the kind gentleman I walked by, but many others have hard faces, betraying a life of independence lived in parched places.

President Lincoln once turned down a job applicant, citing as his reason, "I don't like his face."

One of his Cabinet members expressed surprise and let the President know that he didn't think the reason given was a sound one.

But Lincoln wouldn't bend, saying, "Every man over forty is responsible for his face."

A man's face betrays whether he has lived a life of independence or dependence.

The Dependent Man

> But blessed is the one who trusts in the LORD,
>> whose confidence is in him.
> They will be like a tree planted by the water
>> that sends out its roots by the stream.
> It does not fear when heat comes;
>> its leaves are always green.
> It has no worries in a year of drought
>> and never fails to bear fruit.
>
> Jeremiah 17:7–8

If the independent man will be miserable, we are pleased to learn the dependent man will be blessed. The simile of a tree close to water conjures up an image of lush, tropical surroundings, replete with succulent fruit—an oasis. A life spent in trusting God must be a real cakewalk. Or is it?

When we look more closely at this passage, we read, "It does not *fear* when *heat* comes," and "it has no *worries* in a year of *drought*." Is Jeremiah describing an oasis? Hardly. He is describing hard times. The Christian is not exempt from hard times. God causes rain to fall on both the wicked and the good. Hard times come to all men—it's just part of life. "There I was standing around minding my own business, and then, all of a sudden—life happened!" Everyone suffers and goes through hard times.

The difference between the man who trusts in God and the man ⟨who trusts⟩ himself is not in the *circumstances*, but in his *response*. ⟨They m⟩ay get the same kind of cancer but handle it totally different. ⟨Th⟩e man who trusts God has a positive attitude. He knows hard times will come, but he does not fear them; he doesn't despair when life's inevitable trials strike.

That's the difference between the faces of the independent and the dependent men—one dreads the future, while the other believes God will take care of him.

The closer the tree grows to the water, the greater its nourishment. As water is the source of our physical life, trusting God is the source of our spiritual life. We are never far away from the source of life when we depend on God.

■ ■ ■

The winds howled and the rain blew sideways. New Orleans had not seen such a storm in fifty years. Mike huddled his family under the staircase, and they listened intently to a portable radio, waiting for some word that the storm was letting up.

Mike had planted two trees in his yard many years ago. One was an oak, and the other was what they call a "hackberry" tree. They grew tall, and their branches spread shade over half the backyard.

The next morning the storm had passed, and Mike ventured out to survey the damage. To his surprise, the giant hackberry tree had been uprooted and lay horizontal across his neighbor's fence.

"There are no roots!" he exclaimed. His hackberry tree didn't have any roots—no deep roots to provide support. The oak stood alone, a solemn reminder that when the storms of life sweep over us, we need deep roots.

The independent man has the shallow roots of the hackberry tree—a "bush in the wastelands." The dependent man has deep roots like the oak.

THE ILLUSION OF POWER

If we were going to be independent, we would need power. This could be brute strength to overcome difficult living conditions, or political power that enables us to have a measure of influence over our lives. Money gives power. Money lubricates the system. And a position of power can qualify a man to be independent from others.

But what is power—*genuine* power? The kind of power we usually think of is impotent. Genuine power is the exclusive province of God and those to whom He imparts it. Without the power of Christ no world would exist.

> For in him all things were created: things in heaven and on earth, visible and invisible, whether thrones or powers or rulers or authorities; all things have been created through him and for him. He is before all things, and in him all things hold together.
>
> Colossians 1:16–17

Without His power the leaves would literally fall off the trees. He created everything. He is Lord over all the world, even over those who reject Him. Jesus said, "Are not two sparrows sold for a penny? Yet not one of them will fall to the ground outside your Father's care" (Matthew 10:29). That is the kind of genuine power Christ has. What kind of power do men have?

The Bible tells us we are without any genuine power apart from trusting Christ. Matthew 5:36 notes we do not have the power to change the color of a single hair. Matthew 6:27 tells us we do not have the power to add a single moment to our life. James 4:14 reminds us we cannot even say with certainty what will happen tomorrow. Acts 27:20 brings to mind that we can't save ourselves from disaster. And Jesus humbles us completely when He informs us that no man can have eternal life unless he believes in Him. So where is our power? We have no genuine power except what Christ grants us.

The games we play to become independent produce dwarf-scale
are miniature, feeble, and impotent. The power we use
er makes us like a bunch of little blind ants. We scurry
rgetically plotting and planning, unaware or having

forgotten that genuine power can never belong to us except by the grace of God.

We have our eye on the hole instead of the donut. We look at tiny bits of life and lose sight of the big picture. We become profoundly concerned about skin-deep problems and neglect the problems of the whole life.

Jesus, and He alone, can heal the sick, satisfy our need to be significant, and grant an eternal extension to our eighty-year-long "inch" of life on earth.

THE TURNING POINT

The turning point of our lives is when we stop seeking the God we want and start seeking the God who is. When we seek our own independent way, we try to remake God the way we want Him rather than know Him as He really is. In history, they called it idol worship.

Today we have many substitute gods (or idols) — money, career, country clubs, influence, prestige, physical appearance, possessions, power, our number of Facebook friends — that require huge investments of time to maintain. These other pursuits, however important they may be, reduce our real time with the one true God.

We Americans tend to individualize God for ourselves by devising our own compact, concise definition of who God is. I'm quite certain our view is far different from the Christians in Romania or Egypt. As John White has written about God:

> During the past half century he has in fact been trivialized, packaged for entertainment, presented as a sort of psychological panacea, a heavenly glue to keep happy families together, a celestial slot machine to respond to our whims, a formula for success, a fund raiser for pseudoreligious enterprises, a slick phrase for bumper stickers, and a sort of holy pie and ice cream.[38]

In some ways, God is like the president of the United States. We hear information about the president; we listen to his news conferences; we read about his positions and ideas. A few have even shaken his hand or perhaps toured the White House. But how much do we *really* know about him? Very little, actually.

In the same way, we only have a small glimpse of God so far. But we could know more about Him if we made the commitment. We don't know Him as He is, because we have never really made the effort to get to know Him as He is. The difference between the president and God is that with God we can get to know Him as intimately as we want. All we have to do is invest the time.

Erno Rubik, a Hungarian architect, invented the brain-torturing Rubik's Cube puzzle, which has forty-three quintillion possible positions. Sometimes understanding the Bible can seem as difficult as cracking a Rubik's puzzle.

When we read the Bible, we must confess, if we are totally honest, that we are frequently confused. We don't understand much of what we read. Some of it seems to be written in codes and ciphers. For example, "If your eye causes you to stumble, gouge it out" (Matthew 18:9). What does that mean? How are we to interpret Scripture? How do we break the code?

We should not be surprised that our finite, geographically limited, experientially influenced minds come to different conclusions about who God is. Demosthenes said, "Nothing is easier than self-deceit. For what each man wishes, that he also believes to be true." Our error is not so much the conclusion we reach, but that we deceive ourselves with the information that He makes available to us.

The ultimate escape from the treachery of trying to lead an independent life is to start seeking God as He really is. When we know the God who is, He will help us decipher His mysteries and show us how to attain the goal of trusting completely in Him.

Are you ready to stop seeking the God you want and start seeking the God who is? For us to find our own turning point, we are required to seek God exactly as He is, without embellishment. He requires that we forsake our desire to be independent.

CONCLUSION

From our earliest memories, we recall how we were thrust into the real world. We were raised to be independent, to take charge of our lives, and to chart our own destiny.

As men, we want to control our lives; it's our training and our nature. If we can be in control, then we can be independent of everyone and do our own thing. The human potential movement fans the embers of our self-reliance. The temptation is to take charge of our lives and make our own rules.

Yet God has established moral and spiritual principles and absolutes. Our puny little power is no power at all when compared with the power of God. Who can add a moment to his life or save himself?

The man who trusts in himself or human institutions is destined for a miserable life, while the man who trusts in God will be blessed. Trusting God is depending on Him, whereas trusting in ourselves is acting on our desire to be independent.

The turning point of our lives is when we stop seeking the God we want and start seeking the God who is. God will reveal Himself to any man who sincerely desires to abandon his rebellion and know Him as He is.

Earlier in this book there was an opportunity to receive Christ into your life. Perhaps you were not quite ready at that point, but you have been thinking things over as you have read along.

Or perhaps you are a Christian already, but realize as you've read these pages that you have been playing games with God—that you don't know Him as He really is, that you are just a cultural Christian. Maybe you have reached a turning point in your life. You realize there is more to knowing God than you thought, and you would like to go to the next level with Him and become a biblical Christian.

If you are ready to make the commitment to surrender your life and follow Christ and seek the God who is, whether for the first time or as a deeper commitment, then the following prayer is one way you can express your desire to Him. We receive Christ by faith as an act of the will. It is a decision; it isn't a prayer. Yet prayer is an excellent way to express the desire and attitude of your heart and mind. Here is a suggested prayer:

Lord Jesus, I confess that I have sinned against You by seeking my own independent way. I have rebelled against You and trusted in myself. I have not known You as You really are but, instead, have sought the God I wanted. I am now beginning to realize the difference. Forgive me, Lord. I open the door to my life and receive You as my Savior and Lord. Thank You for dying on the cross for my sins. Take control of my life and make me into the man You want me to be. Amen.

Does this prayer express the desire of your heart and mind? If it does, then why not kneel wherever you are and express your faith in Christ to Him through this prayer? When you do, the Bible promises He will hear you and answer your prayer and come into your life. In Revelation 3:20, Christ says, "Here I am! I stand at the door and knock. If anyone hears my voice and opens the door, I will go in and eat with that person, and they with me."

Share what you have done with someone close to you. Go to a church this weekend where Christ is honored and the Bible is held in high regard.

—————————— FOCUS QUESTIONS ——————————

1. Why do most men want to control their own lives?

2. In what ways have you acted as the "master of your own fate"?

3. Read Deuteronomy 5:7. What kinds of things do we make into "gods" in our culture?

4. What action can you take to memorialize a commitment to stop seeking to control your life and "trust in the LORD with all your heart" (Proverbs 3:5)?

5. Have you been kidding yourself about your ow
   power? What kind of power do men really have? W
   of power does God have?

6. Most men remake God the way they want Him. What ca
   be the turning point of a man's life?

7. Did you pray the prayer at the end of the chapter? If yes,
   what are the next two or three steps you should take? If no,
   what are the next two or three steps you should take?

CHAPTER 20

AVOIDING SUFFERING

God prepares great men for great tasks
by great trials.
J. K. Gressett

We sent Timothy ... to strengthen and encourage
you in your faith, so that no one would be
unsettled by these trials. For you know quite
well that we are destined for them.
1 Thessalonians 3:2 – 3

I had fought off the wolves for months and months, but every day was just another day in the jaws of financial turmoil. The pressure of my problems had turned my love for God and my family into a stale loaf of bread. I would have done anything to avoid more suffering.

Weary from the business blues, I went home early one afternoon, something I had been doing more and more often. Driving down the highway, my heart quickened when a gigantic bolt of lightning flashed on the horizon. If the road had continued straight, that scorching rod of lightning would have burned a hole right through the asphalt pavement.

To be completely honest, I couldn't help but wish, if only for a fleeting moment, that I was under that lightning bolt. How wonderful to go out in a literal blaze of glory. That would solve all of my problems, and then I would be with the Lord.

I would never *seriously* want that, but if natural causes could take me away, well, I would have been grateful to escape from all the suffering.

THE PROBLEM

Life is a struggle. The desire of most men is to be happy, to avoid pain and suffering, and to escape from the bleak life that so many men seem to lead.

We all want to live the good life. And why not? What fool would seek out a life of suffering? And God *does* want to bless our lives with abundance. Yet the Bible also teaches that suffering is part of God's order. We shouldn't go looking for it, but neither should we be surprised when it finds us. *Everyone* is going to suffer. The only decision is whether you are going to suffer with Christ or without Him.

A unique fellowship with Christ comes into our lives when we suffer:

> Dear friends, do not be surprised at the fiery ordeal that has come on you to test you, as though something strange were happening to you. But rejoice inasmuch as you participate in the sufferings of Christ, so that you may be overjoyed when his glory is revealed.
>
> 1 Peter 4:12–13

Martin Luther put it this way: "No man ought to lay a cross upon himself, or to adopt tribulation ... but if a cross or tribulation come upon him, then let him suffer it patiently, and know that it is good and profitable for him."

The questions that float through our minds when we suffer tell the story:

"Does God care about me?"

"Does He know how much agony I am going through?"

"Does He want to help me?"

"Is He able to help me?"

"What is His will for me? Is it to help me or let me fall?"

The plain truth is that when life goes our way, we don't carefully examine our ways. God can't receive the glory for blessing us because we often take the credit. If nothing else, suffering does get our attention. But why do men suffer? Does God cause it? Or does He just allow it? Or does it happen independently of Him?

SEVEN REASONS MEN SUFFER

Picture a loving father comforting his teary-eyed son. We don't know exactly why the boy has been crying, but we do notice how concerned the father is. The son tells his dad exactly how he feels, though we can't make out the words. Finally, the father embraces his son, and the comfort and consolation of the father's love begin to flow into his boy. If only we could get a little closer to hear the words.

In the same way, we come into the presence of our heavenly Father when we suffer, and He dries our tears. "Humble yourselves, therefore, under God's mighty hand, that he may lift you up in due time. Cast all your anxiety on him because he cares for you" (1 Peter 5:6–7).

What could possibly have been the reason for those tears? Seven reasons come to mind that might explain not only this father/son scene but our own reasons for suffering as well:

1. An innocent mistake
2. An error in judgment
3. An integrity problem
4. A change in environment

5. An occurrence of evil
6. Discipline from God
7. Testing by God

Let's explore these reasons. Assume our little boy — let's call him Billy — has been playing baseball in the street with his friends.

First Reason: An Innocent Mistake

Perhaps through carelessness, his baseball rolled down the storm sewer, gone forever. Billy did nothing wrong — it wasn't anyone's fault — but he still suffered. And he went running home to his dad, crying over his disappointment.

Jack invested in a speculative oil venture that checked out great, but he lost all his money and had to pay taxes on some phantom income. We all make innocent mistakes but still suffer the consequences. An innocent mistake is unpredictable, and no one has done anything wrong, but nevertheless, we suffer.

Second Reason: An Error in Judgment

Another possibility: Young Billy may have hit the baseball through the neighbor's window. This is different from an innocent mistake; Billy knew he shouldn't play so close to Mrs. Johnson's window because his dad had told him not to. But still he did nothing dishonest. Not knowing what punishment might result, he fearfully told his father. Dad explained how he had to go tell Mrs. Johnson what happened and pay for the window replacement from his allowance.

Andrew cosigned his brother-in-law's banknote for a car loan. Six months later, the bank was leaning on Andrew to make the payments. Did he do wrong? Yes. To cosign a loan for a friend is an error in judgment according to the Bible, though no command or law was violated, but a principle.

If a bank doesn't think someone's credit is good enough, you make an error in judgment to think you can judge the facts better.

This is evidenced by a Federal Trade Commission study that found 50 percent of the people who cosigned bank loans ended up repaying the debt themselves.[39]

An error in judgment differs from an innocent mistake in this: Some form of guideline, if followed, would prevent an error in judgment, while no guideline exists to prevent the innocent mistake.

Innocent or not, you still suffer. We all use poor judgment from time to time.

Third Reason: An Integrity Problem

Our little Billy may be crying because he stole the baseball bat from the kids down the street and got caught. He's crying because he received a sound spanking.

A man lied about the features of his product to a prospect, who bought on that basis. Later, when the buyer realized the salesman had lied, he phoned the salesman's boss, and the deceptive salesman was fired. Sometimes men do wrong with malice—they "sin"—and they must bear the moral and other consequences of their decisions.

Men often do the wrong thing by innocent mistake or poor judgment, but sometimes we get into trouble because we were dishonest—we sinned. In addition to principles to live by, the Bible also describes the sins we are to avoid. And we must also submit to civil laws.

Fourth Reason: A Change in Environment

Billy could have been enjoying a great game of baseball in the street, only to have a policeman run them off after telling them about a recently passed municipal ordinance that prohibits playing in the street. Upset over the change, he ran home to dad bawling.

Sometimes we are just standing around, minding our own business, and then all of a sudden, life happens. Congress passes a tax reform package that threatens to put you out of business, or the stock market crashes and you face a margin call you can't pay. A disabling traffic accident strikes a daughter or son. When the environment changes beyond our control, we may suffer dire consequences, even though we may have done nothing wrong.

Fifth Reason: An Occurrence of Evil

Billy may have been having a perfectly enjoyable game of baseball when, out of nowhere, the bully from down the street sneaked up from behind and punched him in the face.

Ron worked for months on the sale of an insurance policy to an executive who had purchased several other policies from him over the years. The day before Ron was to close the sale, an unscrupulous agent convinced the executive to cancel all of his old policies and replace them with far inferior ones.

Did Ron or Billy do wrong? No. No matter how much we wish it wasn't so, evil exists in this world. Unfair things do happen. It's not a perfect world, and there are wolves out there who will eat us alive if they can.

Sixth Reason: Discipline from God

Billy's father sent Billy to his room as punishment for knocking the ball through the neighbor's window.

After serving as an elder for eight years, Ted became overly proud of himself. He acted as though if he said it, that settled it. God led the other elders to quietly ask him to step down.

Even though those in authority may not catch a man doing wrong, or even though no one else is aware of a man's sin, God knows. And what God knows, God disciplines.

Regardless of the reason for our suffering, God uses such situations to mold our character:

Endure hardship as discipline; God is treating you as his children. For what children are not disciplined by their father? If you are not disciplined—and everyone undergoes discipline—then you are not legitimate, not true sons and daughters at all.

Hebrews 12:7 – 8

Seventh Reason: Testing by God

The father told Billy he couldn't go out and play baseball until he helped his mother clean the dishes. Interested in his character and conduct, Billy's dad wanted to know how much Billy was willing to be a contributing member of the family.

Genesis 22 tells how God tested Abraham, instructing him to take his knife and sacrifice his only son Isaac:

> When they reached the place God had told him about, Abraham built an altar ... He bound his son Isaac and laid him on the altar ... Then he reached out his hand and took the knife to slay his son. But the angel of the LORD called out to him from heaven, "Abraham! Abraham!"
>
> "Here I am," he replied.
>
> "Do not lay a hand on the boy," he said. 'Do not do anything to him. Now I know that you fear God, because you have not withheld from me your son, your only son' "

Genesis 22:9 – 12

God tests us to see if our character is pure. "The crucible for silver and the furnace for gold, but the LORD tests the heart" (Proverbs 17:3).

You may remember the story of Job. Satan had been roaming the earth and accused Job of being upright and fearing God only because he had so much of the good life. God gave Satan a green light to test Job. He lost his business conglomerate, his children died, and his health failed. Yet in all this, Job did not sin, and this pleased God.

■ ■ ■

If you are getting the idea that suffering is not easily avoided, then you have the right idea. We can suffer because it's our own fault, or because it's someone else's. We can suffer by an innocent mistake or as a consequence of our sins.

Sometimes God tests us, and other times He may discipline us. Sometimes the environment changes on us, and sometimes evil overtakes us.

Whatever the reason for our suffering, we can humble ourselves under God's plan for our lives, or we can resist, but we cannot avoid suffering. Suffering is as much a part of life as eating, and we must consume some of it. Like eating spinach or some other disliked vegetable, if we are to be fully nourished, we must accept it.

RESISTING SUFFERING

Before we humble ourselves when we suffer, we often go through different stages of resistance or rebellion in an attempt to avoid suffering. To avoid or resist suffering blocks us from learning from our pain.

Suffering doesn't teach us anything unless we penetrate our anguish. Anne Morrow Lindbergh wrote:

> I do not believe that sheer suffering teaches. If suffering alone taught, all the world would be wise, since everyone suffers. To suffering must be added mourning, understanding, patience, love, openness, and the willingness to remain vulnerable. All these and other factors combined, if the circumstances are right, *can* teach and *can* lead to rebirth.[40]

There are five ways we attempt to avoid suffering and escape its grasp:

1. We plead. When we suffer, one of our first reactions is to plead with God about His sense of fairness. Is it fair for God to treat us differently than we desire? Our pleading often reflects that we don't think so. His promise to us is that "the righteous person may have many troubles, but the LORD delivers him from them all" (Psalm 34:19).

2. We compare. We compare ourselves to others, pointing out that we are better men and, therefore, deserving of mercy. Or we compare ourselves to other men and wish we were them instead of ourselves. But the psalmist reminds us, "Do not be overawed when others grow rich, when the splendor of their houses increases; for they will take nothing with them when they die" (Psalm 49:16–17).

3. We pout. We become discouraged over our circumstances and have a pity party. We pout about the suffering we have to undergo and feel sorry for ourselves. We lament, as the psalmist did: "This is what the wicked are like—always free of care, they go on amassing wealth. Surely in vain I have kept my heart pure and have washed my hands in innocence. All day long I have been afflicted, and every morning brings new punishments" (Psalm 73:12–14).

4. We shout. We become angry and shake our fist and raise our voice at God because of the pain of our suffering. Will He give us no relief? But this is futile, "because human anger does not produce the righteousness that God desires" (James 1:20).

5. We doubt. After our suffering settles in on us and we realize how devastating our anguish can be, we doubt that God is real and become afraid. But as we read the Scriptures, we find so much is written about His faithful mercy and compassion that we cannot help but be encouraged. "So do not fear, for I am with you; do not be dismayed, for I am your God. I will strengthen you and help you; I will uphold you with my righteous right hand" (Isaiah 41:10).

AFTER THE PLEADING, COMPARING, POUTING, SHOUTING, AND DOUBTING

Obviously we don't go through all of these stages every time we suffer, but it's only human to experience a range of emotions and negative thoughts when we suffer.

The solution to our suffering, however, is not only figuring out how to get over it but also learning how to enjoy the fellowship of sharing in Christ's suffering, to not falter in times of trouble, to not be anxious about anything, to endure patiently, and to walk in the power of the Holy Spirit.

Sometimes God will deliver us according to our desires, but more often He has bigger plans for us, and He doesn't deliver us quickly. Our part in His plan for us is to cast all our anxiety on Him.

Take, for example, this psalm of David:

Do not withhold your mercy from me, LORD;
may your love and faithfulness always protect me.
For troubles without number surround me;
my sins have overtaken me, and I cannot see.
They are more than the hairs of my head,
and my heart fails within me.
Be pleased to save me, LORD;
come quickly, LORD, to help me.

Psalm 40:11–13

EMPATHY FOR OUR SUFFERING

When we suffer, we can be confident Jesus knows exactly what we are going through:

For we do not have a high priest who is unable to empathize with our weaknesses, but we have one who has been tempted in every way, just as we are—yet he did not sin. Let us then approach God's throne of grace with confidence, so that we may receive mercy and find grace to help us in our time of need.

Hebrews 4:15–16

Because Christ suffered just as we do, we can look to Him as the model for our own attitude, just as the apostle Paul did. Paul said, "I want to know Christ—yes, to know the power of his resurrection and participation in his sufferings" (Philippians 3:10). He knew from experience the empathies of Christ in his own suffering.

THE PRIVILEGE OF SUFFERING

Through the ages, Christians worldwide have undergone persecutions and indignities unknown to most Americans. In fact, religious oppression formed the foundation of America.

But in many countries still today—Iran, Iraq, and Afghanistan among the most visible ones—Christians are severely persecuted or imprisoned if they discuss their faith in public. In countries like North Korea, Christians meet in secret to avoid arrest and execution by secret police. Around the world, many Christians live in constant danger, and many are killed for their beliefs.

What was the apostle Paul's attitude about his own suffering? Scripture tells us Paul had some physical infirmity, perhaps his eyes, which he referred to as his "thorn in the flesh." Three times he asked God to take it away. But God told Paul, "My grace is sufficient for you, for my power is made perfect in weakness" (2 Corinthians 12:9).

Paul's response? "Therefore I will boast all the more gladly about my weaknesses, so that Christ's power may rest on me. That is why, for Christ's sake, I *delight in weaknesses, in insults, in hardships, in persecutions, in difficulties.* For when I am weak, then I am strong" (2 Corinthians 12:9–10, italics added).

Remarkably, Paul delighted in suffering. But not just suffering for the sake of suffering—suffering for the joy of sharing fellowship with Christ.

Suffering for doing good is part of the Christian experience. That is why Paul exhorts us, "For it has been granted to you on behalf of Christ not only to believe in him, but also to suffer for him" (Philippians 1:29).

Frankly, until we have suffered, not in some superficial way—like not getting that new car we wanted—but as a Christian, filled with anguish over whether God cares about us or not, we will not have a full understanding of how personal the ministry of the Holy Spirit can be.

Until you have been up against the wall, totally backed into the corner, all your resources expended, no more ideas from your own ingenuity, no more wise counsel from friends, all favors owed having been called in; until you have been totally exhausted and without hope, not just for a moment but for weeks and months or even years on end—not until then will trusting the Lord ever move entirely from abstract to personal.

You may know it in part, but until you come to the point where you feel you will die unless Jesus shows you some compassion, only then will you ever trust Him completely. Once you pass through this threshold of His grace, you will have incredible power to overcome anxiety. The tempter cannot terrorize you with any uncertainty that you have not already known, for you have felt the hands of God reach down, embracing you in response to your faith.

THE RESTORATION OF GOD'S PEOPLE

Avoiding suffering is impossible. Even the man who is so security conscious that he never sticks his neck out will sooner or later find the sorrow of suffering knocking on his door.

Our posture is to look favorably on our suffering:

Consider it pure joy, my brothers and sisters, whenever you face trials of many kinds, because you know that the testing of your faith produces perseverance. Let perseverance finish its work so that you may be mature and complete, not lacking anything.

James 1:2–4

No matter how rough your life gets, remember that it isn't over till it's over. Never quit. Until your heart stops beating and your wrist no longer registers a pulse, there is always another way. God will *always* restore His children. That's why Job was able to maintain his integrity before God when he suffered, because he trusted God completely; he knew God was in control.

Our promise from God is a promise for restoration. "And the God of all grace, who called you to his eternal glory in Christ, after you have suffered a little while, will himself restore you and make you *strong, firm* and *steadfast*" (1 Peter 5:10, italics added).

The good life includes suffering, that unique participation in the sufferings of the Lord Jesus. We suffer for many different reasons, but we have one hope. We can try to resist or avoid suffering, but every man is marked for suffering; it is a part of life that can be sweet if we don't try to run and hide.

READY TO DIE

At the beginning of this chapter, I told you how I thought about death as the ultimate escape from suffering. Sometimes we ache so much that dying sounds good. Like Paul, we can say, "For to me, to live is Christ and to die is gain" (Philippians 1:21). Dying for Christ is frankly a lot easier than living for Him. But death is no answer.

When Paul was on his way to Jerusalem near the end of his ministry, Agabus prophesied that Paul would be bound and thrown in prison. The people pleaded for Paul not to go. Paul answered, "Why are you weeping and breaking my heart? I am ready not only to be bound, but also to die in Jerusalem for the name of the Lord Jesus" (Acts 21:13).

Paul lived and suffered for Christ as perhaps no other man ever has. He didn't seek death as an escape to his own suffering. Yet he knew that death would be sweet for him—a union with the Lord Jesus. And it will be sweet for us too. The Christian is ready to die for Christ, but, that said, it is more important that we enter the pain of our suffering and live for Him.

———————— FOCUS QUESTIONS ————————

1. Is one of your goals in life to avoid suffering? Why, or why not?

2. Read 1 Peter 4:12–13. Are you surprised when you suffer? How can you rejoice when you suffer? Doesn't that seem a little unrealistic?

3. Describe a recent or current situation in which you have suffered. Which of the seven reasons men suffer do you think may have caused your suffering?

    1. An innocent mistake
    2. An error in judgment
    3. An integrity problem
    4. A change in environment
    5. An occurrence of evil
    6. Discipline from God
    7. Testing by God

8. What is your typical reaction to suffering? Do you resist it? Review the five ways we attempt to avoid suffering and comment on which one(s) you employ.

9. Read 1 Peter 5:10. What is our promise as Christians when we suffer? Do you believe God will always restore the suffering Christian? In what ways?

PART 6

SOLVING OUR INTEGRITY PROBLEMS

CHAPTER 21

INTEGRITY: WHAT'S THE PRICE?

If you tell the truth, you don't have
to remember anything.
Mark Twain

Enemies disguise themselves with their lips,
but in their hearts they harbor deceit.
Proverbs 26:24

Kyle was a small building contractor known for the high quality of his work. A sizable company awarded him the bid on a
project larger than any he had ever done before.

Thousands of minute details required exacting coordination to
meet the completion schedule. As the deadline for the grand opening
approached like an unstoppable barge, he drove his men to the brink
of mutiny. He swore he would be done on time, and he was.

The top man at the company who hired Kyle realized Kyle didn't
have the pull of a large outfit, so he withheld the final payment. The
straw man he used was that the quality of the work wasn't right, so
he deserved a discount. He refused to pay. Kyle desperately needed

the final payment for payroll. He finally gave in and lowered the invoice, which meant he had to give up his profit on the job.

THE PROBLEM

Have you ever gone to the pantry looking for a particular thing — say, peanut butter — only to be frustrated that it was nowhere to be found? You yell out to your wife, "Where's the peanut butter?"

Then she walks over to the pantry, reaches onto the second shelf, and hands you the jar with a "you lose" grin on her face.

Sometimes things are so obvious right before our eyes that we miss them. Dishonesty is like that. It is so obvious that we often miss how wholly and completely it tints every aspect of life. If we take off our rose-colored glasses, however, we see a world painted in a whole different hue — the washed-out shades of dishonesty.

Frankly, dishonesty is so prevalent that we have accepted it as the norm — and it is. But while it may be normative, it's cutting men off from God.

Watch the news or read the headlines:

"Pentagon probe aims at payoffs."

"Mr. _____ admits cheating on wife."

"The Ethics Committee of the House issues censure."

"Twenty percent of GDP goes unreported to Uncle Sam."

"College cheating ring uncovered."

As heinous as the crimes of the headlines, the dishonesty that tints the daily life of the Christian grieves God just as much and perhaps more. Most men are trapped in the life of maintaining a "Christian image" for honesty, when in reality they wink at integrity every day. Albert Wells Jr. found this quote:

> Honesty was always rare. Diogenes, the Greek philosopher, lighted a candle in the daytime and went around looking for an honest man. Blaise Pascal said he didn't expect to meet three honest men in a century. The Institute of Behavior Motivation found that

ninety-seven out of one hundred people tell lies—and they do it about one thousand times a year.[41]

When we are all alone, with no peer pressure keeping us on the straight and narrow path, that's when our real character is put to the test.

■ ■ ■

A man sitting next to me on a plane ordered a drink—a bourbon and Coke. The busy flight attendant said she would come back to collect his money, which he left lying on his tray table. She passed up and down the aisle several times. It became obvious the flight attendant had forgotten about his money. After she made a half dozen trips past us, my aisle-mate reached over, picked up his money, and slipped it back into his coat pocket. Integrity—what's the price? Sold for a $6 drink.

This issue is so important because unless we hold on to absolute integrity in every situation, no matter how big or small, we grieve God and cut ourselves off from the larger blessing that we want and that God wants to give. Luke 16:10 warns, "Whoever is dishonest with very little will also be dishonest with much."

THE COMMON THREAD

The great heroes of the Bible came from diverse backgrounds. Some were kings. Others, like Gideon, came from the worst families. Samson was a powerful figure, while timid Moses practically feared his own shadow. Jonah doubted, yet David had unswerving faith.

What, if any, common trait or characteristic did these men possess besides their faith in God? What attracted God to these men of such diversity? The answer will be painful to some of our ears: *God knew that He could trust these men when they were all alone.*

Some of these men willingly obeyed God and were faithful, but others were like pouty children, scoffing and kicking and protest-ing all the way. But they each had integrity. In the final analysis, after they had fussed and fumed, they settled on the honest way. *After their faith, this characteristic of integrity, more than any other, distinguished the lives of Bible heroes.* Their honesty was the common thread that attracted God's blessing on their lives.

THE LOWER END OF THE SCALE

When we think about dishonesty, we usually think of the gross indiscretions—cheating on taxes, stealing from our company, lying to a prospect, cheating on our wife.

If we limit our thinking to major matters, we will miss the point that to be trustworthy with much, we must first prove trustworthy with little. In God's eyes we are as guilty when we stuff our suitcase with motel towels as if we had robbed a bank. To be sure, the *conse-quences* are different, but the verdict is still guilty.

One evening I stopped by the home of a business colleague to drop off some papers. Next to his phone was a notepad with the company logo on it. The company policy manual stated that no office supplies were to be consumed for personal use. From that day forward my confidence in him was never quite the same. For him, that was an expensive pad of paper.

In one of Jesus' parables, he says to a dishonest manager, "So if you have not been trustworthy in handling worldly wealth, who will trust you with true riches? And if you have not been trustworthy with someone else's property, who will give you property of your own?" (Luke 16:11–12).

■ ■ ■

A cab driver offered me a blank receipt. "You fill it in however you want," he said.

"No, that's okay. You see, I'm a Christian. That wouldn't be right."

After a long, blank stare, he just shrugged his shoulders and said, "Okay, buddy, whatever you say."

We must demonstrate our honesty at the lower end of the honesty spectrum before God will let us have greater responsibilities. The first part of Luke 16:10, cited above, promises a reward when we're trustworthy with little things: "Whoever can be trusted with very little can also be trusted with much." When we are honest, a surprised world will give a second thought to the possibility that Christ can make a difference in a man's life.

THE EASE OF BEING GREATLY USED

A man became very successful in the real estate brokerage business. A hopeful protégé asked him how he was able to excel to such heights.

"I'm just an average, hardworking, honest broker. I'm nothing special," he said. "You see, it's just that so many people in this business cut so many corners that an honest and average man like me all of a sudden looks great!"

God is looking for a few good men. You don't have to be the smartest, best-looking, most articulate man to get a job on God's team; you just have to be faithful. God is looking for faithful, honest men—men He can trust.

Most men are so mired down in the quicksand of dishonesty that an average, hardworking, honest man looks very good to God. God will use you if He knows He can trust you. Can He?

THOU SHALT NOT STEAL

After God observed mankind for a while, He decided to set down ten rules—rules for our benefit. Lying, cheating, and stealing made the Top Ten. Honesty permeates all of the Ten Commandments. So anytime we disobey one of the Ten Commandments, it is an act of dishonesty. The gravity of our obedience to these Ten Commandments is carefully prescribed:

> So be careful to do what the LORD your God has commanded you; do not turn aside to the right or to the left. Walk in obedience to all that the LORD your God has commanded you, so that you may live and prosper and prolong your days in the land that you will possess.
>
> Deuteronomy 5:32–33

Our prosperity has everything to do with our obedience in being honest. But as we all know, we can't be honest—or any other virtue described in this book—in our own strength. But Christ in us can. For those of us surrendered to Christ, we take a pledge to let Him work in us to transform us to increasingly become more like Him. "Do not conform to the pattern of this world, but be transformed by the renewing of your mind" (Romans 12:2).

THE LITTLE WHITE LIE

John told Bill he would be at the open house for Bill's new office. But John didn't show up. Later Bill learned that before saying yes to the open house invitation, John had already scheduled an appointment for the same time, an appointment he kept. "Why didn't he just tell me he had already scheduled something else?"

That put a wedge in their relationship that has never gone away. Relationships are built on trust. The fragile thread of trust on which relationships depend can be easily broken, and the *white lie* fractures trust in all kinds of relationships:

"I'm glad you called. I was just getting ready to call you."

"Let's have lunch sometime."

"I'll be praying for you ..."

"The white lie doesn't hurt anyone," goes the logic. That's not entirely true, for the teller of the white lie is always a victim, robbing himself of God's blessing.

In the end, the white lie will get you. As the nineteenth-century English art critic John Ruskin writes, we lie in so many ways:

> The essence of lying is in deception, not in words; a lie may be told by silence, by equivocation, by the accent on a syllable, by a glance of the eye attaching a peculiar significance to a sentence; and all these kinds of lies are worse and baser by many degrees than a lie plainly worded; so that no form of blinded conscience is so far sunk as that which comforts itself for having deceived, because the deception was by gesture or silence, instead of utterance.[42]

THE NARROW ROAD

The American comedian and actor George Burns once said, "The most important thing in acting is honesty. If you can fake that, you've got it made."

As in so many aspects of the spiritual pilgrimage, the right way is often the path least traveled. The street named "Honest" is a narrow, uncrowded path. To distinguish yourself before God requires only that you differentiate yourself from the mass of men, a task easily accomplished.

Christ said the way to eternal life is a narrow road:

> Enter through the narrow gate. For wide is the gate and broad is the road that leads to destruction, and many enter through it. But small is the gate and narrow the road that leads to life, and only a few find it.
>
> Matthew 7:13–14

Dishonesty is a wide road. The abundant life on earth, which is ours for the "obeying," is found by so few because our dishonesty stands in the way.

Moral relativism finds safe harbor in the area of dishonesty. The basic ethic goes like this: If no one sees you cheating (or lying or stealing), then you won't get caught; and if you won't get caught, then it's all right, because unless you are caught you haven't technically done anything wrong.

Whether it has to do with hotel towels or income taxes, returning extra change or running a yellow light, leaving work early or coming in late, the guiding principle is this: The narrow road leads to the abundant life, and only a few find it.

THE THREE REASONS
A DEAL GOES BAD

Let's examine in greater detail one arena—business—where deals go bad for one (or more) of three reasons: an error in judgment, a change in the environment, or an integrity problem.

Error in Judgment

The western extension of a major boulevard was to be completed in three years. The road didn't open until fifteen years later. The investors counted on being in and out of the land deal in two or three years. When the road plans were delayed, everyone decided to throw in the towel.

Everyone makes mistakes, and everyone I've ever known is pretty tolerant of a business deal that doesn't work out, provided good communication takes place. Few men are arrogant enough to believe all their investments will work out as planned. We all know that men are human and make errors in judgment.

Change in the Environment

At the end of World War II, three brothers (one of whom is my father-in-law) started a flying school for veterans under the GI Bill. They taught thousands of returning soldiers how to fly. Without warning, four years after the end of the war, Congress amended the

GI Bill so flying lessons no longer qualified for tuition assistance. The brothers' business immediately went under, and they had to liquidate in pieces, one propeller at a time.

Regardless of how good you are, the vagaries of the business environment—competitive or regulatory—can sneak up on you like a lion stalking its prey. Before you know it, you are face-to-face with calamity, and there is nothing to do but make the best of a bad situation. Tax reform and other legislative changes have suddenly put companies out of business for decades.

Integrity

The third reason deals go sour is the problem of integrity. Men who cut corners to put transactions together are like the first of the three little pigs. The house built with straw collapses at the first sign of a high wind.

Lying to prospects, concealing information that would probably kill the sale, squeezing for a better price by using a competitor as a stalking horse (when you know you really won't buy from the competitor), withholding pay increases from those who are deserving, not paying your bills as agreed when you are able—these are of chief importance to God, a God who is looking for a few good men.

ONCE AND FOR ALL

One dilemma we all face is deciding whether or not to be honest on a case-by-case basis. During the course of a normal day we each have scores of opportunities to lie, cheat, and steal.

If we must decide each time we make a decision whether we will be honest or not, we consume a lot of energy and run the risk of making a sloppy decision and compromising our integrity. Instead, why not settle the integrity issue? Why not decide once and for all that you will *always* be honest?

That's what God liked so much about Job. After Job lost his family and his business, he did not sin by charging God with wrongdoing. Then God said to Satan, "Have you considered my servant Job? There is no one on earth like him; he is *blameless* and *upright*, a man who fears God and shuns evil. *And he still maintains his integrity*, though you incited me against him to ruin him without any reason" (Job 2:3, italics added). Because of Job's integrity, "the LORD blessed the latter part of Job's life more than the former part" (Job 42:12).

By settling the issue once and for all and deciding to always choose the narrow road, to always have integrity, we can liberate ourselves from the bondage of making dozens of daily decisions — those tiny decisions that, like water dripping onto a rock, can wear down our character. We can remove the tint of dishonesty that shades the lives of so many men.

Like the housewife who didn't know how dingy her whites were until she tried the new, improved detergent, we will see a noticeable difference in the brightness of our souls. And God will know that He can trust us, in little and in much, and He *will* trust us, like Job, with true riches.

————— FOCUS QUESTIONS —————

1. Most men cut corners on the little things (e.g., running yellow lights, speeding, taking office supplies home, promising two-day delivery when knowing it will take a week).

   ❏ Agree ❏ Disagree. Explain your answer. Give examples, personal and observed.

2. Read Luke 16:10. The principle is, "As it goes with the little things, so it will go with the big things." Do you agree with this principle? Do you think it's possible to maintain two sets of standards — one for the "little" and one for the "much"? Why, or why not?

3. What is an area of your life in which you struggle with being completely honest and trustworthy? What are you willing to do about it?

4. Read Luke 16:11–12. Jesus asks two rhetorical questions in these verses. How would you answer them? Why?

5. Read Leviticus 6:1–5. Is restitution a valid scriptural principle in modern times? Do you need to make restitution to anyone?

6. Most men make dozens of integrity decisions each day. But we can settle the issue by making a once-and-for-all commitment to always choose the honest way. Are you willing to make a once-and-for-all commitment to integrity?

CHAPTER 22

LEADING A SECRET THOUGHT LIFE

*The secret thoughts of a man run over all things,
holy, profane, clean, obscene, grave, and light,
without shame or blame.*
Thomas Hobbes

*We take captive every thought
to make it obedient to Christ.*
2 Corinthians 10:5

The three of us were eating deli sandwiches at a sidewalk table on the picturesque main street of town. The paper-thin, translucent leaves glistened as the sun diffused through the new growth of an early spring day. The crisp air made the mind feel pure!

As we were about to leave, a very lovely woman passed by on the sidewalk; she was beautiful, fresh, and sophisticated. She seemed a perfect match for the day. Many heads turned as she walked by, including the two men I was with. I watched their eyes follow her, and I could tell they had mentally undressed her in the secrecy of their private thought world. Not a word was spoken, and we headed back to the office.

I found myself on the horns of a dilemma. I brooded with

indignation over the obvious lust of these two, but at the same time, I was keenly aware that the only difference between them and me was that I had more carefully controlled my eye movement.

Because Christians are *expected* to not lust over women, I carefully concealed my thoughts. Yet I knew my pretending not to notice was counterfeit. I knew I was leading a secret thought life different from the image I projected. I didn't like the pressure of leading these two lives, but I was embarrassed about it. I thought it was exclusively my problem (maybe my sins were not forgiven after all, or maybe I wasn't even a Christian).

It never occurred to me that other Christian men might struggle with the same problem. Who wants to talk about a secret thought life anyway? Why couldn't I gain control over the secret thoughts of fantasy, envy, lust, jealousy, wild ambition, a desire for money and power, and the resentments that floated in and out of my mind?

THE PROBLEM

Are you living a secret thought life that portrays you as a significantly different man from the "you" that is known by others? Would you be embarrassed if your friends and associates knew what went on inside your mind? If your thoughts were audible, would your wife want a divorce?

Each of us leads a secret thought life, an invisible life known only to us. This secret life is usually very different from the *visible* you—the you that is known by others. Yet it is the *real* you, and it is the you that is known by our God.

For some of us, our secret thought life consists of a dreamworld of fantasies, which concocts intricate plans that would make us wealthy, famous, and powerful. Others of us fabricate chance meetings with beautiful women who seduce us. We each invent a secret image of how we wish we were, which we would be embarrassed for others to know.

Some of us boil in a hate-world filled with bitterness and resentment over a life that hasn't turned out like we planned. We seethe with jealousy and envy over the lucky break dumped in the lap of the other guy. We find the words of the rich man contemptible to us, not because the words are wrong, but because we despise him for his success.

There seems to be no relief from the perpetual stream of negative thoughts that flows through our minds. Because talking about our secret thought life can be touchy, far too little attention has been devoted to the subject. Why do men lead a secret thought life? What is happening up there in the recesses of our minds?

THE BATTLE FOR THE MIND

One morning I was driving to speak at our men's Bible study. I like driving alone; it's one of the few places where I can think without those incessant interruptions that break my train of thought.

The thick traffic flowed steadily. As I slowed for a traffic light, I was relieved to see that I would make it through the intersection on the next green light. As I braked, the car next to me saw a "hairline crack" in front of me and, without warning, swerved over. I slammed on the brakes and checked the rearview mirror. So far, so good. Anger swept over me, but since I was on my way to speak at a Bible study, I quickly recovered and kept my spiritual glow. I even forgave the jerk, who was obviously a spiritual degenerate.

The light turned green, and the long line inched toward the intersection. Guess which car was the last one to make it through the light? You guessed it. He made it, but I was stuck in line at the red light. That did it for me, Bible study or not. I let out an audible expletive that came from a part of me not surrendered to God.

If this were an isolated incident, I would not be too concerned. But every day we each battle for control of our thought life. The real battlefield for the Christian is the mind.

The apostle Paul, you may be glad to know, lamented over this struggle with sin, just like we do. He wrote:

I do not understand what I do. For what I want to do I do not do, but what I hate I do. And if I do what I do not want to do, I agree that the law is good. As it is, it is no longer I myself who do it, but it is sin living in me. For I know that good itself does not dwell in me, that is, in my sinful nature. For I have the desire to do what is good, but I cannot carry it out. For I do not do the good I want to do, but the evil I do not want to do— this I keep on doing. Now if I do what I do not want to do, it is no longer I who do it, but it is sin living in me that does it.

So I find this law at work: Although I want to do good, evil is right there with me. For in my inner being I delight in God's law; but I see another law at work in me, waging war against the law of my mind and making me a prisoner of the law of sin at work within me. What a wretched man I am! Who will rescue me from this body that is subject to death?

Romans 7:15–24

What encouragement to know that one of the greatest Christians in history struggled just like us! Still, if we don't understand this battle for our minds, then little hope exists for actually winning the war. Our victories can be more accidental than planned.

But when we begin to grasp the simplicity of this battle for our minds, we can equip ourselves with some firepower to retake control of our secret thought lives. Christians today are often ill-equipped for this struggle. It's a little like conscripting civilians into the army and sending them to war, without ever teaching them how to fire their rifles.

Paul, by the way, answered his own question, "Who will rescue me from this body that is subject to death?" He went on, "Thanks be to God, who delivers me through Jesus Christ our Lord!" (Romans 7:25). How does God, through Jesus Christ our Lord, equip us to win the battle for our minds? It's almost as if we have two minds.

MIND X AND MIND Y

One interesting business management theory developed by Douglas McGregor, a professor at MIT, goes by the name "Theory X and Theory Y." The Theory X manager believes people are basically lazy and irresponsible and will do a poor job unless constantly supervised. Theory Y managers believe people generally want to do a good job and will respond to clearly defined objectives. If only supported and encouraged, people will get the job done.

There may be some biblical basis for this theory. The Bible depicts two parts to our mind—one controlled by the flesh, or the sinful nature, which we might call *Mind X*, and a second controlled by the Spirit, which we might call *Mind Y*. As followers of Christ, we are not left on our own to squirm with the sinful nature of our Mind X, but we have been given the Holy Spirit to teach and guide our Mind Y. The Holy Spirit is how God has equipped us to win the battle for our minds.

If we understand the workings of our two minds, we can conquer our secret thought life. Here's the decoder:

> Those who live according to the flesh have their minds [their Mind X] set on what the flesh desires; but those who live in accordance with the Spirit have their minds [their Mind Y] set on what the Spirit desires. The mind [Mind X] governed by the flesh is death, but the mind [Mind Y] governed by the Spirit is life and peace.
>
> Romans 8:5–6

Let us be clear here that we surely don't have two distinct physical minds. But we do have two distinct natures—a sinful (or carnal) nature, which responds to sinful influences, and a "new creation" (or spiritual) nature, which responds to the Holy Spirit of God. The sins of the secret thought life incubate in our Mind X—the sinful nature.

We each have both a Mind X and a Mind Y. We can live by the

sinful nature—"according to the flesh"—and be a Mind X man, or we can live by the Spirit and be a Mind Y man. Too often we vacillate from one to the other, and we risk being branded a double-minded man who is unstable in all he does (see James 1:8).

Part of the problem is that sometimes the difference between a thought and a sinful thought can be a little fuzzy. When do our Mind X thoughts become sins?

THE FUZZY LINE

Little Johnny drew a line in the sand and said to his brother, "You'd better not cross that line or I'll beat you up!"

Little Jimmy, up to the dare, immediately and defiantly stepped across the line and folded his arms across his chest in triumph. Johnny hesitated for a moment, drew another line in the sand, and repeated, "You'd better not cross that line or I'll beat you up!"

Where is the fuzzy line that separates *temptation* from *sin*? Is it a line etched in stone or in shifting sand? Is it one that we can continue to redraw when we don't like the immediate results? What is the difference between a temptation and an actual sin in our thought life?

Many of us don't clearly understand the difference between temptation and sin, so we often feel like we are treading water without knowing where the bottom is; we are like a six-foot man who drowns in four feet of water.

Knowing where this fuzzy line is drawn can be likened to turning up a light dimmer. If you walk around in a dark room, it's pretty hard to distinguish where you can walk or where you will trip over a table. But if you slightly turn up the light, you can make out fuzzy objects in the room—enough to maneuver around, though slowly and without much confidence. Then, when you turn up the full power of the light, you can clearly distinguish where it is safe to walk or not.

To understand the difference between temptation and sin is to understand where it is safe to walk or not. The light comes from

God's Word. The rheostat is our own understanding of what the Word says. The more we know, the brighter the light. The brighter the light, the less fuzzy the objects and the more confident we are about where to walk.

TEMPTATION IS NOT A SIN

The thoughts that enter our lives are not sin. In fact, the Christian may very well be tempted with more negative thoughts than before his conversion, because the tempter would like nothing better than to discourage us about our faith.

We find ourselves asking, "How could I be a *true* Christian and still have these thoughts. I must not have a genuine faith." If we think like that, guess who wins? But we have no more control over our thoughts than we have control over the vulgar language of the man sitting next to us at a restaurant. We hear them both, but we don't control whether or not we hear them.

Many men beat themselves up mentally because they have recurring thoughts of temptation. *Thoughts are not sins!* True enough, we can put so much junk into our minds that it predisposes us to tempting thoughts. Even so, thoughts are merely thoughts. Tempting thoughts can become sinful thoughts, but only if we let our Mind X have its own way and cross the line.

WHEN TEMPTATION CROSSES THE LINE

When does a temptation in our thought life become an actual sin? The best example is sex. Since all men are physically attracted to women, when does mental attraction become sin? Is there some definable threshold over which we cross from mere temptation to actual sin? Can we mark a line over which we are not to cross?

When our *normal* observations become *abnormal* preoccupations, then we have crossed the line. Dr. R. C. Sproul, in his book *Pleasing God*, wrote:

> Lust is not noticing that a woman is sexually attractive. Lust is born when we turn a simple awareness into a preoccupied fantasy. When we invite sexual thoughts into our minds and nurture them, we have passed from simple awareness into lust. Luther put it this way: "We cannot help it if birds fly over our heads. It is another thing if we invite them to build nests in our hair."[43]

One friend said, "Temptation is sexual attraction to a beautiful woman. Sin is walking around the block for another look."

When our chest swells in pride for a job well done, we feel better about ourselves as human beings. When does feeling good about our accomplishments become sin? When we begin to compare our accomplishments to other men and begin to elevate ourselves above others, we have crossed the line.

Dwight L. Moody once said, "When Christians find themselves exposed to temptation they should pray to God to uphold them, and when they are tempted they should not be discouraged. It is not a sin to be tempted; the sin is to fall into temptation."[44]

CONCEALING SIN

Tom's hobby was girl watching. Whenever he traveled, the part he enjoyed most was sitting in the airport terminal and checking out the women who came and went. After Tom became a Christian, he sensed his obsession displeased God, but it was his one private secret. *Besides*, he reasoned, *everyone's entitled to a minor vice, aren't they? Nobody gets hurt. It's a victimless crime.*

Not really, Tom.

No secrets are kept from God; He knows every word we will speak before it is even on our lips. No one else may know, but God knows. The goal of our secret thought life, since it is no secret to God, should be to live a life of personal holiness.

When we do cross over the line into sin, what should we do about it? Simply confess it, apologize to whomever you have offended (if applicable), correct the situation if you can (if applicable), receive Christ's forgiveness, and move on. "Whoever conceals their sins does not prosper, but the one who confesses and renounces them finds mercy" (Proverbs 28:13).

Why do we seem to have such a struggle to conquer our thoughts?

Visibility to Others

Going to a bar is no sin, but I would rather go to jail than be seen in a bar. Frankly, the reasons are not spiritual, but selfish. I don't want my reputation to be tarnished, so I categorically avoid bars. This has less to do with what Jesus might think than what my friends might think.

The *visibility* of our speech and actions helps us keep these in line. Visibility brings a certain level of self-discipline. Sometimes I think peer pressure actually has a greater influence on us toward righteous living than does the fear of a holy God. We all want to get along with others and have a good reputation, and these ambitions keep our behavior in check.

The nonbeliever doesn't have control of his *high visibility* sins because he doesn't have the Holy Spirit to make him aware of his sins and bring him under conviction, nor does he have the peer pressure of a church family. He lives a Mind X life.

Of course, the peer pressure of visibility isn't bad. If no peer pressure existed, then I would have no accountability and the temptation to sin would be more alluring.

But the *low visibility* of our thought life has no peer pressure, no accountability of any sort — save our own self-discipline and dependence on the Spirit — which puts us at a higher risk. The result of low visibility? We lead a secret thought life, often unruly, which we would find embarrassing for others to know about.

My Own Awareness

While our high visibility sins may be obvious to others, we may not be aware of them ourselves.

As new Christians, we brought all of our excess baggage with us to our newfound faith. Regrettably, we were full of anger, resentment, bitterness, self-centeredness, lust, envy, and jealousy.

Even before becoming Christians, we disguised much of our secret thought life, but once we became Christians, we became skilled concealers of these secret thoughts. We carefully controlled our speech and actions to keep in step with our perception of the new job description, mostly because it served our purposes. *Low awareness* sins are blind spots. These low awareness areas are where some of the fiercest battles for our minds are fought. The psalmist inquires, "Who can discern their own errors? Forgive my hidden faults. Keep your servant also from willful sins; may they not rule over me. Then I will be blameless, innocent of great transgression" (Psalm 19:12–13). It's hard to beat an enemy of which we are unaware.

The Visibility/Awareness Connection

Figure 22.1 shows the relationship between the *visibility* and our *awareness* of our sins. Visibility is oriented to the external world—"others"— while awareness is oriented to the internal world—"me." Notice how our *high visibility* sins are usually sins of *speech* and *actions*. Occasionally we can discern how another man's secret thoughts are causing him to sin, but usually he has to *do* something before we notice.

On the other hand, *low visibility* sins are usually the sins of our private thoughts. Our language in public cleans up pretty well when we become Christians, but no peer pressure motivates us to come to terms with the subtle pride of thinking of ourselves more highly than we ought. We must dig deeper into the spiritual life to find the desire to overcome our secret thought life.

While the visibility of our sins provides some motivation for us to become more aware and change, we can't change that part of us of which we are not aware. Our awareness of our sins revolves around the degree to which we are leading an unexamined life. *High awareness* can result from adopting group mores in our speech and actions, but in our thought lives we must rely on the Holy Spirit to make us aware of our "errors" and "hidden faults."

Before I received the Lord, every other word I spoke had four letters imaginatively arranged. I became acutely aware of the sinfulness of this coarse language, aided, no doubt, by its high visibility. Through prayer, God dramatically changed this area of my life.

VISIBILITY/AWARENESS RELATIONSHIP

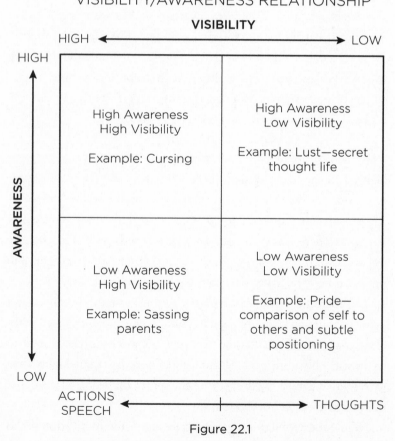

Figure 22.1

But my ambition to control my own destiny and be my own boss without anyone's help, including God's, escaped my awareness for many years, aided and abetted by its low visibility. Let's look at what happens when visibility and awareness are combined.

High Visibility/High Awareness

As you can see in Figure 22.1, high visibility/high awareness sins are the most blatant ones—sins that anyone (even the nonbeliever) would recognize as wrong.

Once, a friend started an affair that everyone, including his wife, knew about. He was approached by some of his friends to abandon his highly visible tryst. He was very aware of what he was doing, and because of its high visibility, so was everyone else. (No, he didn't give it up.)

High Visibility/Low Awareness

These sins are often the sins of nonbelievers, but not always. A man became a Christian, but after several years he still was known for temper tantrums at his place of work. When approached about it, he commented that he thought it was perfectly normal to let off steam. No one had ever made him aware of how anger can be a sin. He has made substantial progress since then.

Low Visibility/High Awareness

Now let's turn to low visibility problems, where the secret thought life can smolder with little or no accountability. Low visibility/high awareness sins are the nemesis of the Christian man. "I know this kind of thinking is wrong, but I'm just not willing to give it up." Or, "I just can't help myself."

Once, a friend offered to help me obtain a business loan through one of his contacts. But when I went for his help, I couldn't get him to follow up on it. My feelings were wounded. I was angry beyond forgiveness. For months I brooded over my anger, and I soon found myself bitter and resentful. I didn't have the courage to confront him, so I just festered.

I was highly aware of the sin in my secret thoughts, but the low visibility didn't require me to account to anyone. Finally, the conviction by the Holy Spirit became so strong that I reconciled the relationship.

Low Visibility/Low Awareness

The slyest sins of all are the low visibility/low awareness ones. Not only does no one else see them, but we don't see them either. And since we rarely give our lives introspective self-examination, we can be oblivious to the wrongness of our wrong thinking.

One day I realized I am a critic. I critique everything—people, paintings, buildings, cars, clothes, landscaping, colors, etc. Nothing escapes the critique. That alone would be no problem, but I also realized I add to my *critique* a *comparison* to myself. So, very subtly, I would constantly put others down to make myself feel better.

This is the essence of the sin of pride. We have said in chapter 16 that pride is a sin of comparison, though Scripture instructs us to not think of ourselves more highly than we ought (see Romans 12:3).

If we will make a commitment to become more aware of our thought life, if we will pause and occasionally ask *"Why?"* when our thoughts don't seem to be our own, then we will have taken a giant stride toward conquering our secret thought life.

THE MIND THAT PLAYS TRICKS ON ITSELF

A brewery that made regular and light beer surveyed people known to favor its brand. "Do you prefer regular or light beer?" they asked. Amazingly, people reported they preferred light beer three to one. For years, the brewery had produced nine times as much regular beer as light beer! They determined that, in essence, people interpreted

345 SECRET THOUGHT LIFE | 345

the question to mean, *Do you prefer the beer of refined, discriminating people, or do you only drink regular beer?*[45]

We have a remarkable capacity to kid, trick, and fool ourselves. Our self-image is so important to us that we will believe almost any reasonable explanation for our failures, as long as we end up as the hero. The prophet Jeremiah noted this when he wrote, "The heart is deceitful above *all* things and beyond cure. Who can understand it?" (Jeremiah 17:9, italics added.)

Unless we develop a solid understanding of how our thoughts, motives, and ambitions are shaped, we will have impure secret thoughts, wrong motives, and selfish ambitions. If we don't leave a sentinel posted in the watchtower, our enemy can slip into our thoughts under the cover of low awareness.

Solomon understood this when he wrote, "To humans belong the plans of the heart, but from the LORD comes the proper answer of the tongue. All a person's ways seem pure to them, but motives are weighed by the LORD" (Proverbs 16:1 – 2).

John decided to buy a new car because the gas mileage on the old one wasn't very good. The new car John bought depreciated $4,000 the first year, but he saved $400 in gas! What John really wanted wasn't better mileage, but more prestige.

CONQUERING THE SECRET THOUGHT LIFE

By now you may be thinking it's hopeless to master your secret thought life. Quite to the contrary, the Holy Spirit will search our spirit (our Mind X) and point out our errors, if we will only ask Him. "The lamp of the Lord searches the spirit of a man; it searches out his inmost being" (Proverbs 20:27 NIV, 1984 ed.). King David asked rhetorically, "Where can I go from your Spirit? Where can I flee from your presence?" (Psalm 139:7). We can run from God, but we can't hide. The answer to winning the battle for our mind — the secret thought life — is to open up ourselves to examination by ourselves and by the Spirit. Our prayer should be the prayer of King David:

> Search me, God, and know my heart;
> > test me and know my anxious thoughts.
> See if there is any offensive way in me,
> > and lead me in the way everlasting.

Psalm 139:23 – 24

TAKE CAPTIVE EVERY THOUGHT

Raising children is tough work. What makes it so difficult? Children always test the limits of rule and order. Whatever boundaries we set for them, they always want to test and retest the limits of our patience.

Some friends had a rule that their daughter could not go to PG-13 movies until she was thirteen. All her friends could go when they were ten and eleven. Every weekend she would ask her parents if she could go to this or that movie — always one that was rated PG-13. She always tested the limits.

Our thoughts are like this girl. Every day they ask us to let them cross the boundaries of rule and order we have established. Our thoughts always test the limits. It takes discipline and effort in our thought lives to keep our Mind Y in gear and our Mind X disengaged. How do we do that?

"Take captive every thought to make it obedient to Christ" (2 Corinthians 10:5). No thought should be allowed to have its own way. Like the daughter who wants to test her parents, our thoughts want to have their own way, but we must take captive each and every one of them. Why? Because, in the words with which Solomon concluded the book of Ecclesiastes, "God will bring every deed into judgment, including every hidden thing [our secret thought life], whether it is good or evil" (Ecclesiastes 12:14).

Of course, you already know you don't have enough willpower

to make this happen. But Christ in you does. When Christ is in control of our lives, the Holy Spirit is in power. When we let the old man — the sinful nature, the flesh — be in control, then the Spirit is quenched. The solution is to take captive every thought — and if we find we have sinned, to confess it and ask Christ to again take control. That's the essence of living by the power of the Holy Spirit.

——————— FOCUS QUESTIONS ———————

1. Each of us leads a secret thought life — an "invisible" life — which is significantly different from the man we project to others.

   ❏ Agree ❏ Disagree. Why?

2. Read Jeremiah 23:24. Do you believe that God knows your thoughts? Why do men put emphasis on living right among their peers, who are mere men like themselves, but do not make living right in their thought lives an equally important priority?

3. What is an area of your thought life with which you really struggle (e.g., lust, fantasies, hate-world)?

4. Read Romans 8:5–6. The real battlefield is the mind. According to these verses, what are the two influences on our thinking we choose between (verse 5)? What are the results of choosing each one (verse 6)? Have you ever heard of "Theory X and Theory Y"?

5. What is the difference between a temptation and a sin? Are thoughts sins?

6. When does a temptation in our thought life cross the line between temptation and sin?

7. Read 2 Corinthians 10:5. What does it mean to "take captive every thought"?

CHAPTER 23

ACCOUNTABILITY: THE MISSING LINK

Our society displays far too little correlation
between what we say we believe and how we
actually behave. There's a disconnect somewhere.
Anonymous

Wounds from a friend can be trusted,
but an enemy multiplies kisses.
Proverbs 27:6

AN OPEN LETTER TO MEN AND THEIR PASTORS

Dear Pastor,

You know me well. I sit toward the front of the church every Sunday—I'm always there. On the way out I always greet you with a handshake and a smile. You seem glad to see me too.

But you don't know the "real" me very well. Behind my happy smile is a life that is somehow unbalanced. Occasionally, you have asked me how I am doing, and I have told you, "I'm fine; how are you?" (I've learned the easiest way to keep to myself is to refocus the attention back on the other person.)

The truth is, I'm not sure you really want an answer. I know you deal with a lot of real pain and real suffering — people losing jobs, their homes, their families, loved ones. Frankly, I'm a little embarrassed to talk to you about where I am spiritually. I'm supposed to be on top of things — after all, I'm a successful businessman.

I've tried to take a look at my life, to examine my ways, but the plain truth is I don't know how. I really enjoy your sermons. They move my emotions and spirit, but on Monday morning at nine o'clock when the phones start ringing and the customers start complaining, I just can't seem to make the transition. I really need help.

Somehow I sense that my problems are really spiritual problems, but I can't find spiritual answers. I know my marriage looks like the picture of success, but behind the closed doors of my private castle, life is very different — I would be ashamed for you to know.

My children don't seem to like spending time with me anymore. Frankly, I've shut them out of my life for so long that I can't really blame them. I've wasted more nights in empty motel rooms than I care to remember. At first, I thought I was doing it for my family — to provide them a better standard of living. But now I realize I was really doing it for me — for my own self-gratification. Maybe I thought it would make me feel more significant. Anyway, I got the ends and the means mixed up, and now I really don't think they like me very much anymore.

I know lots of people, but I am really a very lonely man. I wouldn't know who to talk to if I could even put my frustrations into words. There is no accountability in my life whatsoever. Nobody knows, or even seems to care, how I am doing financially, in my business, with my wife, with my children, or spiritually. I know you are interested at the group level, but I'm talking about just me—personally, individually. I don't expect you to personally spend time with me, but I wish we had some way of linking men together to talk about these things. I think it would happen if you really got behind the idea.

Frankly, I've done some things in business that I regret. I've cut corners and compromised my integrity. I feel guilty about it, but since nobody knows the difference, I just go on pretending everything is okay.

I'm really not much different from anyone else. I often wonder if behind those plastic Sunday morning smiles, other men might feel the same way I do.

Oh, well, I never planned on mailing this letter anyway, but I just had to get some things off my chest. I really wish I could tell you about these things. There is so much I want to know, and I need someone to talk to. But I guess I'll see you Sunday.

Sincerely,

James

THE PROBLEM

I played men's doubles tennis with a partner who always became angry when I netted the ball. Finally I told him, "Look, give me a break. I would never intentionally hit the ball into the net!" Nobody who trusts Christ with their life *intentionally* disobeys the Scriptures. Men don't fail on purpose. James, the fictitious author of the pastor letter, didn't want his life to misfire. Yet we see men falling short of their full potential every day—the wheels seem to come off their wagons. Why? Christians don't fail because they *want* to fail. The truth is that all genuine Christians want to live an obedient life through faith in Jesus Christ. Alas, "the spirit is willing, but the flesh is weak," and temptations beset us at every turn.

My friend, Howard Ball, once said, "Sometimes people remark

that living a faithful Christian life is difficult. That's not true at all. It's not difficult—it's humanly impossible."[46] No man has the strength of will and purpose to *always* make the right choices. Just when we think we are getting ourselves under control—zap! "So, if you think you are standing firm," wrote the apostle Paul, "be careful that you don't fall!" (1 Corinthians 10:12).

One of the biggest reasons men get into trouble is that they don't have to answer to anyone for their lives. Ask around. You will learn that very few men have built accountability into their Christian lifestyle. It is the *missing link* of Christianity. In the three decades I've worked with men as a vocation, I've found that maintaining accountability relationships is one of the hardest things for men to do. Why is that?

Some of us have invested our whole life toward the very goal of "being our own boss" so we *won't* have to answer to anyone. Others of us, confidential by nature, don't want someone else intruding into our private lives. And still others of us have an interest, but we are unsure of what accountability actually is, and how to go about it.

Every day men fail morally, spiritually, relationally, and financially—not because they don't want to succeed, but because they have *blind spots* and *weak spots*, which they believe they can handle on their own. They can't. And they lose their families, their businesses, their jobs, and their savings, and they damage their relationship with God because no one is there to ask, "How? Why? What? and Who?"—the hard questions.

Some men have spectacular failures where in a moment of passion they abruptly burst into flames, crash, and burn. But the more common way men get into trouble evolves from hundreds of tiny decisions—decisions that go undetected—that slowly, like water dripping onto a rock, wear down a man's character. Not blatantly or precipitously, but subtly, over time, we get caught in a web of cutting corners and compromise, self-deceit and wrong thinking, which goes unchallenged by anyone in our lives.

God's Word teaches us how to stand firm in the faith and to guard against falling away. "Solid food [God's Word] is for the mature, who by constant use have trained themselves to distinguish good from evil" (Hebrews 5:14). Yet men *do* fall away because they don't have to answer to anyone for their behavior and beliefs.

In a world in which evil always lurks, and often triumphs, how can a man so order his life that he has the greatest likelihood of succeeding? The answer—the missing link—is accountability.

THE PURPOSE AND DEFINITION OF ACCOUNTABILITY

The purpose of accountability is nothing less than to become more Christlike in all our ways each day and to grow in intimacy with Him.

It is Jesus, and Him crucified, who is the object of our search, our devotion, our sacrifice, and our affection. He is the one we love, and anything less than intimacy with the living Christ will be a pallid achievement. In our accountability we will yearn and strive and sweat for the fullness of His power and presence in the everyday experiences of our lives. To more carefully appropriate His grace toward us is our object in asking someone to assist us in becoming more obedient and devoted to the Lord Jesus.

Has anyone ever asked you to hold them accountable for an area of their life? Have you ever asked anyone to hold you accountable for an area of your life? And just exactly what is accountability anyway?

Accountability is like nuclear fusion. Everyone has heard of it, and everyone knows it's important. But very few people actually know how to explain it.

Here's a useful working definition of accountability for Christians: *To be regularly answerable to qualified people for each of the key areas of our lives.*

Let's explore the four aspects of this definition: *answerable, key areas, regularly,* and *qualified people.*

Answerable

In commerce, every man is accountable to someone. Even the self-employed owner is accountable to his customers and clients. I owned my own business, but I still had to give financial and management accountings to limited partners and lenders.

The most successful formula for business accountability I've ever known calls for a monthly meeting in which goals for the next thirty to sixty days are negotiated and agreed on. Then the subordinate has the freedom to run with those goals and make things happen. But the price of that freedom is accurate reporting (i.e., accountability). At the next monthly meeting the subordinate must give a report of the results achieved for the past month before new goals are set for the future.

Unless we are answerable on a regular basis for the key areas of our personal lives, we, like sheep, will go astray. Yet to submit our lives for inspection to someone else grates on our desire to be independent. While we desire to live like a Christian, we often want to keep it "just between me and Jesus." But the way of the Scriptures points to accountability among believers:

> Brothers and sisters, if someone is caught in a sin, you who live by the Spirit should restore that person gently. But watch yourselves, or you also may be tempted. Carry each other's burdens, and in this way you will fulfill the law of Christ.
>
> Galatians 6:1–2

> Do nothing out of selfish ambition or vain conceit. Rather, in humility value others above yourselves, not looking to your own interests, but each of you to the interests of the others.
>
> Philippians 2:3–4

A new command I give you: Love one another. As I have loved you, so you must love one another.

John 13:34

Two are better than one,
    because they have a good return for their labor:
If either of them falls down,
    one can help the other up.
But pity anyone who falls
    and has no one to help them up.

Ecclesiastes 4:9 – 10

Wounds from a friend can be trusted,
    but an enemy multiplies kisses.

Proverbs 27:6

As iron sharpens iron,
    so one person sharpens another.

Proverbs 27:17

What kinds of "answers" should we give? The answers we give in an accountability relationship are primarily for the *goals* we set and the *standards* we should live by.

We should each set goals to help us accomplish our understanding of God's *purpose* for our lives and the *priorities* He has for us. We need someone to whom we can be answerable—to give an accurate report to—about how we are progressing toward meeting these goals.

The Bible delineates general guidelines for our *character* and *conduct* that apply to all Christians. We also need people in our lives to challenge and encourage us to live up to those standards.

Here's what we should want to be answerable for in outline form:

- goals
- purpose

- priorities
- standards
- character
- conduct

Key Areas

The British steamer *Titanic* was considered by experts to be unsinkable. Yet one of the largest sea disasters in history occurred when the *Titanic* struck the hidden part of an iceberg on its maiden voyage during the night of April 14, 1912. More than fifteen hundred people perished as the submerged part of a mountain of ice ripped open a three-hundred-foot-long gash in the hull of what was then the greatest ocean liner in the world.

An iceberg is one of nature's most beautiful and dangerous phenomena. What we see of these masses of broken-off glaciers is beautiful — like the "best foot" each of us puts forward with our friends. But only one-eighth to one-tenth of an iceberg is visible. The rest is hidden below the surface of the water. And that is where the danger lurks.

Like an iceberg, the beautiful part of our lives is the 10 percent or so we let people see. What's below the surface, however, is where we live the majority of our real lives — lives often hidden from the scrutiny of other Christians. The jagged, subsurface edges of our secret lives often rip open our relationships and damage our spiritual lives. What is unseen and not carefully examined can sink us when we are unaccountable in those areas of our lives.

Figure 23.1 shows how most of our conversation revolves around the cliché level of life — news, sports, and weather. But this is the tip of the iceberg — the "visible" you. The "real" you wrestles with gut-wrenching issues in the key areas of our lives every day, and we each need someone to help us navigate around the submerged dangers of an unexamined life.

THE ACCOUNTABILITY ICEBERG

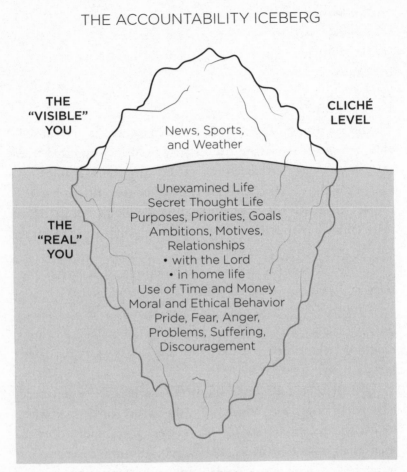

Figure 23.1

The areas of our lives that need accountability can be examined from different angles. One distinction is between *personal* and *professional*. The men we pick to help us be accountable in our careers and ethics may not be the same men we ask to help us maximize our relationships with our wife and kids.

Another distinction zeroes in on the difference between those areas *all men* need to address and *personal high risk* areas—those areas where we have a special struggle. For example, if you are a credit card junkie, addicted to pornography, have a gambling problem, are a drug addict, have become an alcoholic, or experience same-sex attraction, you would be smart to make yourself accountable to someone who has struggled in that area themselves. Otherwise, you know you'll be able to "work" them.

Perhaps the most useful distinction is *categorical*. The key areas in which all of us need accountability are:

- relationship with God
- relationship with wife, if married
- relationship with kids, if you have them
- use of money and time
- moral and ethical behavior
- areas of personal struggle

What is something you really struggle with? What are your weak spots? Wouldn't you like to know your blind spots? In which areas of your secret thought life do you struggle? What is your personal high risk area? These are questions an *accountability partner* should be *regularly* asking.

Regularly

"Regularly" suggests that the interval between contacts with our accountability partners should be frequent and somewhat systematic. For thirty-two years, until his death, I had a weekly meeting with a friend thirty years my senior. We held each other accountable for our relationships with the Lord and, to a lesser degree, with our families (we also had great fellowship and prayer).

My own experience is that men who don't have a standing meeting eventually stop meeting altogether. I'm sure it's possible to meet biweekly or monthly, but I recommend weekly meetings. Figure 23.2 illustrates a checklist of the questions you'll want to cover in those regular meetings. You can add whatever other areas of accountability you feel are appropriate.

The Weekly One-Hour Accountability Checkup

Use these questions as a guide. It is not necessary to ask every question, but be sure you cover each area every week.

Questions to Start
- How has God blessed this week? What went right?
- What problem consumed your thoughts this week? What went wrong?

Spiritual Life
- God's Word: Have you read it consistently? (How often? How long? Why not? Will you next week?)
- Prayer: Describe your prayers for yourself, others, praise, worship, confession, gratitude. How is your relationship with Christ evolving?
- Temptation: How were you tempted this week? How did you respond?
- Confession: Do you have unconfessed sin?

- Church: Did you worship in church this week? Was your faith in Jesus strengthened?

Home Life
- Wife: If applicable, how is it with your wife? (time, meaningful conversation, attitudes, intimacy, disappointments, irritations, her relationship with Christ)
- Children: If applicable, how are your children? (giving encouragement, quantity and quality time, values, education, spiritual welfare)
- Finances: How are your finances doing? (debt, sharing, saving, spending, stewardship)
- Time: Have you given your time to the ones who deserve it?

Work Life
- Job: How are things going? (career, relationships, temptations, stress, problems, working too much)

Ministry Life
- Making Disciples: What have you done this week to (1) *call* someone to live "in" Christ—salvation or abide, (2) *equip* them to live "like" Christ—grow or train, or (3) *send* them to live "for" Christ—make disciples, love, serve others.
- Witness: How have you shared your faith?
- Service: What have you done for someone else this week that can't be repaid? (the poor, encouragement, mercy, service to others)

Critical Concerns
- God's Will: Do you feel you are in the center of God's will and sense His peace?

- Thought Life: What secret are you wrestling with?
- Priorities: Are your priorities in the right order?
- Integrity: How is your moral and ethical behavior?
- High Risk: How are you doing in your personal high-risk area?
- Transparency: Are the "visible you" and the "real you" consistent in your relationships? (If not, in what ways?)
- Faithfulness: Have you been faithful in the key areas above? If not, what's your plan?

Prayer
- Close with ten to fifteen minutes of prayer. Focus on concerns of the week.

MIM
Phone: 407-472-2100
Fax: 407-331-7839
www.maninthemirror.org

Figure 23.2

You can also get these questions on a business card. One day I showed the card to a friend. He read it slowly, became quiet, and just stared at it for the longest time. Finally he looked up and said with great feeling, "Isn't it interesting that everything a man needs to know to keep his life on track will fit on the front and back of a business card?" You can order these checkup cards by calling Man in the Mirror at 407-472-2100 or by visiting maninthemirror.org and searching for "accountability cards."

These questions may seem stilted, especially at first. Unless personal concern, compassion, and friendship accompany the questions, they will be awkward. They can be asked creatively. The most important aspect is to give each man all the airtime he wants in order to give an accurate report. Remember, the ultimate purpose is to become more like the Lord in all our ways and ever more intimate with Him.

Qualified People

An extremely successful county commissioner asked me if I would be part of an accountability group. As we discussed the role of this group, we both realized that what he needed was not a *political* accountability group but a *spiritual* one.

Most of the men he asked to be part of his group would quickly concede they were unqualified to help him politically, but everyone was vitally interested in helping him stand for Christ in the public square.

What does it mean to give an answer to *qualified people*? The overarching qualifications for accountability partners are that they love Christ, want to see you succeed, and also sense a need for accountability. Answering to the right person can make a dramatic difference in the quality of your spiritual life. What kind of man would make the ideal accountability partner?

Pick men who have skill and wisdom, men you respect, men with whom you feel compatible and whose judgment you trust. The last thing you want to do is end up second-guessing the person you have given authority to ask you the hard questions. "Walk with the wise and become wise, for a companion of fools suffers harm" (Proverbs 13:20).

As already mentioned, you may want to have different men hold you accountable in different areas. Don't automatically expect that a man who can help you with your relationship with the Lord will also be able to help with your finances.

Chances are high that an existing friend is a good candidate for an accountability partner. Even if you pick a total stranger, the likelihood of becoming friends is certain. For that reason, you may want to reread chapter 10 ("Friends: Risks and Rewards") in the context of accountability.

A word of caution at this point: You should not have accountability relationships with any woman other than your wife. The temptation of having a close relationship with any woman other than your own wife is an invitation for disaster.

Wives are particularly helpful in areas of personal weakness, where vulnerability is a sensitive issue. I believe every man should invite accountability into his marriage, including as many areas as possible. When I have a decision and I'm not sure about my own judgment, I like to pass it by my wife, Patsy. She knows what I am trying to stand for, and she always asks me a question or two that provides an angle or insight I hadn't considered.

Be sure to pick someone to cover every area — *moral, spiritual, financial,* and *relational.* How tragic to achieve a high degree of success in your relationships with your family and the Lord, only to go bankrupt because of foolish financial decisions. In accountability, two out of three is not good enough.

Sadly, we all have been stung by leaks of confidential information. "If it's said, it's told" often describes how we feel about our secrets. One reason men don't want to reveal themselves to other men is *confidentiality.* This is serious business, and if I am going to share the real me with someone, I want to be absolutely sure I can *trust* him. The fear of betrayal by a friend keeps many of us from taking the risk of being accountable. Be sure to talk over this aspect of the accountability relationship with your prospective partner.

Look for someone you can go into partnership with. In other words, instead of looking for a "boss," look for a fellow struggler so you can help each other. "If either of them falls down, one can help the other up."

Avoid asking men to help you if there may be other agendas. If you owe someone money, that person probably isn't the right choice to hold you accountable in the area of money. If someone has been after you for years to join a golfing group that will take you away from your family on Saturdays, don't ask him to help you be accountable to spend more time with your wife and kids.

How big should your accountability group be? When I first started challenging men to start accountability groups, I put them in pairs. That didn't work as well as I had hoped. In several cases, two men led each other astray. The best-sized group for accountability is at least three and no more than four men. Fewer can spell trouble, and more doesn't allow enough time for every man to have airtime.

Finally, don't go overboard. Time is limited, and since you will probably meet regularly (try weekly), you don't want to have so many accountability relationships that you feel bogged down in the "paperwork" of life. If you form a group of four men, the different skills of the other men will probably help cover all the key areas.

Why is accountability so important, anyway?

HERE AND THERE

The ultimate reason we should be interested in our accountability *here* is our accountability *there*. Each of us is accountable to God for every aspect of our lives.

> But I tell you that everyone will have to give account on the day of judgment for every empty word they have spoken.
>
> Matthew 12:36

> So then, each of us will give an account of ourselves to God.
>
> Romans 14:12

> God "will repay each person according to what they have done." ... This will take place on the day when God will judge people's secrets through Jesus Christ.
>
> Romans 2:6, 16

We all one day will be accountable to Jesus Christ. The more faithful our walk here, the more God will reward us when we stand before the judgment seat of Christ. Accountability relationships can help us live here in a way that is pleasing to God.

On a practical level, the peace and joy of our daily lives spring forth from the integrity and balance we maintain in the key areas of our lives. Whether moral, spiritual, relational, or financial — the "big four" for failures — when we handle our lives with skill and wisdom, we experience a sense of personal satisfaction. Without the help of others in accountability relationships, none of us can attain our full potential.

Senator Bill Nelson from Melbourne, Florida, the home of the Kennedy Space Center, flew on the Columbia space shuttle mission — the mission just prior to the ill-fated *Challenger* disaster. In his book, *Mission*, he described his space experiences. He explained how maintaining a proper orbit is a delicate affair. Since there is no resistance in space, a man could literally turn the huge orbiter over by himself. To maintain a proper orbit, the on-board computers constantly make course and altitude corrections. Small rockets fire to make these adjustments. Larger jets burn to make major changes.[47]

It's said that the space shuttles were actually "off course" 90 percent of the time. If those rockets didn't fire, or if they overcompensated, the space vehicle would veer off its orbit and go tumbling into space.

We men are probably off course a lot of the time too. To keep our lives on a proper orbit we also need to *constantly* make course and altitude corrections. The questions of our accountability partners can act as small rockets and thrusters and jets to help us make the course corrections that will keep us in the right orbit. If we don't, the risk is that we will spin out of control.

THE DIFFERENCE BETWEEN COUNSEL AND ACCOUNTABILITY

Many men get into trouble because they seek Christian counsel and think they have fulfilled their duty. Plainly, seeking counsel adds value to our decisions (most of us should seek more of it), but *seeking counsel alone does not go far enough.*

When I seek counsel, I rarely give all the details, facts, and background. Usually, I only give my counselor what is, in my own estimation, enough information for them to be able to give me an answer. Often, I must confess, I tailor and shape the information in such a way that my counselor will come to my preconceived conclusion.

The counselee has no obligation to tell the counselor what he decides to do. So we can obtain excellent counsel but still do our own thing (which may or may not be the right decision).

Unless our counselors have the right to ask us the hard questions, we have not gone far enough. Unless we have some people who love us enough to hold us accountable in the key areas of our lives, we *will* lead a secret life, a life that is not being held answerable to the teachings of Christ.

Let there be no error in our thinking: No man can live the Christian life alone. Left to our own devices, we will convince ourselves of our own infallibility. "The heart is deceitful above all things and beyond cure. Who can understand it?" (Jeremiah 17:9).

Seeking counsel is at our initiative. Being held accountable gives another person the right and responsibility to take the initiative. To seek counsel is to look for answers to the questions we have. To be accountable is to give answers to the questions we are asked. In your life, does anyone ask you questions?

THE DIFFERENCE BETWEEN FELLOWSHIP AND ACCOUNTABILITY

In most relationships we never get past the cliché level of conversation — news, sports, and weather.

We ask someone, "How are you doing?"

"Great, just great!" they say. Their kids are struggling at school, their wife isn't speaking to them, and they are two months behind in their rent, but everything's "just great!"

Accountability doesn't evolve naturally in a relationship; it results from a purposed decision to live our lives in a "goldfish bowl" before a few men we learn to trust. Not only does accountability give someone permission to ask us hard questions, but asking those hard questions forms the basis for the relationship. Sometimes things can get sticky, but the friendship side of the relationship cannot be allowed to mute the accountability role.

Fellowship, on the other hand, doesn't probe with questions about the key areas of our lives because it has never been asked to do so, nor does it presume to have permission to intrude into the private areas of another's life. Rarely will a Christian brother ask you or me a hard question without invitation, even though they may want to.

One of my most disturbing experiences as a Christian came early in my spiritual pilgrimage. Six of us committed to meet together weekly. Frankly, I was so new in the faith that I had never even heard of accountability. We discussed a wide range of subjects, but we mostly met for fellowship. One of our group members, Howard Dayton, was in the process of writing a Christian book on how to handle money and possessions. Part of our time was spent looking over his ideas.

Totally out of the blue one day, we learned that a member of our group had quit his job, divorced his wife, abandoned his three infant children, and married his secretary—all of which came as a total surprise. None of us had any idea he was even having problems. *How could we possibly not know?* you ask. It was easier than you may think, because we simply didn't ask each other "accountability" questions. That experience taught me that fellowship without accountability has a very limited value, if any at all.

The high number of moral and spiritual failures among us suggests men do have problems, and men do need to have accountability in their lives. Why don't more men answer to others?

WHY MEN ARE NOT ACCOUNTABLE

The human spirit, left to its own devices, will always seek its own independent way. Even after we are captured by Christ, we continue in a lifelong power struggle between the old man of the flesh (the Mind X) and the new man in the Spirit (the Mind Y). Our old man really doesn't want to be held accountable and resists the notion with all of his resources. Here are the common reasons we don't have accountability in our lives.

The Problem of Willingness

Many professional sports leagues regularly have to suspend players for violating their substance-abuse policies. From Lance Armstrong to Roger Clemens, these men thought they could manage their lives on their own. The great Lawrence Taylor, perennial All-Pro linebacker with the New York Giants who was suspended by the league in 1988, once said:

> God, I didn't mean for it to happen. I wish it hadn't, but I did make a bad decision and I'll pay the price for it ... I really wasn't allowing the Giants to help me. I wasn't allowing my wife to help me. I was doing it by myself and trying to make it happen by myself because *I wanted to say I could do it on my own* [emphasis added]. It don't work like that. Boy, I found that out.[48]

Before an alcoholic or drug addict can be helped, the first step he must take is to admit he has a problem. Denial of the problem blocks any hope of overcoming the disease. Any counselor dealing with alcoholism or substance abuse will attest to how critical this first step is.

My mom and dad raised four rambunctious boys. When one of us would argue with one of Mom's suggestions, she would just roll her eyes and say, "You can lead a horse to water, but you can't make him drink." To be accountable we have to be a willing party.

Unless we face our own propensity for sin and self-deceit and acknowledge we need the help of others, we will never stick with a program of accountability. We may start one, but after a few testy moments, we will abandon those nosy, uncomfortable questions.

The Problem of Strong Personality

Once I tried to develop an accountability relationship with another man that really bombed. We were both neophytes and tried to be all things to each other. After a short time, I sensed he wasn't interested in what I had to ask or say.

He was willing to meet, but he failed to submit his ego to the pruning character of the hard questions on how he was doing with the Lord, his wife, and his kids. Instead of asking, "Do you have any ideas for me?" he defended his positions.

A day came when I thought to myself, *Why argue? If he doesn't care, why should I be the only one interested in his spiritual success?* One day I called him on his attitude, and that was the last time we met for accountability. His strong ego wouldn't let him admit failure and humble himself before another man.

The Problem of Success

One day I asked a successful businessman if anyone held him accountable for his decisions.

"It's interesting you should ask that question," he said. "Over the last several years I have become aware that I have no one to whom I must answer. As I have become more successful, everyone assumes I must have my act together. The worldly prestige that comes from success intimidates most people from asking how I am doing. There appears to be the presumption that since I am successful in business, every other area of my life is in order. Frankly, I operate without answering to anyone."

Successful men are high risk. Confident of their own abilities, they tend to think no problem is too big for them to handle alone. Competent and self-assured, they take the bull by the horns and make things happen. Everyone, though, has blind spots and weak spots.

A friend passed along some sound advice for the man who runs his own business. Pick a man in your organization who is secure in his position. Then give him the authority to come to you any time he feels you are getting off track, close your door, and tell you what's on his mind.

The Problem of Personal Vulnerability

The price of friendship is personal vulnerability. The price of an effective accountability relationship is also personal vulnerability. In friendship, personal vulnerability is *voluntary*, but in an accountability relationship, it must be *mandatory*. To get past news, sports, and weather, a man must be willing to reveal that part of him which is hidden below the surface.

To be vulnerable means to risk the disapproval of our accountability partner. Let's face it — none of us will naturally go looking for someone to whom we can exhibit our warts and blemishes. Instead, accountability is a decision of the will because we sense we will receive a higher reward from the Lord Jesus when we pay the price of having a brother sharpen us as "iron sharpens iron."

None of us want to be rejected — that's one of the great fears in revealing ourselves to another man. We want his respect, not his rejection. My guess is that most men who take up the challenge to begin an accountability relationship will go slow in becoming personally vulnerable. That's okay. But be careful not to lie to your partner and just play games. Rather, tell him up front that you want to ease into accountability — that you want to see how the relationship gels. But keep in mind that until you become transparent and vulnerable, your partner can't hold you accountable in that "below the surface" area. Don't kid yourself into thinking an area is covered when in reality it's not.

I have done many things in my life for which I am deeply ashamed. We all have. To have an accountability relationship, we don't need to air all of our old dirty laundry to be personally vulnerable with someone. If we are clear with Christ about an area, I think some things are better left alone. Yet for those areas with which we *continue* to struggle, we do need the help that can only come from making ourselves vulnerable to an accountability partner. If any guilt remains from the past, talk about it—Jesus wants us to be healed.

Even in an accountability relationship it is possible to deceive our partner in an area, unless we make the commitment to be personally vulnerable.

THE PROBLEM OF STRUCTURE

The reason men get into trouble isn't so much that they don't understand what they are supposed to do, but rather that they have no structure to give them the discipline to do that which they already know they should do.

One day I asked a group of men about the frequency of their golf game. The few who said they played regularly also said they have a standing game—a structure. Among the majority who didn't play regularly, not a single one had a standing game.

If we are going to beat the "old man" in each of us, we are going to have to organize to do it. The only men who are consistently having accountability relationships have planned and committed themselves to a specific structure or program—they have a "standing game." Our accountability checkups need to have the priority and consistency of a weekly allergy shot.

Meet at the same time and place for convenience. And when you put it on your calendar, schedule it as a recurring weekly appointment.

GETTING STARTED

Pick out a few men with whom you think you would be compatible. Tell them you are trying to build some accountability into your life. If they also seem interested in the subject, have them read this chapter. Then get together with them, plan a weekly meeting time and place, and start meeting. Discuss *The Weekly One-Hour Accountability Checkup* and see if the iceberg analogy makes sense to all of you. Copy or tear out the *Weekly One-Hour Accountability Checkup* (or get the wallet-sized cards), and use it as a track to guide your discussion.

If it sounds simple, don't be fooled. If it were, more men would be doing it. Where accountability has been promoted, no more than 15 percent of men have taken the action step and stuck with it. Accountability requires hard work, commitment, and lots of patience. The payoff, though, is worth the price.

CONCLUSION

The missing link in most of our lives is accountability. We get off track because we are not regularly answerable for each of the key areas of our lives to qualified people to whom we have given permission to ask the hard questions—questions about the *goals* we set and the *standards* God has established.

We have learned that accountability here and now is important because God will ultimately hold us accountable for everything we do. Accountability goes far beyond mere counsel or fellowship; it requires answers to the questions—sometimes hard questions—we are asked.

If you are part of the vast majority of men who don't have anyone asking them, "Who? What? Why? and How?" then let me challenge you to fill in this missing link in your life. It may be the component that enables you to synchronize your behavior with your beliefs and keeps you from spinning out of control.

THE WEEKLY ONE-HOUR ACCOUNTABILITY CHECKUP

Accountability is to be regularly answerable for each of the key areas of our lives to qualified people.

Suggested Guidelines

1. Use the questions in Figure 23.2.
2. Try to ensure each person gets equal airtime. However, if one of you has a particularly hard struggle one week, be flexible enough to focus on that issue, even if it takes the entire hour.
3. Let each person work through a section at a time, and then let the others answer. This will keep things moving better.
4. Don't neglect the prayer time.
5. Try a small group of three or four men. It will work well if everyone speaks succinctly (one hour will go by very quickly).
6. Reread chapter 23 ("Accountability: The Missing Link") at least once every year and discuss the questions at the end of the chapter. You will be surprised how your understanding of accountability will change over the years.
7. Stick it out. You will want to quit, perhaps often. Ask God to strengthen you when you want to give up.
8. Hold each other accountable for the *goals* you each set for yourselves and to the *standards* of God's Word.
9. Never forget the purpose of accountability—to each day become more Christlike in all of your ways and ever more intimate with Him. Remember, it is Jesus who is the object of our search, our devotion, our sacrifice, and our affection. Anything

less than intimacy with the living Lord will be a pallid achievement of your time together.

10. If you are uncomfortable with the format, feel free to alter these questions and type up your own accountability checklist. The substance is more important than the form. You may want to divide the key areas among more than one accountability partner or group.

11. End your accountability checkup time with ten to fifteen minutes of prayer. Focus on concerns of the week.

FOCUS QUESTIONS

1. How many men do you know who have regularly scheduled time with Christian brothers for accountability? Why do you think so few men have accountability relationships?

2. How could some of the spectacular public moral failures of the recent past have been avoided?

3. Respond to this statement:

   Some men have spectacular failures where in a moment of passion they abruptly burst into flames, crash, and burn. But the more common way men get into trouble evolves from hundreds of tiny decisions — decisions that go undetected — that slowly, like water dripping onto a rock, wear down a man's character. Not blatantly or precipitously, but subtly, over time, we get caught in a web of cutting corners and compromise, self-deceit and wrong thinking, which goes unchallenged by anyone in our lives.

4. How would you define accountability? What are the important ingredients in order for accountability relationships to work?

5. What is the difference between accountability and counsel? Between accountability and fellowship?

6. What are the key areas in which a man should be held accountable?

7. How would you go about selecting accountability partners?

8. Are you ready to establish an accountability relationship? Why, or why not?

PART 7

CONCLUSION

CHAPTER 24

HOW CAN A MAN CHANGE?

Few people think more than two or three times
a year. I have made an international reputation
by thinking once or twice a week.
George Bernard Shaw

The knowledge of the secrets of the kingdom
of heaven has been given to you, but not to them.
Whoever has will be given more, and they will
have an abundance.
Jesus, Matthew 13:11–12

The turnpike from Miami to Orlando stretches endlessly and monotonously for over two hundred miles—the world's most tiring highway. We had just finished a wonderful, but compact, two-day visit with Patsy's parents in Miami. On the drive back to Orlando a frustration with life swept over me.

I began to ask God questions. Nonstop, for an hour and a half, plaintive questions poured out—one right after the other. I had no idea where they were coming from.

It's as though God said, *Oh no, here we go with another one!* And then He let me vent. Frankly, I couldn't tell you today what any three of those questions were. Patsy saw the full spectrum of emotions—from top to bottom. We had only been married for a few months, and I feared Patsy would think I had flipped. I was a brand-new Christian, and my head reeled with questions for God. Then, as quickly as it began, the gush of questions stopped.

When I finished, the impression I had was, *Look, I appreciate your concerns, but you just don't need to know all that right now. Don't worry about it. Just trust Me. I'm all you need. You can't solve those problems. That's what I'm here for.*

A peace swept over me, even though not a single question had been answered.

I'd like to be able to report that this was all I needed and I've never questioned God since, but you know that's not true. But it was enough for that moment. I knew no more than when I started my inquisition, but I knew it wasn't important. I sensed He loved me—that's all that mattered.

Life is a big question mark. God is a big answer. Whatever the question, He is the answer. No matter how down or up, tired or strong, betrayed or befriended, dishonest or upright, hurt or happy, rich or broke, successful or failed, famous or unknown—God is the answer. He is all we need.

I felt my resistance melt away, that sense of wanting to be in control, and I surrendered to Him in a deeper way that morning out on the turnpike. As I've done many times since, I found a deeper level of pilgrimage—a deeper sense of relationship. And my life began to change.

Perhaps you are at a point in your life—because of this book or for some other reason—that you want to change. You want to go deeper into the spiritual life.

THE PROBLEM

As we began this book together, we posed the question, "Why do men think the things they think, say the things they say, and do the things they do?" By now we both have a much better understanding of the answer to this important question.

But in a few minutes you will set this book aside, and you will move on to the next chapter of your life—a life lived in the crucible that is this world. Tomorrow morning, when the phones start ringing and the customers start complaining, life gets real. We live in a demanding, challenging world, but it is not a world we are to shrink away from, nor can we.

Americans have come to expect simple, streamlined solutions to perfectly packaged problems—"the three easy steps to a happy this" or "the four foolproof ways to be a successful that." Life is more complex than "this and that." We didn't become the men we are overnight, and we don't change quickly. Patient, trial-and-error effort, diligently grinding it out on a day-to-day basis—that's the pathway to change.

In this final chapter, let's outline some practical daily steps we can take to change and take our lives to the next level. Let's answer the question, "How can a man change?"

FAMOUS LAST WORDS

The last words or late-in-life words of men are fascinating. Men's last words often reveal that the positions they took and the priorities they lived by early in their lives didn't satisfy their longing for meaning and purpose. Some men attain great esteem in this world—their accomplishments are significant in the eyes of men. But at the end of their lives, how many of these men rest in peace? How many of these men satisfy that deep hunger each of us has for purpose, meaning, and significance?

You may be surprised to learn in what state of mind some great men have gone to their graves:

> Even in the valley of the shadow of death, two and two do not make six.
>
> Leo Tolstoy, Russian novelist

It is a bit embarrassing to have been concerned with the human problem all one's life and find at the end that one has no more to offer by way of advice than "Try to be a little kinder."

Aldous Huxley, humanist and author
of *Brave New World*

How were the receipts today in Madison Square Garden?

P. T. Barnum, American showman
and founder of Barnum & Bailey Circus

President McKinley was assassinated in Buffalo. At his deathbed, his wife pleaded, "I want to go too, I want to go too."

He replied, "We are all going."

William B. McKinley, twenty-fifth president
of the United States

All my life I have been seeking to climb out of the pit of my besetting sins and I cannot do it and I never will unless a hand is let down to draw me up.

Seneca, Roman philosopher and statesman

All of the wisdom of this world is but a tiny raft upon which we must set sail when we leave this earth. If only there was a firmer foundation upon which to sail, perhaps some divine word.

Socrates, Greek philosopher

I am about to take my last voyage, a great leap in the dark.

Thomas Hobbes, English philosopher

I'm looking for a loophole.

W. C. Fields, American comedian
and lifelong agnostic, explaining why
he was reading a Bible on his deathbed

The meager satisfaction that man can extract from reality leaves him starving.

Sigmund Freud, Austrian founder of psychoanalysis

I die before my time and my body shall be given back to the earth and devoured by worms. What an abysmal gulf between my deep miseries and the eternal kingdom of Christ. I marvel that whereas the ambitious dreams of myself and of Alexander and of Caesar should have vanished into thin air, a Judean peasant—Jesus—should be able to stretch his hands across the centuries, and control the destinies of men and nations.

Napoleon, French military and political leader

THE CASE FOR DAILY EFFORT

You can save a fortune by using rechargeable batteries. But if you don't recharge them on schedule, they won't do the job. In the same way batteries need recharging, the Christian must recharge his spiritual batteries every day. If we don't, we will start at 100 percent the first day, but the next day we will only operate at 85 percent power, the day after that—70 percent, then 50 percent, then 25 percent, and, before long, we don't even have the strength to plug ourselves back into our source of power.

The Christian pilgrimage is a moment-by-moment, daily journey. It requires daily effort, without which we will stray. "Stop listening to instruction, my son, and you will stray from the words of knowledge" (Proverbs 19:27).

The kingdom of God starts here—this is God's world. Yet good and evil live side by side; they are enemies. This struggle between good and evil dominates all of our literature, our news, our movies, and our television shows. It dominates because it's one of life's most real characteristics. To the extent we don't stand guard daily, the other side plots ways to break down the walls of our resistance.

Jesus told it this way:

"The kingdom of heaven is like a man who sowed good seed in his field. But while everyone was sleeping, his enemy came and sowed weeds among the wheat, and went away. When the wheat sprouted and formed heads, then the weeds also appeared.

"The owner's servants came to him and said, 'Sir, didn't

you sow good seed in your field? Where then did the weeds come from?'

"'An enemy did this,' he replied.

"The servants asked him, 'Do you want us to go and pull them up?'

"'No,' he answered, 'because while you are pulling the weeds, you may root up the wheat with them. Let both grow together until the harvest. At that time I will tell the harvesters: First collect the weeds and tie them in bundles to be burned; then gather the wheat and bring it into my barn.'"

Matthew 13:24–30

This world is God's field, and He has styled it so that the good and the evil, the wheat and the weeds, live alongside each other. But the weeds will choke out the wheat unless we daily attend to watering, fertilizing, and tilling the soil.

Few lives are static and unchanging. Usually our spiritual lives either march forward or slip backward. Life is like the treadmill at your gym. If you stop walking forward, you lose ground. How do we keep walking forward? By recharging daily. The wheat is gathered up and brought "into the barn"; the weeds get burned.

What are some practical daily steps we can take to assist us in making the right choices?

PRACTICAL DAILY STEPS TO CHANGE

Each year the Houston Astros and the Atlanta Braves come to the Orlando area for spring training. Over the course of several weeks, what do you think these million-dollar thoroughbred athletes do? Do they come to Florida to learn about obscure, rarely used baseball strategies? No. They practice fielding, running, and batting, and they do conditioning—they focus on the basics. Every day they hit, run, and field. In the same way, the Christian should return to the basics daily.

Daily Preparation

A man's first spiritual discipline is to prepare daily for life among the "weeds." Whether done in early morning or in the evening hour, daily *Bible reading and study* coupled with *prayer* comprise the first essential building block for helping a man to change. Personally, I've never known a man whose life has changed in any significant way apart from the regular study of God's Word. Current research indicates four or more days a week really makes a difference.[49]

Underline passages that capture your interest. *Memorize* passages for strength, courage, and faith. As an act of discipline and an expression of faith, *establish a daily routine* of seeking God as He really is.

Write down impressions, ideas, and prayers. *Keep a journal* of what you pray about, and record the answers in it. I use the acronym ACTS to help me pray:

- "A" is for adoration—praising God for his attributes.
- "C" is for confession—asking forgiveness for the sins I have committed. Learn to keep short accounts with God.
- "T" is for thanksgiving—expressing gratitude for His blessings and answers to my prayers.
- "S" is for supplication—asking for anything and everything that comes to mind for myself and for others.

Be persistent in prayer (see Luke 11:5 – 13). I also pray the Lord's Prayer and often dwell on one phrase to pray about in greater detail. For example, I might name the sins I'm asking forgiveness for when I pray, "Forgive us our sins."

Daily Temptation

Everyone is tempted to sin every day. God promises He will provide an escape—a safety valve—if we will choose it. When tempted, reject the thought and thank the Lord for giving you the power to have victory over temptation. The apostle Paul wrote:

> No temptation has overtaken you except what is common to mankind. And God is faithful; he will not let you be tempted beyond what you can bear. But when you are tempted, he will also provide a way out so that you can endure it.
>
> 1 Corinthians 10:13

Whatever thought pops into our minds, we should take it captive to make it obedient to Christ. And remember, thoughts alone are not sins! It's what we let God do with those thoughts that counts.

Daily Sin

Everyone sins. Seneca once said, "We have all sinned, some more, some less." Inevitably, we are overcome and give in to temptation. When you become aware of a sin, confess it to the Lord and thank Him for forgiving your sins — past, present, and future — according to His promise in 1 John 1:9. Invite Christ to again take control of your life, and then get on with the next part of your life. This is the essence of living in the power of the Holy Spirit. As John wrote:

> If we claim to be without sin, we deceive ourselves and the truth is not in us. If we confess our sins, he is faithful and just and will forgive us our sins and purify us from all unrighteousness.
>
> 1 John 1:8–9

DAILY POWER

When Jesus controls our lives, the power of the Holy Spirit is at work in us (see John 14:26; 16:13; Romans 8:9). The Holy Spirit is given to *all* believers (see 1 Corinthians 3:16).

Not all believers enjoy this power because they resist Him or otherwise sin. Even more, most Christians do not understand how to live in a moment-by-moment, daily fellowship with God. The fruit of God's Spirit—love, joy, peace, patience, kindness, goodness, faithfulness, gentleness, and self-control—belong to the surrendered man who yields control of his life to the mind of Christ every moment.

If we crucify our own ambition, confess our sins, and give Jesus Christ first place in our lives, then the power of the Holy Spirit is available to meet every need. Living by the power of the Holy Spirit is that intense, moment-by-moment love relationship with the living Christ in which we soar on wings like eagles, or, having sinned, we tearfully confess and are restored.

Daily Witnessing

If Christ is truly preeminent in our lives, then we will want to tell others about Him. Every Christian has the *command* and the *power* to witness (see Acts 1:8). The Great Commission does not say, "Therefore, *37 percent* of you go and make disciples of all nations"— it just says "go." Do you have the *desire* to see others come to faith in Christ? If not, why? Do you have the *ability* to show someone how to trust Christ for the first time? If not, obtain training (see 1 Timothy 2:3–4; 1 Peter 3:15).

After all has been heard and considered, it is the human soul alone that passes from this world to the next. Can anything else matter, then, unless we address the need of the human soul first?

Daily Pilgrimage

Life is a struggle. Each day is part of a pilgrimage that prepares us for our eternal destiny. Each day we should set apart Christ in our hearts as Lord. Focus on the good you see and hear. Testify, just as a witness before a jury, about the *changes* occurring in your own life.

Encourage those around you, and meet together regularly for friendship, accountability, Bible study, and prayer. To encourage someone is to inspire them to have courage. Attend a weekly worship service at a church where the Bible is believed and Christ is honored. Join a weekly Bible study group with a leader who shares Christ's vision for "becoming and making disciples." Form accountability relationships. Pursue your job as a holy vocation. Remember the poor when you give your resources. Be a faithful steward. Stand against bigotry and racial prejudice. Increase your love for God and for people. Remember, no amount of success at work can compensate for failure at home.

THE SIN OF PARTIAL SURRENDER

When asked about his attitude toward whiskey, Fuller Warren, thirtieth governor of Florida, once answered:

> If you mean the demon drink that poisons the mind, pollutes the body, desecrates family life, and inflames sinners, then I'm against it. But if you mean the elixir of Christmas cheer, the shield against a cold winter chill, or the taxable potion that puts needed funds into public coffers to comfort little crippled children, then I'm for it. This is my position, and I will not compromise.[50]

Many of us go back and forth like this between the life with Christ and the life in the world. We compromise because we have only partially surrendered to the Lord Jesus Christ. The challenge is to be a certain kind of man—the kind we have described in these pages, a man committed to the Christian worldview, a biblical Christian.

CONCLUSION

Is it time for you to stop just going through the motions and get serious about your eternal destiny and earthly purpose? The examined life *is* worth living! Determine to let Christ explore every inner room of your mind. Christ wants to empower us to break out of the mold of this world and lead an *authentic* Christian life. But it requires daily effort on our part.

My father once had an employee who said, "Mr. Morley, I need to make more money. If you will just pay me more money, I promise I'll work harder."

With a twinkle in his wise eyes, my dad responded, "I can see you really have a need. I'll tell you what; I'd like to help. Why don't you go ahead and work harder, and then I'll pay you more money?"

We often want God to increase our "pay" without putting forth any effort. To receive the higher wage, though, we need to take some daily steps to know Him as He is.

The pen is in your hands now, so go ahead—write the next chapter! And may God grant you every desire of your heart.

───────────── FOCUS QUESTIONS ─────────────

1. What makes people resist change? What makes you resist changing to become more like the man Scripture calls you to be?

2. Do you have complaints against God? Do you have unanswered questions you would like God to answer? What do you think of the statement, "Life is a big question. God is a big answer. Whatever the question, He is the answer"? Do you really need to have all the answers, or is God enough?

3. Record what you would like to be remembered as your last words:

   _____

   _____

   _____

   _____

   _____

4. Are you prepared to put in the daily effort required to change? In what ways can you personally identify with

the statement, "Americans have come to expect simple streamlined solutions to perfectly packaged problems"?

- What specifically are you prepared to commit to do in daily preparation?
- How specifically are you prepared to deal with daily temptation?
- How specifically are you prepared to handle daily sin?
- Do you understand how to walk in the power of the Holy Spirit? Explain.

5. Do you have the desire and training to see others come to a saving faith in Jesus Christ? If not, what are you prepared to do to correct that situation?

6. Have you been guilty of partial surrender—trying to have your cake and eat it too? Are you willing to make a clean break with the ways of the "old man"?

A NEW AFTERWORD
FROM THE AUTHOR:
NOW WHAT?

Where do you go from here? Our nation and world face a devastating "men problem." Legions of men have grown up without a clear understanding of how to execute their manhood. The collateral damage in marriages and families has been staggering. Of course, no man fails on purpose. Yet if the next twenty-five years are like the last twenty-five, life as we have known it will be no more.

No matter how we got into the current situation, the only solution is to disciple our way out. Making disciples is God's designated way to release the power of his gospel on every problem we face.

Notice that Jesus did *not* say, "Go and *become* disciples." He said, "Go and *make* disciples." Of course, you can't give what you don't have, so becoming a disciple is important. But for at least one generation, we have emphasized "becoming" at the expense of "making." The result? Most Christians today are not contagious. We sneeze, and nobody catches what we have. We have created a generation of spiritual overeaters who don't "pass it on."

So where should you go from here? I have taken a step to disciple you in this book. Now it's your turn to go and disciple others. Be sure to disciple your family first. That's your most important priority. After your family, the place on the battlefield where you are most needed today is to disciple men. Be sure to teach them to "pass it on," since you're not making disciples until your disciples are making disciples.

According to Jesus, making disciples is the one thing that's guaranteed to make a difference twenty-five years from now.

DISCUSSION
LEADER'S GUIDE

A ny man interested in starting a group to discuss *The Man in the Mirror* can successfully do so and lead a lively discussion by following these guidelines:

1. Decide how many weeks your group will meet, and pick the chapters to read and discuss each week. Groups may be formed from existing Bible studies, fellowship groups, prayer groups, or adult education classes (women can be included). Or you may want to start a new group.

2. *How to Start a New Group*: Copy the Contents pages in the front of *The Man in the Mirror* and the questions at the end of a couple of chapters, and give a copy to the men you want to meet with. Ask them if they would like to be in a discussion group that would read the book and answer the discussion questions at the end of each chapter. This can be a group from work, church, your neighborhood, or any combination. The optimum-sized group would be eight to twelve men (assuming some men will have to miss a week occasionally). Decide to meet for a set number of weeks. Consider starting with a six-week commitment to meet and discuss the first six chapters. That's because more guys will commit to a six-week group than to a longer one. Then in weeks five and six, offer each man the option to keep going through the rest of the chapters. But don't make men feel guilty if they need or want to stop after

six weeks. If the group gels, you may want to suggest the group continue to meet after you are finished studying *The Man in the Mirror.*

3. *First Week*: Distribute a copy of the book to each member, along with a schedule. Assign the first chapter as next week's reading assignment, and ask them to be prepared to answer the questions at the end of the chapter. Then go around the room and ask each man to take three minutes to share briefly with the group where he is on his spiritual journey right now. This is a great icebreaker, and the men will be encouraged and enjoy learning about where other men are on their journeys. Be sure to point out that there are no wrong answers to this question. Some may just be starting out; others may be well down the road. Close with a prayer. Always adjourn exactly when you said you would.

4. *Typical Week*: Begin with an icebreaker question. As an alternative, you may ask a different man each week to give a maximum five-minute personal testimony of how he became a Christian. During a one-hour meeting a good schedule to follow would be:

   - icebreaker question (5 minutes)
   - discussion questions (45 minutes)
   - group prayer (10 minutes)

5. *Alternative Typical Week*: Prepare a twenty-minute lecture based on the chapter. After your presentation, spend thirty minutes discussing the questions and ten minutes in prayer. Use your creativity to think of other ways to help men deal with the man in the mirror.

6. *Refreshments*: Have coffee, water, and maybe soft drinks available. If you meet over lunch or breakfast, allow an extra fifteen minutes for eating, if possible.

7. *Leading a Discussion*: The key to a successful discussion group

will be your ability to ensure that each member gets airtime. Your role is to encourage each man to render his thoughts and ideas on the subject of the day. If off-the-subject questions are asked, simply suggest that you discuss those at a separate time. If someone rambles too much, privately ask them to help you draw out the more shy members of the group. If you have a shy member, take the initiative and ask, "_____, how would you answer question number three?" Take each question in succession, and make sure everyone has the opportunity to comment—but not every man has to answer every question. If you run out of time and don't get through all the questions, don't worry about it. Giving men an opportunity to open up is the goal, not necessarily answering every question.

8. You don't have to be an experienced Bible teacher to lead a discussion about *The Man in the Mirror*. If someone asks you a question that is beyond your ability to answer, simply say so and move on.

9. The pleasure and added understanding you will experience from a group discussion will prove to be well worth the effort on your part.

ACKNOWLEDGMENTS

I want to express a deep sense of gratitude and affection to the men who have had the greatest influence on my spiritual growth. In chronological order from their initial impact: Bob Morley, my father; Ed Cole, my wife's father; Jim Gillean, my first Bible study leader; Tom Skinner; John Morley, my son; Chuck Green, my pastor until he retired; R. C. Sproul; Bill Bright; Jay Simmons, my son-in-law; Joel Hunter, my pastor today; and Davis Cole Morley, my grandson.

The man in my mirror has also been deeply influenced by four women: my mother, Alleen; my wife, Patsy; Patsy's mother, June; and my daughter, Jen. Thank you.

A special word of thanks to my pastor for twenty-five years, Chuck Green, and to my wife, Patsy, for reviewing the manuscript to test its integrity and compassion toward the readers. Thank you, Jamie Turco, for proofreading the new manuscript and for your many helpful suggestions.

I will always be grateful to Robert Wolgemuth and Mike Hyatt for agreeing to publish an unknown author. And thank you, Robert, for remaining my champion as my literary agent, along with Erik, for these twenty-five years and twenty books.

My colleagues and friends at Zondervan, especially John Sloan and Dirk Buursma, have been so encouraging about this update. Thanks to your entire staff.

I owe so much to so many, but I would never forgive myself if I neglected to acknowledge the wonderful *team*—a word not selected lightly—at Man in the Mirror, who skillfully advance our vision of making it possible "for every church to disciple every man." Without your love and support, none of this would be happening.

NOTES

1. Vance Packard, *The Hidden Persuaders* (New York: Pocket Books, 1981), 17.

2. Quoted in James Heiser, "Ted Koppel's Absurd Lament Over Media Bias," *The New American*, www.thenewamerican.com/usnews/politics/item/3532-ted-koppels-absurd-lament-over-media-bias (accessed February 13, 2014).

3. Wilson Bryan Key, *Subliminal Seduction* (New York: Signet, 1974), 61.

4. Cited in Jean M. Twenge, W. Keith Campbell, and Elise C. Freeman, "Generational Differences in Young Adults' Life Goals, Concern for Others, and Civic Orientation, 1966–2009," *Journal of Personality and Social Psychology*, vol. 102, no. 5 (2012): 1045–62.

5. Francis A. Schaeffer, *A Christian Manifesto* (Westchester, IL: Crossway, 1981), 17–18.

6. Allan Bloom, *The Closing of the American Mind* (New York: Simon and Schuster, 1987), 41.

7. Reprinted from Lane Cooper, *Louis Agassiz as a Teacher*, copyright © 1945 by Cornell University. Used by permission of the publisher.

8. Francis A. Schaeffer, *How Should We Then Live?* (Westchester, IL: Crossway, 1976), 205.

9. Frank Grenville Beardsley, *A History of American Revivals* (New York: American Tract Society, 1912), 211; U.S. census data.

10. Research shows U.S. household debt in 2012 totaling approximately $11.4 trillion, and the U.S. Census Bureau lists about 115 million households. See Lam Thuy Vo and Jacob Goldstein, "Household Debt In America, In 3 Graphs," National Public Radio online, www.npr.org/blogs/money/2012/11/21/165657931/household-debt-in-america-in-3-graphs (accessed February 14, 2014); "State & County Quick Facts," U.S. Census Bureau online, http://quickfacts.census.gov/qfd/states/00000.html (accessed February 14, 2014).

11. See C. S. Lewis, *Mere Christianity* (New York: Macmillan, 1943), 10.
12. "State of the American Workplace: Employee Engagement Insights for U.S. Business Leaders," Gallup, Inc., 2013, www.gallup.com/ strategicconsulting/163007/state-american-workplace.aspx (accessed February 18, 2014).
13. "Cat's in the Cradle," words and music by Sandy and Harry Chapin, copyright © 1974, Story Songs, Ltd.
14. "The World Fact Book," Central Intelligence Agency, www.cia.gov/ library/publications/the-world-factbook/fields/2127.html (accessed February 18, 2014).
15. Michael Foust, "70 percent of High School Students Are Virgins, Study Reports," *Baptist Press*, www.bpnews.net/BPnews.asp?ID= 33877 (accessed February 18, 2014).
16. Cited in James C. Dobson, *Straight Talk to Men and Their Wives* (Waco, TX: Word, 1984), 35–36.
17. Matea Gold, "Kids Watch More Than a Day of TV Each Week," *Los Angeles Times*, http://articles.latimes.com/2009/oct/27/entertain ment/et-kids-tv27 (accessed February 18, 2014).
18. Myron Magnet, "The Money Society," *Fortune*, July 6, 1987, http:// money.cnn.com/magazines/fortune/fortune_archive/1987/07/06/ 69235/index.htm (accessed February 18, 2014). Reprinted by permission.
19. Anne Marie Miller, "3 Things You Don't Know About Your Children and Sex," *Church Leaders*, www.churchleaders.com/youth/ youth-leaders-articles/169715-anne-marie-miller-things-you-know-about-your-children-and-sex.html?p=1 (accessed February 18, 2014).
20. Gordon MacDonald, *The Effective Father* (Wheaton, IL: Tyndale House, 1977), 79.
21. Quoted in Ann Landers, "Too Soon, Children Are Grown, the Years Gone," June 2, 1988, *Chicago Tribune*, http://articles.chicagotribune. com/1988-06-02/features/8801040158_1_dear-ann-landers-brain-kids (accessed February 18, 2014). Reprinted by permission.
22. Cited in Carol Kent, *Speak Up with Confidence* (Nashville: Nelson, 1987), 89.
23. "I Am a Rock," words and music by Paul Simon, copyright © 1965.

24. Charles Lamb, "The Two Races of Men," in *The Prose Works of Charles Lamb*, vol. 2 (London: Edward Moxon, 1836), 50.

25. Terence P. Jeffrey, "U.S. Government's Foreign Debt Hits Record $5.29 Trillion," August 16, 2012, *CNS News*, http://cnsnews.com/news/article/us-governments-foreign-debt-hits-record-529-trillion (accessed February 18, 2014).

26. Bernard M. Bass, *Bass & Stogdill's Handbook of Leadership: Theory, Research, & Managerial Applications*, 3rd ed. (New York: Free Press, 1990).

27. "A Talk with Brzezinski," *New York Times* Opinion, April 22, 1981, www.nytimes.com/1981/04/22/opinion/a-talk-with-brzezinski.html (accessed February 22, 2014).

28. Quoted in Louis B. Barnes and Mark P. Kriger, "The Hidden Side of Organizational Leadership," *MIT Sloan Management Review*, October 15, 1986, http://sloanreview.mit.edu/article/the-hidden-side-of-organizational-leadership/ (accessed February 22, 2014).

29. Peter F. Drucker, "Getting Things Done: How to Make People Decisions," *Harvard Business Review* (July–August 1985), 1.

30. Leo Tolstoy, "Three Methods of Reform," in *Pamphlets: Translated from the Russian* (Christchurch, Hants, UK: Free Age Press, 1900), 29.

31. Theodore Roosevelt, "The Man in the Arena," excerpt from the speech "Citizenship in the Republic," April 23, 1910, www.theodore-roosevelt.com/trsorbonnespeech.html (accessed February 22, 2014).

32. Dale Carnegie, *How to Win Friends and Influence People* (New York: Simon & Schuster, 1936), 93.

33. C. S. Lewis, *Mere Christianity* (New York: Touchstone, 1996), 112.

34. Discovery Channel, "How Often Does the Average Person Tell a Lie?" *Cognitive Neuroscience*, http://curiosity.discovery.com/question/average-person-tell-lie (accessed February 24, 2014).

35. John Witherspoon, *The Works of the Reverend John Witherspoon*, vol. 2 (Philadelphia: William Woodward, 1802), 562.

36. S. I. McMillen, MD, *None of These Diseases* (Westwood, NJ: Spire, 1973), 72.

37. "The Effects of Stress on Your Body," *Mental Health Center*,

WebMD, www.webmd.com/mental-health/effects-of-stress-on-your-body (accessed February 24, 2014).

38. John White, *Putting the Soul Back in Psychology* (Downers Grove, IL: InterVarsity, 1987), 79.

39. Howard Dayton, founder of Compass—*finances God's way*, personal correspondence.

40. Anne Morrow Lindbergh, *Hour of Gold, Hour of Lead: Diaries and Letters of Anne Morrow Lindbergh, 1929–1932* (New York: Harcourt Brace Jovanovich, 1973), 3.

41. Quoted in Albert M. Wells Jr., ed., *Inspiring Quotations: Contemporary and Classical* (Nashville: Nelson, 1988), 90.

42. John Ruskin, *The Works of John Ruskin*, vol. 5 (New York: Wiley, 1885), 268.

43. R. C. Sproul, *Pleasing God* (Wheaton, IL: Tyndale House, 1988), 79.

44. Dwight L. Moody, *Life Words: Selections from Gospel Addresses of D. L. Moody* (London: John Snow, 1875), 53.

45. Cited in Packard, *Hidden Persuaders*, 12–13.

46. Quoted in "Standing for the Faith," International Diocese, Anglican Church in North America, www.idio.net/content/standing-faith (accessed February 25, 2014).

47. See Bill Nelson, *Mission* (New York: Harcourt Brace Jovanovich, 1988), 120.

48. "Taylor Says He Made a 'Bad Decision,'" September 1, 1988, *New York Times*, www.nytimes.com/1988/09/01/sports/taylor-says-he-made-a-bad-decision.html (accessed February 24, 2014).

49. See Arnie Cole, EdD, and Pamela Caudill Ovwigho, PhD, "Understanding the Bible Engagement Challenge: Scientific Evidence for the Power of 4," December 2009, Center for Bible Engagement, www.centerforbibleengagement.org/images/stories/pdf/Scientific_Evidence_for_the_Power_of_4.pdf (accessed February 24, 2014).

50. Jacksonville Jaycees, "The History of the Jaycees," www.jacksonville-jaycees.org/jaycees_history.html (accessed February 24, 2014).

ABOUT
PATRICK MORLEY

For decades, Patrick Morley has been regarded as one of America's most respected authorities on the unique challenges and opportunities facing men. Through his speaking and writing, he is a tireless advocate for men, encouraging and inspiring them to change their lives in Christ.

In 1973, Patrick founded Morley Properties, which for several years was one of Florida's one hundred largest privately held companies. During this time, he was the president or managing partner of fifty-nine companies and partnerships.

In 1989, he wrote *The Man in the Mirror*, a landmark book rooted in his own search for purpose and a deeper relationship with God. With over three million copies in print, *The Man in the Mirror* captured the imaginations of men worldwide and was selected as one of the one hundred most influential Christian books of the twentieth century. Altogether, Patrick has written twenty books and more than 750 articles. He has appeared on several hundred radio and television programs.

In 1991, Patrick founded Man in the Mirror, a ministry that has helped thirty-five thousand churches impact the lives of twelve million men worldwide. Their vision is "for every church to disciple every man" through local area directors who help churches disciple men more effectively. He speaks to men daily through the

398 | THE MAN IN THE MIRROR

radio program *The Man in the Mirror Radio Minute*, which is carried on seven hundred stations nationwide.

In addition, Patrick teaches a Bible study every Friday morning to approximately ten thousand men — 150 men gather in Orlando, Florida, and the others are reached through a webcast in all fifty states and throughout the world.

"The ministry of Man in the Mirror exists," says Patrick, "in answer to the prayers of all those wives, mothers, and grandmothers who have for decades been praying for the men in their lives."

Patrick Morley graduated with honors from the University of Central Florida. He has earned a PhD in management, completed postgraduate studies at the Harvard Business School and Oxford University, and graduated from Reformed Theological Seminary. He lives in Winter Park, Florida, with his wife, Patsy. They have two married children and four grandchildren.

His weekly video Bible study, articles, daily devotionals, radio program, books, and e-books can be found at PatrickMorley.com. Follow him on Facebook at facebook.com/PatrickMorleyAuthor and on Twitter @patrickmorley. Check out his ministry websites at maninthemirror.org and areadirectors.org.

WANT TO READ MORE BY PATRICK MORLEY?

The Man in the Mirror

Devotions for Couples

Devotions for the Man in the Mirror

Discipleship for the Man in the Mirror

Second Half for the Man in the Mirror

Seven Seasons of the Man in the Mirror

Ten Secrets for the Man in the Mirror

Coming Back to God

Understanding Your Man in the Mirror

The Dad in the Mirror (with David Delk)

The Young Man in the Mirror

The Marriage Prayer (with David Delk)

No Man Left Behind (with David Delk and Brett Clemmer)

How to Survive the Economic Meltdown

Pastoring Men

A Man's Guide to the Spiritual Disciplines

A Man's Guide to Work

Is Christianity for You?

Man Alive

How God Makes Men